NC

People Movements in Southern Polynesia

*Studies in the Dynamics of Church-planting
and Growth in Tahiti, New Zealand,
Tonga, and Samoa*

by

ALAN R. TIPPETT

"Shall not the isles shake at the sound of thy fall?"
(Ezekiel 26:15)

MOODY PRESS
CHICAGO

People Movements in Southern Polynesia has been produced in connection with a nondegree research project undertaken at the Institute of Church Growth, Eugene, Oregon, with the help of a church growth fellowship from Northwestern Christian College and a traveling grant from the Department of Overseas Missions of the Methodist Church of Australia. The rough draft was prepared in Eugene, after which the researcher returned to the Pacific for checking it against library and archival records.

The author expresses his thanks to Dr. Donald A. McGavran and Dr. Homer G. Barnett, whose respective approaches to critical analysis of data and theory are, no doubt, reflected in this book.

© 1971 by
THE MOODY BIBLE INSTITUTE
OF CHICAGO

#197720

Printed in the United States of America

CONTENTS

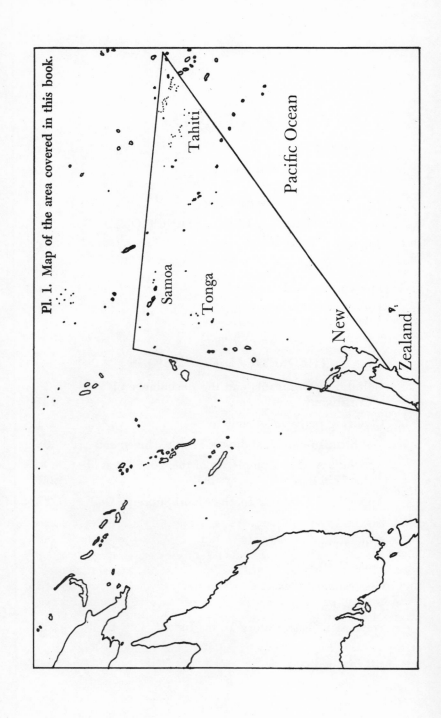

Pl. 1. Map of the area covered in this book.

INTRODUCING THE SOUTH PACIFIC

THIS GREAT ISLAND WORLD, which "primitive" navigators had sailed for centuries and charted on stick-and-fiber frameworks, was at last "discovered" by white men—Magellan, Mendaña, Queirós, Wallis, Carteret, Bougainville, La Pérouse, and Cook. Their fellow countrymen who followed came to exploit. There were the seekers of spices, sandalwood, and bêche-de-mer; whalers to prepare oil and satisfy their instincts in some island paradise; and blackbirders, who kidnapped islanders for work in the plantations of Samoa, or the cane fields of Queensland and Fiji, the mines of Peru and the guano islands off the South American coast—mostly to die quickly and never return. This is the world into which the white man brought firearms and ammunition and new diseases, so that the patterns of island life were thrown into chaos.

Ordinary people of the West learned of this world through the writings of Melville, London, and Stevenson, but there were also numerous popular editions of famous voyages of the last century—Wilkes, Palmer, Erskine, and Wilson.

The first modern missionaries came to this strange and already disintegrating world. They too have left a body of fine writing: John and Thomas Williams, Ellis, Gill, Murray, Cheever, Paton, Chalmers, and many others. These are primary sources for the historian and the anthropologist today. They are essential for any study on the dynamics of church-planting and growth in the area. Although colored by the theological pigments of their day, they describe actual dynamic processes at work. They devote more space to the indigenous servants of the church than did the promotional journals and histories of the time.

The archival records of the last century are superior to those of the present for research material for our purpose. They pulsate with life and record the heartbeat of the young churches.

They were not organized purely for record purposes or to serve any promotional interest. They have long descriptions of dynamic encounters between Christian teachers and pagan medicine men, dramatic accounts of conversion, deathbed testimonies, and accounts of love feasts where indigenous converts shared their religious experiences. Today one combs through thousands of pages of official papers about costs, budgets, staffing problems, building repairs, mission launches, transport, land leases, business conferences, furlough arrangements, and policies on mission trade. Then perhaps after a hundred pages one reads

> There has been a real movement of the Spirit among the A—— tribe in the mountain valley beyond B——. It began in a prayer meeting held on Pentecost Sunday, and within a month had spread through four villages.

There is nothing more for another hundred pages, and then perhaps another sentence which shows the movement is still going on.

> *Some hundreds of people have done an unprecedented thing in their tribal history. They have destroyed the old gods in whom they trusted and turned to Christ.* It is true that they know little about him. But somehow they have come to believe that he has the answer to their need, and as they have turned to him *the things they have feared all their lives have lost their terror.*

What happened? They came in large groups—families, extended families, whole tribes perhaps, or segments. We will study these phenomena in this book, not merely because it is a story worth recapturing from the past, but because Christian missions are encountering these experiences today in Oceania, Africa, and elsewhere. These are not identical, but there are identical features about them all. We will ask how the Holy Spirit used these people-movement experiences to bring men to salvation, to discover what they have to teach us in our missionary methods today. Many present-day Christians have trouble in accepting the idea of people movements to Christ, and therefore I devote a critical chapter to an analysis of the process and leave the reader to determine whether it be of God or not. For my own part I have no doubt that God, who made man to dwell in societies, can speak to men through social mechanisms.

A people movement to Christ is a positive phenomenon in any

discussion on church-planting and church growth. At the opposite pole, we have the negative movement out of the church. The anthropologist may call it a *nativistic* movement. Patterns vary, but they are common with second-generation Christians, who have not personally shared the dynamic experiences of the original converts. They also grow from disillusionment, unsatisfied yearnings, and spiritual voids. They may be triggered by culture contacts and by war in particular. They explain many of the dramatic falls in the line graphs of growth in church statistics. These have been more active in Melanesia than Polynesia in our times, but the long history of the church in the latter permits a wider perspective. I have therefore devoted special attention to one of the Maori movements, which has evolved into a "church." It may be taken as a type and has similarities with the North American Peyote and some of the African prophetic churches.

A dominant element in the backdrop against which these dramas were played was the missionary policy of civilizing to evangelize. A critical theoretical synthesis attempts to show the world dimension of this policy and how it kept recurring in different forms down to the present day. In its old and its modern forms, this theory has often obstructed the very growth its sincere advocates desired, because it loses sight of priorities and promotes Christianity in terms less than the highest. Those whom it seeks to win make their appraisals in those lesser terms. This has something to say to us today.

The theme of comity appears at several points. Clearly there are two sides to this question. The problems that arise differ in different areas. Comity agreements should allow for social structure. In this book I show how a people movement and local social structure wrecked a comity agreement with unhappy results, injuring the quality growth of the emerging church by affiliating it with rivalry in the social segments.

In the study of the conversion of Samoa, the historical reconstruction is followed by an application of anthropological criteria. I hope this has some value to modern missionaries in areas where doors are beginning to open. It shows the relation of social structure, family patterns, value systems, and magico-religious configurations to the acceptance of Christianity and its forms. Many things that worked out for the Samoan church were not consciously planned to fit the culture. Had the culture been studied, the missionaries could have brought the church to a state of indigenousness more rapidly. Furthermore they would have realized the dangers of their denominationalism in a rivalry-orientated society. Of course there was no science of anthropology in those days. There is no excuse today.

If the approach of this book is anthropological, it is not an anthropology. If it is historical, it is not a history. It is a selection of studies from a confined area: Southern Polynesia. Tahiti, Tonga, Maoriland and Samoa belong to one culture area. There is one basic study from each. They reveal different responses to the same gospel, though it was surely the one Holy Spirit who brought them all to God. Environmental, social, political, geographical, and acculturative factors had bearing on the responses —sometimes to obstruct and sometimes to stimulate. The grace and the growth is of God, but man must hear the gospel and make the decision to accept or reject. This book analyzes the nature of those acceptances in a single culture area.

Part One

HISTORICAL RECONSTRUCTIONS

1

THE TAHITIAN WEB

THE FLAG of the London Missionary Society* fluttered at the masthead of the *Duff* on August 10, 1796. On the deck below, thirty missionaries joined with those on shore in singing

> Jesus, at thy command
> We launch into the deep.

The evangelical revival had stimulated the English conscience and brought the idea of the universality of the gospel into focus. A period of humanitarianism had begun which led to reforms in education, factories, and prisons and to the abolition of the English slave trade. At the same time England was learning much about the Pacific through the reports and writings of navigators like James Cook and William Bligh. Concurrently also many persons appeared in England with accumulated funds for investment in religious and humane projects. Much of this was the direct effect of the revivals led by Wesley and Whitefield, which had in fact influenced all England. In this new moral climate, the day of modern British missions dawned.[1] In a thousand ways God was surely in it all.

The *Duff* party was sent to Otaheite (Tahiti)[2] and other islands about which the navigators had written. Cook had been sent there to observe the transit of Venus. Bligh had stayed long enough to establish buildings and prepare a description of the country with its customs and language, both vocabulary and grammar. During the voyage the missionaries studied these and grew into an integrated unit. They instructed each other in their

*Hereafter this body will be referred to as the L.M.S.

respective crafts and learned first aid and anatomy from the doctor in their company. In due course they reached Tahiti, where
eighteen of their number remained. Others went to Tonga and
the Marquesas. The gospel was first preached to the chief,
Pomare I, March 12, 1797. The first attempt at Protestant church-
planting in the Pacific had begun.[3]

There is no doubt whatever about the clear religious emphasis
in the personal lives of these missionaries and the clear instructions they received about their personal devotional habits; yet
equally clear were the instructions that they were to evangelize
the islanders by civilizing them first. They were to establish
communities, each to be a "model civilized society,"[4] and they
were to collect stock and seeds at specific ports en route to establish their settlements.[5] The ancient theory behind this policy was
that an uncivilized pagan cannot understand a gospel of salvation. It was hindering church growth as far back as the fourth
century.[6] The mission party was comprised mostly of artisans
and laborers. That the directors of the Society had a profound
belief in the rightness of "civilization" in terms of Western thought
and concepts may be seen from these instructions which they
gave to the pioneers:

> As an inducement to us to prefer their island, they must give us
> a full title to the land, guarantee us the safety of our property
> from plunder, and enjoyment of our laws and customs and the
> undisturbed exercise of our religion. . . . The land should not be
> purchased but required, as a condition of our remaining with
> them.

The instructions also said:

> In negotiating with the chiefs, you will explain to them the
> advantages which will arise to them from our residence among
> them.[7]

The people in the community organized themselves systematically and devoutly. They moved about only a little, and then
with Pomare I's escort. As a permanent settlement they represented the biggest innovation in Tahitian life since the mutiny of
the *Bounty*. They had opportunities not always open to pioneer
missionaries. Some of their crafts interested the islanders. They
had the manuscript grammar and dictionary before they began.
They had the strength of numbers and further additions to their

staff after three years. Yet for sixteen years there was no church growth whatever on Tahiti, and both the other experiments had failed. Many of their supporters in England had begun to wonder about this project into which they had put their funds for a decade and a half without any conversion returns.

Many reasons have been advanced: the strength of the pagan religion and custom, the bad influence of escaped European convicts, and island wars. But these were universal obstructions to the gospel all over the Pacific. Tahiti was no worse, and considerably better, than many parts which turned to the gospel in a shorter space of time. In Oceanic society if there is no response in six or seven years it may be assumed that there is either some unique obstruction or the missionary technique is faulty.

The *Duff* missionaries were amazingly good observers and recorders, and their records reveal the Tahitians as normal island people. They were open to cultural innovation and were psychologically capable of individual or group conversion. Socio-psychological processes were at work which made it possible for outsiders (i.e., missionaries) to be received into society, or into groups other than those into which they were born. Tahitian society was potentially receptive to the gospel, with no apparent peculiar obstructions. We are therefore forced back to examine the missionary techniques used.

At two major points the Tahiti missionaries may claim our sympathy for being less fortunate than those who followed in other island fields.

In the first place, they did represent the pioneer project. They had no older missionaries to share experience and give advice or suggest the type of problem to be met. Their knowledge of the culture and environment had come through the writings of seamen. Their only other advice was from Society directors who were so very Western.

In the second place, they had no indigenous agents to work with them. As we proceed, the reader will see the significant role of these island evangelists as the spearhead of gospel penetration. The Tahiti mission had none of these.

However, having said this in their defense, it is difficult to see why they delayed so long with their program of Scripture translation during those sixteen barren years. The later L.M.S. missionaries did yeoman service in this respect, but Tahiti certainly got off to a bad start.[8] The personal lives of these men were built on Scripture; but in the policy of "civilize first" early conversions were not expected, though they worked to this ultimate goal. They certainly did not expect the sudden and dramatic people-movement form which put most of the community under their instruction at one time. They were caught quite unprepared.

Scripture translation is also an essential for the pioneer missionary for its reflex value. It forces him to learn the language, to struggle with its idiom, and to discipline himself in the mastery of this essential tool. Without this tool there is no effective communication, whether preaching, teaching, or pastoral encounter.

The "civilize to evangelize" theory created a certain mental set that shifted activity from real priorities. The missionaries themselves, though forced into subsistence farming by their pattern of employment by the Society, nevertheless came more and more to reject the theory as a means of evangelization. The records show this in Tahiti and New Zealand and even among some of the committee leaders at home.[9] As a historian with an abundance of data and looking back after the events, it seems to this writer that a major fault of the theory is that it implies that growth must be slow. In point of fact, the implication is unsound. To put it in biblical imagery, time after time in Oceania "fields ripened to harvest." When the crop yellows, the ingathering must be a speedy program. The success or failure of the mission involved will lie in its readiness, its mobility of resources, its capacity to ingather immediately and to provide the follow-up the ingathering demands. This includes translated Scripture and other aids. Any theory of church growth which implies that it must be slow will leave its advocates in distress when crops ripen suddenly, as in God's providence they often do.

The directors of the L.M.S. had no intention of setting aside their policy. Even when reports of people movements came to hand, the directors turned to the establishment of secondary industries and markets.[10] By the third decade of the century, they had sent a deputation to inspect the work on the field and reaffirmed their conviction in the the priority of civilizing. At the same time some of the Pacific missionaries were pressing for drastic policy change. Before we look at this, we must consider how Tahiti turned to Christ.

THE TAHITI CONVERSION COMPLEX

The winning of Tahiti for Christ must be seen in its correct context and sequence. There has been much superficial appraisal of the conversion of Pomare II—over-simplification, as if one single factor were responsible for the whole dramatic change. Historians, propagandists, and anthropologists have been guilty. This is shown in an appendix to this volume. If we are to study the dynamics of church growth we must see this in its correct cultural perspective as a total complex.

For the first decade of the mission and well into the second there had been virtually no interest in Christianity. Those of the missionaries who had acquired the language itinerated and did some preaching, but they got no hearing.[11] Their prestige was largely maintained by the frequent visits of British vessels, and on one occasion the missionaries actually delayed a vessel for forty-eight hours because of the war situation that endangered the mission personnel.[12]

The directors in London had shown deep concern for the missionaries' failure to convert the people, and this concern was transmitted to Tahiti. The missionaries had discovered that interest in them had declined in England. They felt hurt and neglected—not without some justification.[13]

They had worked at the language and improved their vocabulary, having checked and cross-checked their list, which contained 2,700 words by 1806.[14] Pomare II had learned to read and write, and so had a number of his people.[15] By direction from London the missionaries began teaching in English. It was not a success. For all their discipline and organization there were no converts.[16]

War situations may or may not affect the growth of Christianity. Basically war and Christianity are opposites, and the former stimulates those things which turn men from Christ. At heart the missionaries were pacifist and stated this as their position from the start,[17] but they found the stand difficult to maintain because of local events they did not control. At the same time social dynamics show that war is always a time open for dramatic and extensive change. With their policy one of civilizing it was inevitable that the war situation should enmesh them. Civilizing depended on the cultivation of lands, protection of herds and crops, and the care of fences and storage sheds and manufactur-

ing plants. This in turn depended on some form of stable government. The existence of this type of mission depended on peace.
It was therefore natural that they should seek to maintain the
status quo, and view the "rebels" as rebels, who threatened their
own existence. It is amazing that none of the critics has seen fit
to mention the fact that when the missionaries helped Pomare II,
they were not militarists but opponents of rebellion.[18]

To escape from dependence on this supposed feudalism the
missionaries had pressed for a larger and stronger settlement,
only to be snubbed by the directors for imagining any policy
other than working with the "king" and his officials.[19] There
were ways in which the missionaries worked to restore peace and
save life, but they neither produced converts nor saved their
property.[20] In 1808 a rebellion spread over the whole island and
some of the missionaries had to shift their place of abode.[21]

In 1809 events moved toward a climax. Pomare II was very
much under the control of the prophet Meetia, whose prophetic
inspiration led the harassed king into aggression. Pomare II
was not a good general. Against a superior force that was in a
superior position, Pomare II's forces made war on a basis of
prophetic oracles and omens.[22] The enemy overran three districts,
destroying houses and taking the missionary cattle. It was a large-
scale loss.[23] More warriors arrived from other islands. The struggle continued until October and ended, for the time being, by
Pomare II's forces being ambushed and routed.[24] Tahiti passed
into a period still known to this day as *hau manahune* (rule by
untitled commoners), a period of suspense, both parties being
afraid of the other. Pomare II never surrendered his claim to
rule. By 1811 he was back in Tahiti again, in control of one of
the five districts. Some seven hundred had joined him.[25]

Most of the missionaries were now prepared to admit defeat.
The fortunes of war, loss of property, deaths among their number,
retirements, and some loss of faith had worked together with
the feeling that the church in England had forgotten them.
Because of these factors plus the anarchy they were under and
their failure either to civilize or to evangelize, most of them left.
They took the opportunity offered by the vessel *Hibernia* to
voyage to Port Jackson and abandon the mission.[26] Thus the
political crisis of October 1809, with the defeat of the king, the
extensive destruction of missionary property, and the departure

of most of them from the group, marks a clear-cut end to a period
of missionary endeavor.[27] Of the original party of thirty, only
two remained, and a third, quite neglected, was still at the
Marquesas.[28] The civilizing phase now gave way to a period
of intensely dynamic factors which almost requires a different
value system to appraise.

The defeat of the king and his rejection by the main body of
missionaries opened the way for change in him. Was there, perhaps, some truth in what a missionary letter had once communicated to him—*was* he under the displeasure of their God?
Had he been wrong in following so blindly the oracles of Meetia,
the prophet? The missionaries at least had been loyal and reliable.
Now most of them were gone. Fortunately two or three did
remain in his islands. There is evidence that Pomare II did feel
this way, but he was not constant. Having accepted a peace
which at least secured him one of the five Tahiti districts, he now
set about the regaining of his "kingdom." It was still to his
heathen gods he appealed, with feasting and dissipation and the
same old sacrifices. Many priests were employed in this service,
many prayers and great offerings were made. The missionaries
were not with him at the time, or nearby. One person, high in
his family, took ill and died. Pomare II and the chiefs were vexed
with their gods, for the person was a child in whom they had
great hopes. The parents drowned their sorrows in unbridled
drinking and both died as a result. Pomare II now expressed the
opinion in his chiefly council that it was his mind to turn from
his gods to the God of the missionaries. The issue was debated
but there was a division on the matter.[29]

One anthropologist has questioned the sincerity of Pomare II's
conversion, saying he "flirted" with the missionaries to gain the
help of their God for war. This is speculation. Pomare II, like
his father before him,[30] was a careful man in matters of religion.
As a pagan he was sincere in his dealings with his gods, until in
these years immediately prior to his conversion, he had clearly
lost his faith in them.[31] His behavior follows a normal Oceanic
pattern. He disclosed his intention of changing faith to the social
group to which he was responsible. In the deliberations there
were differences of opinion—in terms of religion, not politics. This
savors of sincerity.[32] When he finally took the eventful plunge, he
did so alone, inviting others, but not drawing back when none

followed him.[33] When not under missionary observation he could
have relaxed, but he preferred to continue with the Christian
prescriptions,[34] and when he finally regained his lost position he
chose to maintain his new faith in a worthy manner. I see no
reason for doubting his sincerity. He was true to type as far as
Oceania is concerned. In the study of dynamics this is important.

The focal point of dynamic encounter was his eating of the
sacred turtle under forbidden circumstances, which I cite at
length from a primary source:

> Pomare had, for some time past, shewn his contempt for the
> idols of his ancestors, and his desire to be taught a more excel-
> lent way. . . . The natives had watched the change in his mind
> with the most fearful apprehension. . . . They were powerfully
> affected on one occasion when a present was brought to him of
> a turtle, which was always held sacred, and dressed with sacred
> fire within the precincts of the temple, part of it being invariably
> offered to the idol. The attendants were proceeding with the
> turtle to the *Marae*, when Pomare called them back, and told
> them to prepare an oven, to bake it in his own kitchen, and
> serve it up, without offering it to the idol. The people around . . .
> could hardly believe the king was in a state of sanity. . . . The
> king repeated his direction; a fire was made, the turtle baked,
> and served up at the next repast. The people of the king's house-
> hold stood, in mute expectation . . . of the god's anger. . . . The
> king cut the turtle and began to eat it, inviting some that sat at
> meat with him to do the same; but no-one could be induced to
> touch it. . . .[35]

This was in July 1812. There is reason to believe that Pomare II,
who had asked for Christian baptism in the previous November
and had been refused,[36] had come to realize that some dynamic
encounter was required, not only to convince his fellow countrymen of the truth, but also to convince the missionaries of his
sincerity.[37] The missionaries kept him waiting seven years for
baptism, not on the score of sincerity, but because he needed
more instruction. This is the first of a series of power-encounter
episodes we are to meet in this study of the dynamic configurations of church-growth. We are able to look back and interpret
it today in the light of scores of similar events all over the
Oceanic world. They fall in line with the biblical encounters on
Mount Carmel (1 Ki 18) and Ephesus (Ac 19).

In the meantime, a number of the missionaries who had de-
parted in the *Hibernia* had returned from Port Jackson. Upon

their arrival in Australia they had received communications from London and under the persuasive powers of the Anglican Samuel Marsden, they repented of deserting their post.[38] But it was a different Tahiti to which they returned. Furthermore they returned with a different spirit, and several of the single men had married. The old station was stilled unoccupied, but they set up at Eimeo instead of Tahiti. They returned, not to a civilizing project, but into a dynamic situation. One does not wonder that the critical anthropologist mistook them for a band of new missionaries.

Even though they established themselves at Eimeo, things were beginning to happen at Tahiti. Pomare II had returned there and the Tahitians had found him different. The character change won him both friends and enemies and brought ridicule and persecution. A missionary visiting him early in 1813 found a new spirit of inquiry that had not been there before. Later they discovered a growing interest.

A young man named Oito had previously had some contact with the missionaries, but it was the change in Pomare II which had impressed him. Oito found Tuahine, and before long several men and youths were meeting together.[39] They organized themselves into a group on a five-point basis:

> to stop worshiping idols
> to live more orderly lives
> to worship on the Lord's Day
> to worship the Christian God
> to meet on the Lord's Day for prayer[40]

It is interesting that they codified their thought of Christianity in this manner. No doubt, as observers of the missionaries, who had left Tahiti, they saw Christianity in this light. If so, then perhaps the effect of civilizing is found in the character of orderliness.

This spontaneous indigenous move toward Christianity was dynamic however in its capacity for growth. The missionaries recognized this and took the party to Eimeo for instruction. This would raise no serious problem, because the Tahitians were familiar with the requirement of instruction groups in their own esoteric cult. It is interesting to speculate on what might have happened to this movement if it had not been immediately channeled into Christian organization by the missionaries. Before long they held a public service to permit those who had come under instruction to make an act of public decision, and some thirty-one responded in this way. A proper instruction class was then established to deal with them. That thirty-one adult Tahitians had made a public confession of faith was certainly news in Tahiti. They became witnesses; and eleven more were shortly added to their number, among them a young chief of Huahine, a principal *Areoi* (a member of a society of cultic minstrels) and an important priest.[41]

Some two hundred persons attended a Christian service held in Tahiti on the last Sunday of June. Davies reported "remarkable attention," such as "had not hitherto been witnessed by the missionaries." Puru, a chief of Huahine, had followed the missionaries from Eimeo, together with some of his own people. Several *Areoi* were present.[42] This interest of the chiefs, priests, and minstrels demands some notice. It was either an official investigation of the new movement, or the movement was penetrating all levels of society. The former would fit the facts but it is also clear there was a deeper personal interest from the small chiefly group from Huahine. In any event Tahiti society was shaken. A static situation had suddenly become dynamic. If I permit myself to make use of the Maori situation we are to meet in the next chapter, we will observe that these groups are the superstructure of society. The popular levels would follow blindly the inspirations of the prophet of Oro. The interest of the upper classes, familiar with the esoteric cult and Polynesian world view (similar to the Hebrew-Christian in many respects) and the hostile inspiration of the popular-level prophet, would both indicate that Christianity had suddenly become a dynamic factor as it had not been before.

We note that this change followed closely on the eating of the sacred turtle by Pomare II without the sacrificial ritual. This encounter had started off two lines of response, one classical and the other popular.[43]

Comparative analysis of the primary source material that has been published reveals both these levels of response. It also reveals specific regional distribution. Clearly the movement toward Christianity was developing simultaneously in various localities: on Tahiti itself in the Pare district (not at Matavai where the original mission settlement had been); an area of a valley near to Eimeo; in Huahine; and as far as Raiatéa. In all four localities it was felt in chiefly circles, but did not include all the people in any of them. These islands are scattered over an area of sea perhaps a hundred and twenty miles across, and which can be encircled on a map as contiguous. They were like fields coming ripe unto harvest at one time. In their later days some of the missionaries had done a little itinerant preaching in these localities, but there had been no settled stations there.[44]

The key to this particular segment of the people movement we are about to discuss was surely Pomare II himself. The leaders of all these localities were interested in the House of Pomare II and in the man himself. Pomare II was born in the line of the chiefs of Pare, and could trace back his ancestors for more than twenty generations to the founder of the line. It was in Pare that he landed when he returned from exile. Oito and Tuahine also came from there, though the latter had been born in Raiatéa. The two wives of Pomare I, his father, came one from the line of the chiefs of Eimeo (Moorea) and the other from Raiatéa. The mother of Pomare I was also from the line of the chiefs of Raiatéa, as was also his own wife. The ruling family of Huahine was certainly more than friend and ally, if not related.[45] Pomare II had personally tried to interest all these subunits in Christianity, though without success. Then he ate the sacred turtle. Pomare II's demonstration was of tremendous interest immediately to all these chiefly connections. The demonstration became a reference point for subsequent action by people who desired to change their religion. What they had heard with no great conviction from the itinerant preachers suddenly became dramatically relevant. A great door opened to the missionaries, and this accounts for the type of inquirer they now met; but it does not account for them all.

The movement of 1813 had not won any converts on the popular level, though the populace was most interested in Pomare II's remarkable behavior. The Hauhaua Valley prayer group from the Pare district of Tahiti had met with contempt and persecution before the missionaries transferred it to Eimeo. Yet the growth of the young church was more in Tahiti than Eimeo. By the end of 1814 Ellis estimated some three hundred were attending worship, two-thirds of whom had actually made a profession. If the other islands be included he thought that from five to six hundred

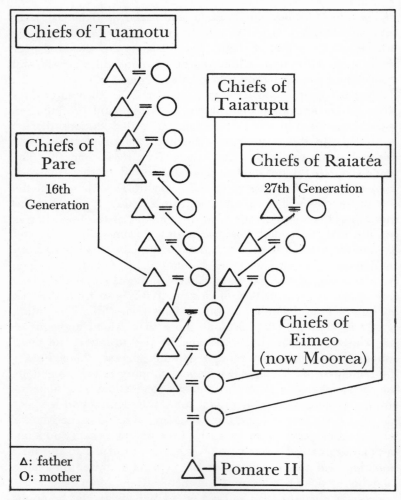

Pomare II (b. 1782, d. 1821) was the second child of Pomare I (d. 1803) by his second wife, a Raiatéan. His connections with Raiatéa were strong. His grandmother was Tetupaia i Hauiri, daughter of Tamatoa III, the ruling chief of Raiatéa. This shows how Pomare II himself was the key to an extensive kin network, and many persons were involved when he ate the sacred turtle. This may also account for early movements to Christianity in Pare, Eimeo (now Moorea), and Raiatéa.

Pl. 2. The ancestry of Pomare II of Tahiti.

had renounced their idolatry.[46] Davies cited the same figure and added, "including most of the principal chiefs,"[47] a valuable reference. Even though chiefs were involved it had not been without opposition and persecution: houses had been fired and some Christians had been driven from their regular places of habitation. It shows Pomare II's authority was not as strong as it might have been at this time. Yet it was in Tahiti that the growth was obtained. At Eimeo there were as yet perhaps no more than fifty Christians. They were found with the missionaries in the district of Papetoai, a stronghold of popular religion. Ellis said they were jealous and cruel and looked askance at Christianity, wondering "whereunto this thing might grow."[48]

Early in 1815 the floodlight on the stage passed from Pomare II to Patii, a chief priest of the popular religion at Eimeo. Patii had been to hear the preaching of Nott, the missionary, and walked home with him along the beach to the mission settlement. He announced that he found the old religion bad and the new way good, and that he would burn his gods to prove his belief.[49] He named the time and place he would do so and discussed the religion of Christ.

Nott was in two minds about Patii's intention. He had no doubt about the opening of the door for Christian expansion, but he very much feared the "agitation and excitement" and the "consequent tumult, devastation and bloodshed that might follow."[50] Patii was as good as his word. The time scheduled was sunset, but preparations began in the forenoon. Patii ordered his attendants to set fire to the pile of carved wooden images covered with finely braided coconut fiber and ornamented with red feathers. Patii himself tore off the sacred cloth that enveloped them and cast the stripped objects into the fire. As each started crackling in the fire, he addressed it by name and expressed his regret at having worshiped it. At times he turned to the spectators and pointed out the inability of these gods to protect themselves[51] —like an early church apologist.[52] They were human figures, properly carved in this case, not fetish objects. They were thought of personally and with pedigrees.

Excitement was intense but reactions varied. Patii was an important regional priest and controlled an important *marae*. It was here that the iconoclasm took place, so that this desecration terminated both the worship of these idols and the efficacy of the sacred area. It was the most startling thing that had ever happened in Eimeo. It was priestly and religious, not political or chiefly. But it had political repercussions. It is important to note that Pomare II was not the key to this event. Patii had become convinced of the falsehood of his old faith and the truth of the new. If we view the primary sources as a whole we are obliged to accept that.[53] Naturally Pomare II would have approved. Indeed Davies thought this probably saved Patii from the angered pagans of Eimeo.[54]

Patii's announcement had led to the assembly of a huge gathering, most of whom expected to see the gods (as Ellis put it) work "sudden vengeance" on this "sacrilegious criminal." Missionaries and island Christians were also there. Ellis likened it all to the encounter of the Lord of Israel with the prophets of Baal. Psychologically it was. When no immediate penalty fell on Patii, the most hardened pagans were ready to wait Gamaliel-like to see what would come of it. Many were indignant and angry because of the impiety and the widespread influence it would have, and some because their crafts and emoluments would be endangered.

Yet the hostility lay more with the pagan chiefs than with the priests and people, who were impressed. Many in Tahiti and Eimeo not only burnt their idols, but destroyed their maraes, stripped altars, and used the wood for fuel in their kitchens.

> His [Patii's] conduct on the above occasion gave idolatry a stab more deadly than any which it had before received, and inflicted a wound, from which, with all the energy subsequently manifested, it could never recover.[55]

Ellis was writing of the effects in Tahiti and Eimeo. This event took place before the Battle of Bunaauia, when, according to Buck, a "lucky shot" *won* Tahiti for Christianity. From this point many priests lost faith in their old gods and the beginning of the popular movement can be traced. This was not concerned with any world view or esoteric cult. It was a dynamic encounter on the level of popular animism. A number of incidents mentioned in the source material reveal it was spreading widely before Bunaauia.[56]

Patii made a good and effective Christian, and his reformed character and natural capacity for leadership led to his election to an important lay office in the church. From the indigenous scale of values at the time, he had everything to lose by becoming Christian. His conversion can be explained only by its genuineness.

Patii's authority, though considerable, was regional.[57] But he set a pattern for other regional priests. The widespread destruction that followed impressed the populace. Unconverted chiefs and priests were startled, but—finding it easier to deal with commoners than chiefs—commenced to persecute the Christian commoners. Persecution became more bitter. It was clear that sooner or later there would have to be a showdown on a national level between *Oro* and the Christian God.

Once Christianity made inroads into the various strata of society and ceased to be confined to family segments, new conflict patterns developed. There is no doubt about the growth of the Christian community before Bunaauia. The pagans, in derision, coined a name for it: *Bure Atua*. The term brings together the words for "to pray" and "God." Under persecution they had developed their capacity for prayer, and were nicknamed because of it. The converts themselves spoke of themselves as *Haapii parau*, which means learners or disciples.[58] There was thus a clear concept of Christian entity, irrespective of the kinship and status segments which belonged to it. Here is the ecclesia being called out of the pagan world, *and being seen as such* by both pagan and Christian. It was the pagan realization of the growth of this community as an entity that led them to engage in persecution on a wide scale.

The *Bure Atua* had some competent leaders and aggressive evangelists, like Farefau, a Borabora man, who had come as a heathen to Eimeo, been converted there, attended school, and went to evangelize the remote part of Taiarabu—somewhat rash in zeal but an indignant opponent of idolatry.

The resort to plots and persecution is virtually an admission of defeat at spiritual levels. Clearly the pagans feared this dynamic Christianity. Pagan chiefs of Matavai, Hapaiano, and Pare plotted to assassinate every individual of the *Bure Atua*. In order to be certain of their armed strength they invited Atehuru and Papara to join them, though these had been their enemies for years.[59]

A large Christian gathering at Tahiti offered opportunity for massacre, but the plot was discovered an hour or so before the scheduled slaughter, and the Christians embarked immediately for Eimeo. Finding the birds had flown, the armed and enraged pagans blamed each other and renewed old animosities. Tahiti was again in a state of war.

About four hundred persons who had been in two minds about the new religion now left Tahiti and joined the Christians at Eimeo. Again I note that the planned massacre and escape of the Christians is dated July 7, 1815—four months before Buna-auia.[60] In Eimeo the Christians held a day of fasting and prayer. More and more attended the missionary school. In September another thirty-nine people became Christian.

Back in Tahiti the war continued until one party was driven into the mountains. In the uncertain peace that followed, the Christian refugees were invited to return. Pomare II accompanied them to restore them in their lands. A pagan party tried to prevent their landing by firing on them, but received no fire in return. Pomare II succeeded in getting some of them established but the situation was uneasy. This was the situation when the Christians planned a united gathering for worship on Sunday, November 12, 1815.

For some months agitation had been coming from the temple of *Oro*. A prophet had been advocating a war party raiding the Christian community at Eimeo and attacking Pomare II. The planned act of worship, with the gathering of some eight hundred Christians from all social groups, was too good an opportunity for the pagans to miss. Because the *Bure Atua* was gathered together and Pomare II and other Christian chiefs from several islands were with them, the pagans prepared for action. Some of the Christians were well aware of their vulnerability and had come ready for action. Others were unarmed.[61]

Pagan warriors planted themselves round the locality and awaited the commencement of worship. On the reading of the opening hymn a musket was fired. Pomare II demanded the service be held in an orderly fashion. After full pagan rites were performed, the Christians were allowed to complete theirs. Both sides then prepared for battle. Ellis provides us with a full description. His best informant was Auna, a converted Areoi, who had read the hymn at that service. Pomare II stationed his forces with the men of deepest religious conviction at the strategic

points. Auna, Upaparu, and Hitote led the front line (*viri*). The
leaders of the *paparia*, or "cheek" were also recognized leaders
of the *Bure Atua*. The Eimeo Christians formed the *tapono*, or
"shoulder." Pomare II placed his force for the battle according
to his reliance on a man's Christianity. The people all knew full
well what would happen if they lost the battle. Pomare II wanted
men at the key points who were ready to die. A strange army
they made—the chief of Huahine beside the daughter of the
chief of Raiatéa. Pomare II himself took a canoe and attacked
the flank of the enemy from the sea. The battle was fought on
the seafront and contested at every point.[62] The Christians were
victorious.

Once the pagan army realized the battle was lost, they scattered
and fled. Pomare II stopped pursuit, prevented the destruction
of villages and property, and protected the women and children.
However, everything associated with the pagan religion was
destroyed. Symbols and idols were taken to the temple of Oro,
where, together with the temple buildings and altars, they were
publically disposed of by Christians whom Pomare II could trust
in the matter. But not a dwelling house, a fence, a plantation, or
a person was injured in the excitement of that battle aftermath.

Several important factors should be noted now. In the first
place there was the staggering realization that Oro worship was
completely wrecked. The ironwood body of Oro had been carried
off to become a common housepost in Pomare II's kitchen, and
to serve thereafter as a reference point in Christian experience.
What Patii had done on a regional level Pomare II had done on
the national level. The destruction of sacred objects became
fixed as a reference point, as a device for demonstrating that one
was casting away his old fears and faith. All over Tahiti, in the
lesser *marae*, the process was repeated. In cases where political
loyalties were involved, the sacred objects might be handed over
to Pomare II or the missionaries, if there was reason for doing so,
but usually local groups became convinced of the truth and took
the initiative themselves. Such occasions were followed by a day
of fasting and thanksgiving. The pattern became fixed. It was
an indigenous pattern. If the missionaries applauded, they did
not inspire it. Its inspiration came from the psychological necessity of knowing that the old feared forces no longer held power
over them. *Where civilizing had failed, dynamic factors had been*

effective; it is a pattern much used of the Holy Spirit in confronting the spirit forces of animism.

Another factor emerged from the events at Bunaauia and left
the pagans as astonished as did the destruction of the temple of
Oro, which was partly expected as the price of defeat. What
they did not anticipate was the Christian behavior of Pomare II
afterward. They had rebelled. They had humiliated him. They
had every reason to expect from him what they would have done
to him had they been victors. Their motive for war was to
exterminate the *Bure Atua* and Pomare II with it. He frankly
forgave them all, spared their food gardens, their houses, their
wives and children. They now knew what Christianity had done
for Pomare II. He certainly hated Oro, the false god, but he had
forgiven them. For a time they took refuge in forest hideouts
and sent out spies to see what fortune was left for them. Only
after some days could they bring themselves to creep out in small
groups and find it all true.[63] *This discovery started the third and
final people movement toward Christianity*: that among the
enemies of Pomare II. Within a few weeks Tahiti was Christian.

JOHN WILLIAMS, CHURCH-PLANTER

It has been said that Tahiti henceforth became the nucleus of
a web. New missionaries started there, learned the language
and something of the customs; and the Polynesian teachers were
trained there before going out into the hundreds of islands that
surrounded them.

This is true only because there came to these islands a man
who was surely born for the situation: John Williams. He dared
to disagree with his brethren on the pattern of their missioning.
He too was a civilizer, but his civilizing was far more culturally
relevant and was always *conditioned by the practical requirements of the primary motive of planting churches.*[64] He built a
ship of purely local materials, in order to sail to Samoa[65] with the
gospel. He introduced new features into housebuilding, using
local materials with which he had to experiment; burnt coral
lime to make plaster; and taught principles that would help the
people drag heavy logs with less effort. He taught reading and
bookbinding, the books being catechisms and Scripture portions.
In doing this he drew close to the people. None of this was
closely related to commerce and markets.

True, Williams was a civilizer, but this was his lesser motive. He had basic ideas on church-planting. He believed that when an island was evangelized the congregation had a duty to reach out in its own missionary effort. He was annoyed with his brethren, who wished to established themselves at sedentary stations in tiny Christian communities, when heavily populated islands lay just over the horizon without the gospel. This was the motive which inspired his boatbuilding and bookbinding and accounts for the impetuosity with which he forced the L.M.S. into new patterns of missioning. Here is an abbreviated extract from a highly impetuous letter he wrote as a young man of twenty-four to the august personages of the London committee. It was critical of his brethren but contains the philosophical core of his lifework.

> I have given myself wholly to the Lord. . . . I have not another desire but to live and die in the work of my Saviour . . . but I regret that I ever came to these islands. . . . I request, then, a removal. . . .
>
> In the first place—the small population of this island, and the comparatively easy life I am now living. . . . Our settlements . . . consist of from 600 to 1000 persons, and our congregations about the same; and there are at Huahine three missionaries and three at Raiatéa.
>
> I saw in some of your publications that there were 34,000 inhabitants on these islands. . . . There were only 5000 or 6000 . . . in Tahiti, with 8 or 9 missionaries, I naturally expected to find about 28,000 persons in the six leeward islands, and was quite angry with my brethren, . . . for staying to windward when there were so many missionaries and so few people. . . . After two years travelling . . . in these leeward islands . . . I can find . . . about 4000 inhabitants. I know that one soul is of infinite value. But how does the merchant act who goes in search of goodly pearls? Supposing he knows where there is one pearl . . . and at the same time, another spot, where there are thousands of equal value; to which would he direct his way?[66]

One can imagine the effect this would have on the London committee, who, though admitting Christians were made only by baptism of the Holy Spirit, still felt that the motive of missionary work was to "make Christian rulers, and Christian artisans and Christian traders,"[67] or as they stated it to the Tahitians, "to advance religion and civilization."[68] After an official deputation had visited Tahiti, their response to this view that is expressed in

Williams' letter was to state the missionary duty as instructing ordinances, disciplines, and duties (i.e., as pastor of a settled congregation) in terms of civilizing:

> He must show them in what manner they may build better houses, more effective canoes, manufacture domestic furniture, cultivate new crops upon the waste ground, prepare soil, sugar, tobacco, cotton, &c., for use and for commerce. In a word, it rests with the minister of religion to form anew the character. . . .[69]

This official statement required mission stations, sedentary labor for the missionary, supervision of agriculture, and manufacturing. One of the matters attended to by the visiting deputationists was the acquisition of a new site for a cotton factory. We can imagine the effect of Williams' appeal on them at the time when he advocated that the three missionary societies in the Pacific cooperate and acquire a vessel for the specific purpose of spreading the gospel farther and farther afield, and penetrating the largest islands, even as far as Melanesia. He had pressed for this in an earlier letter:

> We must branch out to the right and to the left; for how can we, in justice to the heathen world, especially to the surrounding islands, confine the labours of so many missionaries to so few people?[70]

Here was an impetuous young man. The impetuosity of his faith made problems for the London committee, but it made great conquests for the kingdom of God. He himself was not to be held back from those "large places, numerously inhabited" which were to him a "great and effectual door for the gospel." It was to deal with this matter that he built himself the vessel *Messenger of Peace*. It was in obedience to this heavenly vision that he gave his life eventually in Melanesia away on the other side of the Pacific from his starting point.[71]

In reality it was Raiatéa, rather than Tahiti, that was the nucleus of the web of growth. Significantly this was also the nucleus from which the early Polynesian migrations appear to have fanned out.[72] It was certainly the Raiatéa congregation that became the Polynesian sending church, and long before he had a ship of his own Williams insisted that they see themselves in this light. This was part of the genius of Williams' plans: they allowed for an island congregation sending out island evangelists.

On the schooner *Endeavour* in 1823 he started correctly with his island workers, laying down for them a set of rules, with a theological preamble—four points, thoroughly biblical:

1. You are chosen by the Church at Raiatéa (Cf. Antioch)
2. You go to the land to which God leads you (Cf. "the place which the Lord, thy God, shall choose")
3. Christ himself promises to be with you to the end (The Great Commission)
4. What his power has done for Raiatéa, and in your hearts, will be done for others in the lands to which you go (Cf. "unto Samaria and to the uttermost parts")[73]

Then he outlined their practical program, all couched in terms of biblical theology, and in this faith the Polynesian agents went forth.

As they went forth, Williams wrote to his directors:

> I now propose to visit the islands between this and New Caledonia, and to carry as many native teachers as we can. . . . The field is large—the opportunity favourable.[74]

With this the directors were left behind. Williams' sails filled with the winds of faith. The vision and the initiative were his; but he could never have achieved his purpose had it not been for the readiness of the young church and its servants to respond. Church-planting on a large scale had begun.

The day was to come when the representatives of the L.M.S. were to admit from the platform that they had been wrong about civilizing and to have their admissions published under the caption "Wrong Ideas in Evangelism."[75] Williams' criterion had been *relevance*: boats, buildings, food supply, bookbinding. He avoided the commercial type of civilizing because on his arrival he found himself hopelessly involved in it, in priorities that were, to him, all wrong. He was thus a convert from the method, having fought out his position between 1821 and 1823. He set down his views in this way:

> A missionary was never designed by Jesus to get a congregation of a hundred or two natives and sit down at ease as contented as if every sinner was converted, while thousands around him are eating each other's flesh . . . and dying without knowledge of the gospel. . . . For my own part I cannot content myself within the narrow limits of a single reef.[76]

Once Williams, with the help of the people of Raiatéa, had determined on a course of expansion, we may ask, What was the pattern of that expansion?

Approach to a new people was always made through their chief within their own culture pattern. Williams would visit the chief, pay his respects, request permission to leave a teacher under his protection, and then some time later he would return to see how the teacher had fared and whether or not the church had begun to grow. Pages could be written of the splendid service of these island pioneers, their devotion, bravery, and personal sufferings. In the last century these narratives made a dramatic appeal for missionary promotion. The men were effective advocates of the gospel to the fringe of the culture area, where the basic Polynesian language was used. Beyond that they began to meet problems of communication.[77]

The threads of the web made an ethnic net. There was a sameness about the acceptance of the gospel in island after island through this indigenous advocacy. Thus, for instance, Williams took Makea, chief of the Rarotonga, with him to Samoa. There Makea told his experience and what Christianity had done for his homeland: wars had ceased, Scriptures were printed and read, and the people were happy. Something of the happiness of Makea was transmitted to Samoa.[78] Williams recognized that it was not in the civilization from the West but in the inherent capacity to civilize from within their own frames of reference that the important factors lay—the way of peace, the Book to read, and happiness to discover in their own life setting, to use Makea's own points. If things were to be changed the changes ought to be relevant. For instance, many missionaries, with their disciplinary patterns, never discovered the meaning of *relevance* across these cultural frameworks. Many; I did not say all.

The pattern of church-growing was status-conditioned. Status, in such societies, does not mean aspiration to rank; it means knowing one's role. To know what one is, where one belongs, what is expected as one's duty in the group, means mental and social security in island society. To be dragged out of one's place as an individual who has to accept foreign ways and controls, so that he is unanchored and alone, is to lose status. Hence, though people always make individual decisions, they tend to register them in groups. Small or extensive people movements appeared; people would be brought into the congregation in groups, prepared for baptism in groups, prepared for communion in groups. Within the fellowship itself they were classified in groups—adherents, catechumens, members, and so on—on a basis of experience. This status pattern was acceptable on the personal and community level.

In the L.M.S. pattern in Polynesia the movement would gain momentum until it reached a degree of strength and solidarity, under the guidance of a Polynesian teacher. At this point the group would be given a higher status, namely as a full-status congregation with a European missionary as pastor. This was not the policy of other Protestant missions in Oceania and I make a point of stressing the peculiarity. The idea of the appointment of a European, as it was often conceived, as "a reward for good growth" had serious dangers. It was a move toward foreign control and away from indigenousness. May I cite here a single example, for which the statistical data is available: the case of Mangaia.

> A Polynesian teacher has been placed at Oneroa, Mangaia, in 1823. According to pattern a small people-movement developed and after two decades a church of some strength had grown.
>
> The total population of Oneroa was 2000. Polynesian teachers provided schools and teaching for 900 children and young people. 360 adults came into membership. Another 306 were under instruction to this end. Of the remaining 434, some would be infants. There had been 45 infant and 4 adult baptisms that year. The people-movement had slowed down, the congregation was being organizationally consolidated.
>
> This strength was considered adequate to warrant the appointment of a missionary to Mangaia and when he arrived in 1845 the total population of the whole island (not just Oneroa) was 3567, of whom 500 were in full communion and 600 in adult classes for instruction. If we eliminate the 2236 young persons we have a remainder of 1331, from which we subtract the 500 and 600. In the whole island only 231 persons are thus seen to be still pagan. Thus when the discipling of Mangaia was 83% completed a missionary was appointed.[79]

This case illustrates the relative roles of European missionary and Polynesian teacher. In McGavran's terminology the latter were "discipling," the former "perfecting." The task of the missionary was civilizing, character-building, consolidating. Williams' personal policy was for self-propagation of island churches, and he himself supported them. But the structure of the L.M.S. work was against him, and the sequence in congregational status from a Polynesian evangelist to a Western pastor did not help a really indigenous church to develop.

The battle of missionary theory between Williams and his principals over a century ago is not finished yet, though there is a more widespread awareness of its problems. Today we see clearly that where missionaries take over cross-cultural pastorates they frequently close the opening for indigenous leadership and bring about a dependent church. Educational and medical workers can do the same. Every branch of Christian work must produce its own leaders or an attitude of dependence will be built-in. In other words: It leads to static rather than dynamic churches.

We now turn to a critical analysis of some of these problems that emerged in Polynesia after the initial people movements. I call them *problems of consummation*. This presupposes that though the people movement is a good and effective means of discipling, the process is not an end in itself. It requires a follow-up program, as Wesley pointed out after good responses to his evangelism.

Problems of Consummation

The missionaries frankly admitted the superiority of Polynesian agents for breaking new ground and bringing paganism into confrontation with Christ.[80] They accepted people movements per se. The Polynesian capacity for this should also indicate a capacity for pastoral leadership, but opportunities were not adequately provided partly because of the mission system, and partly because education for civilization was still required after conversion.

Nor does one find any reference in the source material available to a spiritual consummating movement. If one took place, the missionaries did not report it. Their perfecting of converts was of a *disciplinary* rather than an *experiential* character. In this Tahiti stands in contrast with Tonga, at the other end of the culture area.

Statistical evidence also demands a probe, because it reveals a huge disparity between the *worshiping community* and the *communicant membership*. This is out of all proportion with other Oceanic patterns. In the Hervey Islands group, after thirty-five years of church growth, only 1,200 of the 11,000 worshipers were communicants. At the same point of time after twenty-six years of church growth in Samoa, when 33,000 were at worship, only 2,000 were communicants.[81] Of 15,000 recorded at worship in Tahiti, only 2,100 had accepted full commitment. Thus at a point of time very soon after midcentury, four decades after the first convert, when the Polynesian web showed 81,000 islanders at worship, only 5,500 had committed themselves fully—less than 7 percent of professing Christians.[82]

At the same time the total Protestant population in the Pacific for all mission fields was 239,900, of whom 45,929 were recorded as communicants—an average of almost 20 percent, in spite of the drag of Polynesia to the east. If we separate the two areas, the 7 percent for the area we are discussing is set against 25 percent for the remainder of the Pacific.[83] We are forced to admit that even after leaving a margin for unaccountable factors, the growth on the "perfecting" level seems to have been defective—and this in spite of European pastorates.

The slowness with which converts were brought to baptism has not escaped criticism. It seems remarkable, for instance, that the man whose personal conviction encouraged him to eat the sacred turtle without pagan rites, and to do it alone, should have been kept waiting seven years for baptism.[84] Or to pass from Tahiti to Samoa (date, 1840)—when a decade of solid people movement had brought some 40,000 out of paganism and under Christian teaching—only 200 of the 40,000 were admitted to the Lord's table, even though there were 718 adult baptisms that year and 20,000 had learned to read.[85] Even by the Eastern Polynesian scale this is mighty small. It shows people being kept "on trial" for over a decade. My natural impulse was to distrust the figures, but it must be admitted that they do reflect the situation.

Joseph King, missionary historian of half a century ago, wrote of Polynesia:

> The Protestant missionary societies of Oceania have not made the profession of faith easy, but the reverse. The approaches to the communion table have been fenced by tests of knowledge and periods of probation.[86]

To turn from physical statistics to the written record of missionary experiences, I wish to discuss two references, one positive and the other negative, which may throw some light on the situation in Tahiti itself.

In the summer of 1835, after almost four decades of his faithful service, Henry Nott (one of the original party of the *Duff*) reported a revival at Papara, Tahiti. It was a revival in the real sense of the word, among people who had been discipled twenty years earlier. Folk came in small groups: twos, fours, sixes. Then larger parties: tens and twenties and one of thirty. They came in waves of genuine repentance. They were not tribal or family groups, but loosely held sodalities on a basis of sex and age. They were individual decisions that should have suited any Westerner. Nott was so impressed with the unusual event that he thought it worth recording that the repentance took place among three types of persons:

1. those who had never made more than a nominal profession when they abandoned heathenism, having gained some communal satisfaction but never having had the decision translated into a real spiritual experience;

2. those who had been baptized as children for training, and who, now in their teen ages, had come face to face with their own sin and wanted to register personal decision; and

3. those of the first group who had been disciplined for behaviour—"back-sliders under repentance," as their Wesleyan brethren would have said.

Nott organized them into classes and dealt with them according to their needs.[87]

In other parts of the Pacific there are many records of missionaries striving for a second work of grace, a consummation of the people movement. They even spoke of two conversions. They were never satisfied that the people movement merely required instructions and discipline to complete it. They sought a dynamic experience, even to the "penitent form." In this book we will meet this in the case of Tonga. The fact that Nott felt he had to analyze the experience of 1835 suggests that it was something new to him. That there had been no recorded consummation movement in Tahiti for twenty years is remarkable, because they were a praying people. However their available scripture portions were few and this would have hindered the personal exploration of their religion. Some of their civilizing was rather secular, and religion itself was legal and formal and its norms were generally Western.

If there is no positive consummation movement, it is always possible for a group negative movement to emerge in any generation not confronted with personal commitment. Many Cargo Cults and other nativistic movements can be partly attributed to this. Situations which lead to nativistic movements are usually also situations open for revival, provided the Christian forces act before the neopagan. Such movements go back a long way in history.

About the same time as the Tahiti revival,[88] missionary reports from Borabora indicated such negative movements at Maupiti— "dangerous and visionary heresies"—from 1831 to 1833.[89] It was played down in the promotional reports.[90] There had been signs of trouble in Tahiti in 1826 but the chiefs, missionaries, and church leaders had kept it under control. The prophets of the movement moved to Maupiti where there was no resident missionary, and there they developed a full-scale nativistic cult, syncretistic and millenarian. They practiced Christian rites but organized immoral exercises as a reaction against Puritan legalism. They claimed the inspiration of Peter, Paul, and Mary and induced spirit-possession. This movement, known as the Mamaia sect, had a moral, theological, and prophetic structure, fortified by some elements of pre-Christian tradition. At each of these points it was a rejection of foreign norms and authority. Psychologically it was a cry for the prophetic voice in a religion which seemed dominantly ethical, with its highest values in terms of industry.

In reality the missionaries were men of prayer and faith, but they had never demonstrated a conviction that they were concerned most for the saving of souls. No doubt they were—otherwise they would not have been in the islands—but the impression they created throughout was that their highest priority was the care for and cultivation of the land, production of good crops and the establishment of markets. One or two of them were aware of the difficulties of changing to "manners and modes of civilized life"[91] and a few found it hard to be "confined within a single reef," but none seem to have realized that their own personal habits were interpreted as *their real values*. They stayed within the reefs too much, plastering houses, cultivating tobacco, spinning cotton, and crushing sugar; so much so that two of them were able to make one thousand pounds in eight months by trading,[92] a huge sum in those days. They had been fifteen or sixteen years in the group and had attempted no serious Scripture translation. The *missionary value system* was seen in terms of hard work and profit-making. It was reinforced by a severe policy of discipline on the basis of a legal code and perfectionist standards which denied the means of grace to most ordinary Christians. The Mamaia sect rejected all this and swung to the opposite extreme of drunkenness, open fornication, and emotional enthusiasm.

In passing we note how white missionaries are themselves appraised by what they do, what they give their time to, and what they appear to set value on. This is why to this day in the outworking of missionary activity in agriculture, medicine, education, and social relief, we should not create the impression that these are the supreme motive. They are the fruit of the gospel, but not the gospel itself. In fairness to the Tahiti missionaries, however, we should remember that they represented the views of the church at large in their day, and of their directors in particular. The official deputationists, Tyerman and Bennet, had thoroughly approved of the legal system of Tahiti.[93]

The *Journal* of the deputation contains valuable observations but findings are weighted by theoretical preconceptions, thereby offending against Durkheim's first corollary of sociological method.[94] The basic presupposition is that evangelism must be by civilizing. Recognizing the genuineness and value of the people movements into the church, they yet stressed the need for civilizing. "The *profession* of Christianity is *not* Christianity, however happily influential in restraining evil" [Italics theirs]. They saw in "the improved character of the whole people and the regenerated character of a great many" (a neat distinction) that the missionary role should continue to be that of a sedentary civilizer.[95] They attributed the Tahitians' long resistance to Christianity to their authoritarian control under an alliance of chieftaincy and priesthood; and in describing this obstruction they spoke of the missionaries' *evangelistic work*.[96] Yet during that unresponsive period there had been no Scripture translation, no preaching to speak of, and virtually no missionary itineration. Working in the expectation of a slow response, the gospel had not been presented as an appeal for decision. They had taught some craftwork, a little reading and writing, cultivation of the soil, and some new housebuilding techniques. There had been the good example of the missionaries' own Christian lives, their diligence in prayer and religious discipline. But not until Oito and his comrades moved toward Christianity of their own volition was any real opportunity for decision presented.

The deputationists projected this concept of evangelism into their ideas of follow-up. When Williams was pressing for expansion, they insisted that the missionary role was still sedentary and civilizing: better housing, better crops, better furniture, and better markets.[97] Settled civil government was essential for this and for an acceptance of moral standards and relationships. Therefore they approved the new law code. The Mamaia sect was a vigorous opposition to this new law. Why?

The acceptance of codified law per se created no problem. The old way had been determined by oral laws that had some down through the centuries. As Tahiti was coming into a day of reading and writing, it was good to have a written law. The changes brought about by whalers, sealers, bêche-de-mer traders, and sandalwooders required a statement of what should and should not be allowed, and most of the criticisms of missions at the time came from seamen who found their license curtailed by such laws. The acceptance of Christianity provided the opportunity for dealing with the problem, and the Tahitians themselves were desirous of having a law code to fix their standards under the new religion. It is therefore important to note that the nativistic resistance was not against law as such, but against the particular contents of this law.

The missionaries considered law-giving to be part of the civilizing process, and had Israel under Moses and the Kingdom of God under the Lord's Sermon on the Mount as biblical precedents. They greatly influenced these particular laws but it is not quite correct to use the popular jibe of "missionary laws." The laws were accepted culturally by the people in a symbolic ceremony under the direction of the chiefs. The missionaries did not draw up the laws but were present in consultation with those who did. The final product of the consultation of chiefs was presented by the "king" in a public assembly of the people for their acceptance. This procedure was observed first in Tahiti, then in Raiatéa and elsewhere.[98] The chiefs and people sat in assembly according to the social structure, the southern Tahitians under Tati; the people of Teorapaa with Utami; those of Eimeo with Arahu; and those of Taiarabu with Veve. The "king" formally asked each chief in turn what he desired. Each replied that he wanted the new laws.

The laws were then read, and each chief assented. The "king" then addressed the people and asked if they were willing to obey. They signified this by raising their hands. The articles were passed and approved.[99] This can hardly be called a missionary imposition, as is sometimes done. There was no objection to law per se or to the mode of its establishment. Even the contents of the laws were approved by the people, although it was here that trouble arose. We must remember that the influences of some traders, sailors, and fugitives from justice in these islands had been very bad. They had hindered the missionary work and some of the laws were intended to deal with their influences. The laws were indeed Puritan in character, yet some scientific observers, like Charles Darwin, were quite impressed by what they saw.[100]

However, law is never a substitute for spiritual experience. The root of the trouble lay in the fact that the people movements to Christianity had never been consummated. There were enough regenerated people to have been set working for a general deepening of experience; but there was a tendency to rely on discipline and laws, and these were tightly held by missionaries supported by chiefs and judges—a select circle. The deputationists had said that the acceptance of Christianity had been resisted by a united authority of chiefs and priests. In point of fact the situation remained exactly the same. The missionaries had taken the place of the indigenous priesthood. Those who had lost their role in society had the choice of becoming church agents under the foreign missionaries or sitting idle at the fringe. We do not wonder therefore that this nativistic movement should commence on the fringe of the Tahiti congregation and come from men who, in their pre-Christian days, had belonged to the priestly segment of society. Under Christian discipline they had never made the grade spiritually according to perfectionist standards and were obliged to remain at the fringe. They had indeed been disciplined by the circle of chiefs and indigenous judges in Tahiti before their moving to Maupiti.[101]

By way of contrast, the people of Raiatéa, under Williams the church-planter, responded to his leading and became the Antioch of Eastern Polynesia; while the Tahiti church formed into parties along family cleavages. Neither civilizing nor discipline will build a church, because they have not the supreme value or concern. A vision "beyond the reef," a daring to build a ship, a readiness to go forth, a dedicated haste to get the Scriptures into the vernacular, and to distribute them in ceaseless itineration, and a stress that every regenerated Christian should be involved in evangelism—these stresses show a different supreme value. It was from this Raiatéa value—not from the official civilizing and disciplining pattern—that the church grew in Polynesia. This type of concern at Raiatéa prepares the way for Pentecost. Graduation into Christianity by civilizing does not do this. The great tragedy of this chapter is that the policy could have been changed in 1823, but those who could have changed it had preconceived notions that were set. Wise after the event, we learn from Tahiti how missionaries transmit unintended values. All social projects, however noble, must be prevented from creating the impression that they are themselves the supreme concern. Our supreme concern is to win men for Christ.

2

THE MAORI WEB

ANGLICAN MISSIONS entered the Pacific by way of Australia and New Zealand. William Wilberforce, who fought the slave trade and worked for the establishment of the British and Foreign Bible Society, persuaded Pitt to establish a chaplaincy for the convict settlement in New South Wales. When the vacancy came in 1793, it was Wilberforce again who persuaded Samuel Marsden to accept the undesirable post. Marsden set up his homestead and model farm at Parramatta, in Australia. The farms of the freed convicts were badly run, so Marsden established a pilot project in farm development and soil husbanding. He promised hope to released convicts. In England he had some contact with wool spinning and weaving, and he recognized the fine quality of Australian wool. After fourteen years he took samples to England, had them washed and spun, and displayed them for the trade and Colonial Office. At the same time he pressed that more convict sentences be remitted, and that released persons receive land grants and be encouraged in farming. He also advocated the sending of mechanics and skilled labor as free citizens to join them, so that a self-supporting colony might be established.

Because of his effective advocacy he returned to Australia with superior breed sheep and by 1811 was able to send five thousand pounds of fine wool to England. A new trade and a new experiment in civilizing had begun. That trade meant more than money; broken lives were rehabilitated and convicts became citizens. Citizens soon required schools. Marsden was grappling with problems of a peculiar colonial environment. One feature that complicated that environment for the chaplain was the fact that Sydney became the major base for South Pacific trade, especially whaling. Many whalers recruited Maoris from New Zealand and brought them in great numbers to Port Jackson.

Marsden welcomed and housed them at Parramatta in special quarters he had set up. Sometimes there were as many as thirty at a time while their boats were in port. Among these contacts was a Maori chief, Ruatara, who was impressed with both Marsden's farming and his Christianity. Ruatara had seen the unseemly side of the white man's influence on his country: arms and ammunition, liquor and disease. He now felt there was another side that might interest his people. Thus it came about that, despite the bad racial tension through the *Boyd* massacre at the time, the chaplain bought a ship (*Active*) and, with horses, sheep, cattle, poultry and the gospel, went to New Zealand. He landed on Christmas Day, 1814, and addressed the people on the text, "Behold, I bring you good tidings of great joy," with Ruatara translating. The *chaplaincy* was expanding into *mission*.

In twenty-three years Marsden made seven visits to New Zealand, exploring, making contacts, opening and supervising missions, fighting the white man trade in arms, and generally building up good relationships. He is known in history as a pioneer, a preacher, a pastor, and a peacemaker. He had some worthy helpers, one a Maori who helped him with the language.

ANGLICAN PEOPLE MOVEMENTS

Thus the work of the Church Missionary Society (henceforth C.M.S.) began in New Zealand. The first station was established at Rangihoua, on the northwest side of the Bay of Islands. Here the first missionaries suffered many privations and undoubtedly could not have lived through the first fruitless decade had it not been for a few influential chiefs who protected them. One of these was the bloodthirsty Hongi,[1] who had been to England, and another was Ruatara. As with Cyrus of Persia, the Lord girded them, though they knew Him not (Is 45:5). New missionaries arrived and new stations were opened round the bay and to the north. Schools were set up but there was little response to the offer of instruction. As we have seen with the L.M.S. in Tahiti, Marsden was an advocate of the policy of evangelization by civilizing. He had demanded for his mission three mechanics: a joiner, a shoemaker, and a smith. The latter being unavailable, his principals sent a schoolmaster who had farming experience.[2] Marsden himself expressed the theory thus:

> Nothing, in my opinion, can pave the way for the introduction of the Gospel but civilization—and that can only be accomplished among the heathen by the arts. . . . The arts and religion should go together. Till their attention is gained and moral and industrious habits are induced, little or no progress can be made in teaching them the Gospel. . . .

And to this statement the C.M.S. historian has added:

> Marsden and the Society were to learn the fallacy of this by hard experience, and it was the New Zealand Mission that was to teach them.[3]

By 1820 the "arts of life" were progressing: wheat harvests were good; horses and cattle prospered; fruit trees were growing well; blacksmith shops, saw-pits, and rope walks were busy—but as yet there was no sign of any conversion. However there had been success in Tahiti by this time, and Marsden was encouraged to continue with his policy.

The appointment of Henry Williams (who had served as an officer in the navy and subsequently had ministerial training and was ordained under the new Colonial Service Act) was an innovation for Pacific missions. It sets the date of 1822 as the point when British missionary policy-makers first recognized their doubts about evangelizing by civilizing. They had watched the L.M.S. work with concern, and had been influenced by the ideas of John Williams of that society. He was just becoming missionary "table-talk" at that time, but had not yet proved his case. Henry Williams received his instructions in these terms:

> It is the great and ultimate purpose of this Mission to bring the noble but benighted race of New Zealanders into the enjoyment of the light and freedom of the Gospel. *To this grand end all the Society's measures are subordinate.* . . . Go forth . . . having no secular object in view, but desirous of bringing glory to God by advancing the Kingdom of His Son [italics theirs].[4]

This important instruction commissioned Henry Williams to a specific itinerant evangel at the expense of a sedentary civilizing station. The C.M.S. policy-makers by no means abandoned civilizing[5] but they safeguarded their ultimate goal by specific provision for itinerant evangelism.

In 1824 the chief, Waitangi, was converted and baptized as Rangi. His conversion led to others within a confined social unit at Paihia, where Henry Williams had been for only one year. By 1831 the cause had grown, twenty adults and ten children having been baptized—individual conversions but within family units.[6] The tendency toward growth was continually obstructed by bad relations between Maoris and the crews of vessels. It says much for the authority of the sympathetic chiefs that they were able to protect the missionaries at all.

Henry Williams was joined by his brother, William, in 1826. They were to be united in this work for forty years.

In 1827 a supply of Maori books, printed in Sydney, arrived. These included Scripture portions, prayers, and hymns.

The friendly Maoris had succeeded in their protective role only by keeping the missionaries confined to the coastal strip. Every attempt to itinerate had been frustrated until the missionaries had effectively established their character as friends, unlike many whites who had come in the same way by sea. In 1830 they were permitted to cross into the Waimate area, which opened to them a strip of forest interior with a series of villages along a thirty-five mile bush track. The population of these villages ranged from one hundred and fifty to two hundred persons each. In many cases their chiefs agreed to the holding of Sunday services and, during the week, instruction classes. This was the beginning of itinerancy.[7]

Henry Williams planned the extension of the mission from the Bay of Islands to Waimate and Kaitaia in the north, the Hot Lakes District, the Waikato River, and the Bay of Plenty. William Williams moved to Turanga, Poverty Bay, and another post was opened at Otaki in the south.[8] Some of these extensions were due to the zeal of Maori converts. The movement toward Christianity preceded the missionary thrusts. Quite often the evangelist was a Maori. Young converts were used from the beginning and often, as at Kaitaia (1834), the church spread because of "the earnest solicitation of the chiefs and people" (in this case of the Rarawa tribes in the vicinity of North Cape). After two decades in this area, known later as the northern district, 624 converts had come into full status as communicants. In the year 1853, at which point we have good statistical data,[9] 136 adult baptisms were recorded, showing the people movement into

Christianity had not yet run out. The power of the movement was in the interior villages rather than along the more acculturated coastline.[10]

The movement spread from the north through the central area into the east and west, and the missionaries organized it into fourteen areas. By 1839 they recorded 8,760 as attending regular worship. Of these 233 had been accepted as communicants. The New Testament was available in the vernacular. Then in a letter dated May 5, 1840, William Williams wrote "the population *as a body* professed Christianity [italics his]." Statistics of those at worship rose from 8,760 to 27,000, and full communicants from 233 to almost 2,000.[11] Four months later, writing of the Eastern District alone (one year after its commencement) he said "almost all the people are enquiring after the truth" and "more than 8,000 assemble regularly for worship."[12] This strong people movement was at its full tide when the first bishop arrived, so that he was able to commence immediately with his plans for development. He had advantages over most pioneer bishops at this point and recognized it: "I seem to see a nation born in a day." Half a century later Bishop Stuart cited these words at the London Conference as

> the testimony of Bishop [G. A.] Selwyn, who, after other men had laboured, came to enter into their labours; that was his generous and honourable testimony to the work he found had been done.[13]

The growth of the church in the eastern district was rapid from the outset. An increase of 878 *at the communicant level* in one year at such an early stage is remarkable, and in extreme contrast with the situation in Tahiti. But here again we find numerous references to "a large proportion of the leading chiefs," so that the people movement was at the classical Polynesian level of intellectual acceptance of the Christian world view as the consummation of Io worship, as well as that of popular animism. We will examine this in a moment.

In the western district also we note the role of the chiefs in the spread of the church. Indeed one elder, a noted warrior from a distant island in Cook Strait, sent his two sons on a five-hundred mile journey for instruction. They reported that the Christians had been observing Sunday, with church form, prayers, and hymns in the worship services. A Maori, Matahau, had gone

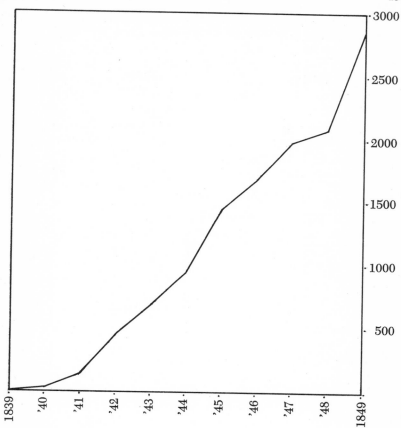

Statistical effect of systematic instruction of converts. This was a relatively new area with only 29 communicants in 1840, 133 the following year, and thereafter between 300 and 400 were added annually for a decade. The progression, however, could have been geometric rather than just arithmetic. Four years later a survey showed four missionaries in this area, doing evangelistic and pastoral work rather than civilizing. Their adult baptismal intake was four times as many per worker as in any other part of the C.M.S. area. This district had only 13 percent of the available staff, but 40 percent of the adult baptisms and nearly 60 percent of communicants. Deployment of personnel might well have produced a remarkable graph of communicant growth that would have stood by the church in the difficult days ahead.

Pl. 3. Regularity in communicant growth in New Zealand, eastern district, 1839-49 (C.M.S. statistics).

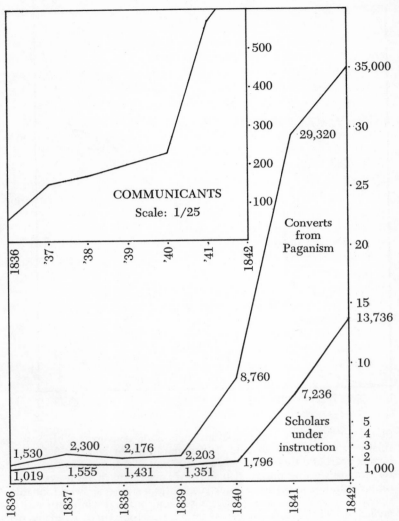

These C.M.S. statistics reflect the character of the early stage of the people movement. The similarity of pattern in the line graphs, converts, instruction, and reception as communicants reveals operational consistency, but the scale of the inset is 1/25, so that only 2 percent of converts were admitted to the Lord's supper in six years.

Pl. 4. C.M.S. growth among the Maoris before the arrival of Selwyn (1836–1842).

there of his own accord and preached the gospel and now the whole island desired a teacher. There are many such reports.

In view of the extreme rapidity of the intake one must comment on the quality of this conversion. The conversions from the pagan system to the Christian system were quite genuine; but the missionaries did not claim moral perfection for their converts. However they did demand sound evidence of spiritual conviction and experience before accepting them as communicants. We may honestly say of both the Anglicans and the Wesleyans (of whom more shortly) that they recognized the two levels and demanded sincerity at both.[14] Their standards for admission to full status were high, but they opened the door wide to all who were prepared to take that important and fearful step of putting away their ancestral gods—the most dramatic thing they had hitherto done in their lives.[15] Bishop G. A. Selwyn appraised the formal change from heathenism to Christianity, as he saw it going on before his eyes, as "an essential change in all their moral habits." The whole land was open to the gospel. He saw also that this situation called for theological and normal training for indigenous workers, and he established institutions for this purpose.[16]

One of the earliest trainees of the teaching institution was sent to the Otaki tribe, most famed for its vicious cannibalism prior to their acceptance of Christianity. They demonstrated the practical application of their new faith by erecting a fine church in the best forest timbers. The furniture was expertly carved in their own craft style, that their crafts might be dedicated to the God of their new experience. With the church went a school. Apart from some guidance on structural matters from an English carpenter, it was entirely Maori work. With the exception of a 30 percent government subsidy for materials that had to be bought for cash for the school, the project was financed by the people themselves. These new Christians were self-supporting from the start, and before long were prosperous farmers, owning their own plows, horses, cattle, pastures, potatoes, and wheat. These things came not as the road *to* the gospel but as the road *from* it.[17]

Forty years after Marsden's visit (or about two decades after the people movement began), the C.M.S. had an organized church with twenty-one stations scattered over four districts,

designated respectively northern, middle, eastern, and western.
Over all, some 50,000 had turned from their old beliefs. Of these,
7,027 were full communicants. Growth from the pagan community was for a period at the rate of a thousand adult baptisms
a year. Ministerial and lay missionaries numbered thirty-one,
and viewing the situation in retrospect on a basis of reports and
statistics, and admitting it is easier to be wise after the event,
we see they might have been more strategically distributed. The
greatest opportunities for growth at the time lay in the eastern
district, but the missionaries were strongly concentrated in the
two older areas, middle and northern. The deployment of staff
to areas of opening opportunity was too slow. The growth was
fast and spontaneous, but it needed shepherding. Strategic redis-
tribution of personnel about 1853 might well have saved a great
deal of trouble a decade later.

THE SOCIAL STRUCTURE OF MAORI PEOPLE MOVEMENTS

The Maori people movements into Christianity took place within a specific cultural matrix which, for purposes of analysis, we
may break down into three units: the segmented character of
society, the widespread network of intercommunications, and the
structure of pre-Christian religious thought.

There are so many references in the early records to the growth
of Christianity among chiefs and slaves, and so often are these
two thrown into contrast, that we are liable to think that as long
as we make the distinction between them this is enough for an
understanding of the situation. In the first place we have to see
the chiefs as a class of persons, not individual heads of tribes.
As long as the tribe continues, the chiefly class is a stable entity,
but it is only one of several stable strata. Slaves come and go,
are an unstable group, dispensable according to the situation
at any time, and may or may not include born chiefs. When confronted by the gospel, the psychology and motivations of these
two groups were two very different things.

The Maori chiefs were frequently prime movers or initiators
in church-planting and growth. When only three or four converts were mentioned they were frequently chiefs. To cite a pair
of quite typical references, Yate recorded (May 4, 1834) that he
"baptized four chiefs and several other persons" and again on
June 8, that he "baptized thirty-eight adults, the greater portion

of them chiefs." They had passed through a long course of instruction, were baptized, and later received as communicants. The chiefly group, as Marsden discovered, was always ready for discussion and the missionaries made good use of this cultural institution.[18] Here radical views could be presented and discussed without fear, so that individual opinions were formed and often group action emerged in time. There is some reason for believing that the possibility of the Christian world view being the consummation of the world view of Io worship was long argued in these chiefly conclaves. Certainly the references to the movement toward Christianity in the chiefly caste suggests conversion not from popular animism but from the rational, classical Polynesian esoteric cult.

Slaves did not belong to the lowest class. They had no class at all, no status, no assembly, no rights. If ever they were able to meet together they would ceremonially lament their captivity and mutilate their bodies as for mourning.[19] They were mostly prisoners taken in war, who happened to have escaped being eaten on the battlefield. When slaves were in short supply, war was made on weaker tribes to replenish stocks; but there was no organized slave system as in classical nations. They could be used for almost any purpose and were degraded and insulted.[20] Fortunate slaves were used for menial service or sold to other tribes for labor. They could be killed as retaliatory satisfaction, or sacrificed on the death of a chief (to go as servant-spirits with him into the afterlife). One can understand the humiliation of this experience to a captured chief. There are also numerous references to them being used merely to satisfy the hunger of a cannibal chief.[21] They were also used in war sacrificial ceremonies.[22] In the enemy locality a wild hope of escape was slight. The conversion of the chiefs changed all this. From the death of Hongi, the use of slaves for a funerary sacrifice was discontinued over a wide area.[23] Widespread manumission shows that Christianity was taking root. With the slaves it was a freedom movement, and a complex one. Many freed slaves made their way home southward and were thus a factor in the spread of the good news.

I have said that Maori society was not a simple dichotomy of master and slave at the time Christianity was injected into it. Some dexterity is required in reconstructing the pattern. The two main classes were chiefs—*rangatira*—and commoners—*ware* or *tutua*—though the latter had "a more depreciatory meaning than the English word." The anthropologist Buck, himself a Maori, admits this is difficult to understand since they came from a common ancestor, but accounts for it because "rank and leadership went by primogeniture in senior families and purity of descent was jealously guarded by selection in marriage."[24] Junior members could only rise in status by marrying above them, and there were social pressures against this; or by opening new lands and forming new tribes. Both procedures had limited possibilities. The craft priests (*tohunga*) were not a separate class but mostly were also chiefs (*rangatira*), though they had a specific role within that group. There was, however, a stratum still more menial than that of the commoners. There were the legitimate servants (*pononga*), who must be distinguished from the slaves (*taurekareka*), war captives of whom we have already spoken. The commoners and servants had a different level of religion from the chiefs. They represented a substructure of popular animism. I feel confident that there was also a movement among these two groups. The evidence is implied rather than direct. It falls in line with other parts of Southern Polynesia, as a popular-level power encounter, distinct from the intellectual movement among the chiefs and priests and the freedom movement among the slaves. Missionary statistics can hardly be explained otherwise, for the Io cult was inaccessible to any but chiefs. Among the Maoris, as in Tahiti, social segmentation figured prominently in the configurations of conversion to Christianity, and each segment had its independent motivation and rationale.[25] This shows that what may seem to a casual observer of the statistics to be a "mass movement" is nothing of the kind. It comprises a configuration of independent and interacting segments, each multi-individual. It has something important to say to us today—that group movements, either into or out of the church, have their social structure that must be understood.

Although the Polynesian people present strong evidence of racial solidarity, there are physical facts that reveal segmentation within that totality. They have sprung from many migration movements and, according to Buck,[26] blood types and skull measurements suggest something of this segmentation. When his argument of the distribution of longheaded and broadheaded types is set beside tribal traditions and historical records, there is a possible cohesion of evidence that at least deserves consideration. An ancient invasion of Tahiti by Raiatéans, which forced the Manahune back into the upper mountain valleys, is supposedly confirmed by a study of head types. The same kind of anthropometric data of ethnic segments exists in New Zealand. Buck speaks of longheaded and broadheaded migrations and of an "absorbed" broadheaded migration. If this physical anthropologist is correct, this is meaningful in the study of the dynamics of church growth when we discover that the people who evangelized the widely dispersed islands of eastern and central Polynesia were broadheaded types, not those of the intellectual longheaded segment. Anthropometric data do not concern us per se, but if the ethnic segments so suggested fall in line with transmission of and response to the gospel they are highly relevant. There is room for further research at this point.

The second unit to be examined in the social structure of Maori people movements is the widespread network of intercommunications. This was itself pre-Christian. In the course of their normal life there were groups of Maoris frequently making journeys. They followed the waterways, and stopped en route at approved allied villages. Their disputes were often settled and healed by intertribal marriages. All Maori warfare required a system of communications, even with the enemy. Inlanders came down to approved places on the coast or rivers for trade. They brought preserved birds, river eels either smoked or cooked in fat in bark bundles, and bird feathers for weaving into chiefly cloaks and regalia. These they exchanged for seafoods. Northerners went south for greenstone to make their sacred weapons. It came from the region of southern lakes. The *tohunga*, the craft priests, built up "banks" or reserves of the stone for craftwork, which was ritually organized. In return they offered *kumera* and taro, root foods, to balance the carbohydrate deficiency of the southerners, whose only food of this type was a fern root. Along all these strands of the Maori web of life, news of Christianity spread before any white missionary began to itinerate.

In one such outpost two missionaries on their first visit called the folk together and began to sing a hymn. To their surprise the group joined in. They began the liturgy and found they got the correct responses. Investigation revealed that three boys, who had been to a mission, had been their teachers.

The Bishop of Australia visited New Zealand in 1839 and wrote of the converts being a considerable proportion of the population in the remote places he visited. In that year the missionary Henry Williams arrived in the eastern district and found three Maori teachers already in active control of the situation, with a chapel built and an orderly congregation of five hundred. No missionary had been there before.

Two factors were involved: the network of communication itself, and the persons who used it. Some of the latter were free persons, but many were released slaves, who had every reason to think kindly of Christianity. Some had received Christian instruction and were able to pass it on, their manumission itself being a source of wonder to their relations at home.[27]

However, a study of the records forces one to the conclusion that there was another factor at work mightily. It was the fruit of the translation policy of the early missionaries. One missionary made a four-hundred mile tour, mostly in new territory. In almost every village he found someone who could read, and in all but one he found some scriptures. Many "teachers" had never been to a mission school. In a report of 1843, which claimed much growth in response to the work of Maori teachers, the phrase "and the circulation of the Scriptures" was added as a second cause. It is amazing how frequently this kind of reference is found at an early date.[28] Clearly the Maori Scriptures themselves did much in bringing the intellectual Io worshipers to God. The Wesleyans also had this same experience.

Vernacular tracts were used in quantity about 1827, and gospel portions, prayer books, and catechisms were in good supply by 1830, the year the people movement began. The four years when the full New Testament was widely distributed saw thirty-three thousand Maoris turn to the church for instruction in the C.M.S. area alone. Wherever scriptures circulated, they were read and discussed and inquiries began. It was a key factor in the complex.

The third feature was the structure of Maori religious thought. We are most concerned with the thought of the esoteric cult of Io worship, as it has been disclosed through its myths and oral tradition. This is a well structured ontology and hierarchy of gods, closely guarded as secret by the cult and kept away from the commoners, whose religion was a dynamic animism, not a structured theism. We have seen how these segments were sharply marked off by social barriers, such as marriage patterns, so that it was difficult for a commoner to aspire to the cult.

Slaves might have been in the cult at home, but were without any social grading in their slavery, mere things for service or sacrifice, and at best an outcaste group. Their gods had failed them and salvation was seen only in terms of freedom.

In all parts of Oceania the virile Christian movement has come on the dynamistic rather than the intellectual level. My own experience has been that the indigenous ministry has more often come from the dynamistic level, though frequently the messiahs of nativistic movements have emerged from the intellectual (especially the priestly) level. At both extremities of Southern Polynesia that we have studied, we have found a dynamic movement on the vassal level (either servant, commoner, or even slave) moving out from underneath the priestly superstructure into Christianity and thus into alliance with the missionaries. The chiefly esoteric cult was threatened and forced to reconsider its position. Security and the dominant role in religion were threatened by this mobility in the religious substructure. Chiefs and priests began to discuss the possible equation of Io and Jehovah. Was there conviction in this intellectualism or was it necessary rationalization?

Io, the Supreme Being of the Polynesian cult, had many similarities with Jehovah of the Hebrew-Christian world view. The members of the cult were in much the same position as the Jews of the day of Christ, worshiping Jehovah and accepting a host of angelic intermediaries. Both Io and Jehovah were remote, isolated, and so holy that the name could not be mentioned. To the converted Jew, Christ made the Unknown known, was "made flesh" and "dwelt among them." As Christianity offered a personal revelation of God in Christ to the Christianized Jew, so it seemed to the intellectual Maori to be the consummation of this esoteric view that they held of the world and the powers that be. This position cannot be proved, but it has many advocates and it fits the known facts. It is the only explanation I can see for those facts. The god of Io worship was a god who hid his face. The Christian Scriptures had much food for thought for such people.[29]

The fact that the cult was secret and segregated limited its ramifications throughout society in general. The whole fabric of the cultus, its ritual and symbolism, was ultimately abandoned without much serious dislocation of society because Christianity offered natural functional substitutes: prayers, liturgical worship patterns, hymnsinging, reading the sacred tradition and responses by the group. It was essentially a participation pattern and acceptable to the Maori.

Changes on the level of popular dynamism were more disruptive. Christianity came into encounter with the basic concepts of *mana* (dynamic force), *tapu* (protective force), *utu* (retaliatory satisfaction), and *muru* (penalty plunder) which were involved in the ceremonials of daily life and discipline and the general cohesion of society. Christianity took a strong stand against cannibalism, human sacrifice, and war. One of Marsden's voyages was almost entirely devoted to resisting the sale of firearms. The one missionary who became involved in this trade was dismissed immediately. The notion of using war as a means of settling disputes between tribes of one blood was rejected and a principle of arbitration for settling disputes was approved. This was long before the commencement of the wars over land.

These features demonstrate that Christianity made a specific impact on levels of intellectual acceptance and belief, of practical worship and devotion, and also of moral application.

Most of the early missionaries considered the war patterns as the most obstructive force against the acceptance of the gospel.[30] These patterns were changed by the introduction of the sale of firearms, which was stimulated by white settlers, whalers, and sailors. Many of the white settlers were themselves a major hindrance to the spread of Christianity, as scientific observers like Charles Darwin observed.[31] As time went on and settlers increased in number, land tenure became the greatest obstruction, but before we deal with this we must look at the Wesleyan people movements that were contemporaneous with the Anglican.

The Wesleyan People Movements

The Wesleyans came into the picture in the following way. Samuel Leigh of the Wesleyan Missionary Society (W.M.S.) worked among the settlers of Australia. Needing a rest from his exacting task, a health trip to New Zealand was suggested. This introduced Leigh to the Maori race and their claims. He talked the matter over with Marsden, had the Maori good will, and received an invitation to commence a mission. The Anglicans, knowing that the dimensions of the opportunity were beyond their capacity and resources, agreed to a policy of cooperation. Thus it came about that a Wesleyan missionary began work at a C.M.S. station in 1821, being assisted in learning the language by Anglicans, at the request of Marsden himself.[32] When other Wesleyans arrived from England they established their own station at Whangaroa (now Whangarei).[33]

At Whangaroa they worked in the open air, teaching letters, catechism, prayers, and hymns. However, they suffered many privations. Their station was plundered and destroyed; they lost their possessions and almost their lives. A bitter struggle continued between two tribes and for some time it seemed the Wesleyan cause would perish altogether. Eventually, through the tribe in this struggle that was favorable to the Wesleyan missionaries, an opening was made for a new station at Mangungu, on the Hokianga River.[34]

For three years (1828-30) the Wesleyans were quietly observed. Early in the thirties a fluttering of interest was felt, a readiness to inquire and listen to instruction, accompanied by a slow but clear weakening of the more vicious forms of heathenism. In 1831 there began a real spiritual movement along the Hokianga. The first Maori Wesleyan class was formed with five members. The experience of one of these class members was so advanced that he was permitted to conduct worship when the missionaries were away itinerating. We may say this marks the commencement of the Maori indigenous agency, which increased in strength and efficiency as time went on. The reader will remember that the Anglicans were experiencing similar things at the same time. Both involved men of the chiefly group.[35] The two missionary bodies drew on the same cultural openings. It had little if anything to do with denominational factors. The door opened suddenly, opened to them both; both made the most of it and rejoiced in each other's successes. Cases of conversion multiplied in 1832. The following year the chief, Haehae, had a clear experience of conversion, was baptized, and admitted as a communicant to holy communion. The Christian community continued to expand during 1833.[36]

The intake was by group movement and multi-individual deci-

sion. Strachan, Leigh's biographer, speakers of *villages* professing conversion.[37]

By 1834 the missionaries were preaching to a full chapel at
Mangungu. Before long large parties were coming by canoe
from as far as forty miles away. By 1835 some two hundred
could answer the catechism questions without error and seventy-
eight could read the New Testament, among them a number of
chiefs.[38] The mission printing press was at work by 1836. The
C.M.S. also had a press, and the programs of the two were co-
ordinated. The latter was working on Scripture and had reached
the gospel of John. A harmony of the gospels, prayers, and hymns
were coming from the former.

In that same year some five hundred were reported as meeting
in the members' class and numerous places of worship were over-
flowing. Matangi, a fierce cannibal, was converted, to become in
a very short time a class leader and exhorter. We have a reference to a communal group of 200 becoming convinced that Christianity was the true way of salvation, and the following year
Patuone and his people turned to Christ as a total group. In
August 1837 the missionary baptized 120 converted adults after
a period of instruction, and in November another 138, among
them some of the leaders who had expelled the mission from
Whangaroa.[39]

By this time the New Testament had been fully translated into
Maori and printed by the Bible Society. The Wesleyan quota
was 10,000 copies. Shortly afterward they had another 5,000. By
this time the Wesleyan press on the field had also produced 5,000
Scripture lessons, 6,700 catechisms and prayers, and 6,700 hymns
and prayers. The C.M.S. press had a similarly formidable list of
publications. In less than a decade the Wesleyan missionary
work had expanded to thirteen stations, with 3,259 meeting in
fellowship and about 4,000 children attending school.[40]

Geographically the C.M.S. and W.M.S. movements had different directions. These have been illustrated on a flow map. It
shows something of how comity may work out as a policy in such
situations. Both drives were distinct, though they had common
features. Both began, as we have seen, in chiefly circles. Whatever feelings for Christianity the unfortunate slaves might have
had could never be expressed until the gospel touched the hearts
of the chiefs and stimulated manumission. But there is no doubt

whatever that once the freed slaves began returning home southward (many of them being chiefs in their own right at home),
the whole country suddenly became open for the gospel. This
is clearly established by John Bumby's *Journal* of 1840. Indeed
Whiteley was being pressed for teachers and books from Taranaki
in 1839.[41]

The W.M.S. London Committee drew two conclusions from
Bumby's communications: (1) the deplorable state of heathen
Maoris as a result of internal wars, and (2) the general desire for
Christian instruction throughout the land. This situation had to
be met in terms of missionaries, instruction classes, and gospel
literature. We may, with profit, pay some attention to this important communication.

Bumby and Hobbs made a southern trip to consider these
openings that were being reported. They took a company of
about twenty youths, southerners who had been captured in war
and enslaved and had now become Christian. At Port Nicholson
at the heathen village of Whanganuiatara, for example, some of
their lads met friends and relatives they had not seen for ten or
twelve years. This opened the way for the preaching of the
gospel, secured them a hearing and inspired a readiness to hear
the message. There were many coastal villages in the area. Ware-
pouri, a superior chief, expressed a desire for a missionary. With
this in mind, according to Maori custom, a piece of land was
tapued for the establishment of a mission station, and the deal
sealed by rubbing noses after the pattern of indigenous land
transactions.[42]

The whalers warned the Maoris that acceptance of missionaries
would mean the termination of their arms supply. In spite of this
hindrance the missionaries were well received everywhere. The
gospel had preceded them. They found fragments of the New
Testament preserved with great care and some nationals who
could already read. Yet they were the first missionaries to visit
these localities. At Mana Island the greatest chief was a notorious
cannibal by choice. Nevertheless he expressed an interest in the
gospel, and one of the Christian lads was left to instruct him.
So they traveled round the south of the North Island, visiting
scores of places until they came to Kawhia, Whiteley's station,
which had been started in 1835 under the patronage of the chief,
Haupokia.[43] Whiteley played a great role in breaking down the

pagan custom of *satisfaction* and establishing Christian *reconciliation* as a substitute, though it cost him his own life in the end.[44] The account of the voyage of Bumby and Hobbs is important in establishing the character of the open doors in 1839-40.[45] It is supported by other missionary correspondence.[46] It shows that the manumission of slaves and circulaiton of Scripture were basic factors in the opening of southern doors.

Another important Wesleyan itineration journal was that of Walter Lawry in 1844.[47] It speaks of changes: the passing of cannibalism and enslavement; the establishment of churches; combined gatherings for fellowship and feasting. Lawry tells of a Christian chief who had built a chapel, lived an exemplary life, and ministered the word of life to his people—a cohesive tribal pattern retained under converted leadership. The Lord's Supper was always a feature of these combined gatherings. The Wesleyans had extended up the river Mokau to form a station at Operiki, where there existed a pocket of about a thousand persons. They planned to avoid the C.M.S. locality and extend a line inland, parallel to the west coast from Kawhia to Port Nicholson, as they had many requests from the south. The main feature of Wesleyan evangelism at this stage was its continual itineration, with catechizing and exposition of the New Testament.

By 1846 there were missionaries on seventeen stations and one post empty. It was a rural post with open doors; wisely, one missionary was removed from a town where the work was more static to deal with the responsive area. Again in 1849 there was a similar deployment.[48] In 1846 Woon was enjoying a strong people-movement intake in Taranaki South at Waimate. Once again the stimulus was the return of freed slaves from the north. It took place in the Ngatiruanui tribe, which had been "stripped and peeled perhaps more than any other tribe in the country" and had now greatly gained by manumission.[49] Smales, at Aotea, was experiencing the same thing. Christianity "as a system" had been received there before 1844. He had over a hundred baptisms after clear conversions, and a good many liberated slaves had returned home. In the three years that followed, about 20 percent of those baptized had come on in Christian growth into a rich full membership. The practical outworking of Christianity was evident on all sides, former disputes had ceased, and worship was constant.[50] By 1851 the general secretary could report that:

Scriptural Christianity has taken deep root in the native mind,
and is generally received throughout the length and breadth of
the land. Very few remain in heathenism. . . . Almost all the
aboriginal families throughout New Zealand read the Scriptures,
and pray together, both morning and evening.[51]

The following table compounds the C.M.S. and W.M.S. figures
as published in 1853:

	C.M.S.	W.M.S.
Stations	21	16
Missionaries	31	20
Indigenous Teachers	440	24*
Schools	113	71
Professing Christians	50,000	10,769
Full Communicants	7,027	4,316

*This figure probably refers to teachers in the sense of catechists. There
must have been others for the 71 schools. The 24 were paid agents. There
were also 293 indigenous local preachers and 521 who helped as Sunday
school helpers.

An Anglican estimate at the time gave the Roman Catholic
figure at about 5,000. If we allow, say, 4,000 for the unaffiliated
pockets of Christians known to have been scattered about in
remote places, it gives us an estimated figure of 70,000 who came
from paganism into one form of Christianity in two decades.

The official C.M.S. report for 1852 estimated the total Maori
population as between 80,000 and 120,000. Another estimate at
the time (Whiteley's) was 100,000, which, we note, is the mean
of the C.M.S. extremes. If these figures be reasonable we may
assume that the movement had absorbed about 70 percent of the
population.[52] We also note that 11.34 percent of the estimated
total population had accepted the commitment of full communi-
cancy. This suggests considerable growth on the level of perfecting, or follow-up. The double experience, mentioned in other
parts of this study, was common also among the Maoris, and the
testimonies in the Wesleyan classes and love feasts were quite
true to type.[53]

FACTORS OBSTRUCTIVE TO INDIGENOUS GROWTH

By this time the people movement from paganism had largely
run its course; but there is both a warp and a woof in the pattern.
We must retrace our steps a little through the records to seek

Flow chart of the approximate courses of the people movements among the Maoris during the 1830s and 1840s. All the places mentioned on this map on the east coast (except Whangaroa) were served by the C.M.S., and all those on the west coast (except Kaitaia and Otaki) by the W.M.S. Where the two streams met in the south later some comity problems arose. This map also shows the importance of regular indigenous lines of communication in the diffusion of the gospel. (Note: The place names are variously spelled in the primary sources.)

Pl. 5. North Island, New Zealand—C.M.S. and W.M.S. flow map of people movement.

the evidence of the forces which were already cutting across the people movement.

After having discussed the deep roots of scriptural Christianity, as cited earlier, the general secretary went on to discuss how "colonization has had its influence in New Zealand; secularizing the natives in some localities."[54] As early as 1839 William Woon wrote, in a letter otherwise full of hope and open doors, of Europeans increasing on every side, of talk of towns, of excitement over land, and ventured the forecast:

> An increase of settlers must affect the aborigines; and if colonization is carried forward in its various ramifications, we fear that . . . the people will soon be swept away.[55]

Moister pointed out later that this influx of Europeans settled round the principal harbors.[56] The New Zealand Land Company had emerged, and both the C.M.S. and W.M.S. actively tried to restrain colonization, but in the end acquiesced in the hope that British Law (for New Zealand was ceded to Queen Victoria in 1839) would be able to control the irresponsible settlers. In anticipation missionary personnel was increased.[57]

A phase of missionary activity ended with the establishment of colonial status. It permitted the appointment of an Anglican bishop, and this immediately affected the relationships between the missionaries. The church became much higher and it became quite apparent to the Maoris that there was such a thing as denominationalism.[58]

The 1840s were years of rapid transition. Both groups enjoyed people-movement intake, and by midcentury such vices as the plundering of food crops, sacrificing of slaves, and cannibalism had virtually ceased. Slavery and polygamy had grown less and less, so that the whole orientation of life had changed quite apart from the influx of Europeans. At certain periods the administration completely failed in legislating for these changes. Much of the subsequent irritation between races, especially in the matter of land tenure, failed to allow for the different outlooks with respect to land transactions. Turton, the missionary, in 1845 described this as "the irreconcilability of Maori and civilized law," showing that each party refused to see the other's point of view. He found a thousand Europeans and six hundred Maoris at New Plymouth, where some of the best land lay, and the Maoris very disturbed. He severely criticized the official acts of Governor Hobson, who plunged into the situation without acquainting himself with the facts. Turton insisted that the situation called for *transitional laws*. He found a wedge being driven between his work with settlers and Maoris and confessed it was defective as a result. His work was hindered in quality growth through fear and distrust and he had premonitions of bloodshed to come. "Let a systematic warfare be once commenced in New Zealand, and farewell to every hope of spiritual and civil advancement for twenty years to come."[59] It was clear foresight.

The same dichotomy of pastoral work was mentioned in Auckland, two years later, by the younger H. Lawry.[60] There was still Maori intake from paganism, and secular development was proceeding apace,[61] but the missionaries found their time divided between two interests, and their work threatened by conflicting loyalties. Wesleyan policy stressed chapel building, the establishment of new circuits, and the meeting of the needs of the new colonists, especially in the emerging towns. In reporting this, Moister felt he had to add that the Maori work was not neglected.[62] This very comment is significant. Inevitably one was increasing while the other was decreasing. Evidence of this is considerable. There was a tendency in the 1840s to establish committees to deal with Maori institutions.[63] These committees were comprised of missionaries and lay colonists who had a deep interest in the Maoris. But the very pattern was paternalistic and tended to compartmentalize the Maori life of the church. It became an adjunct.

A second body of evidence reveals the growth of towns, with an increasing demand for the establishment of circuits and the concentration of missionary activity on the colonists. One Anglican writer described how, until the building of the cathedral, the most imposing building in an area of Anglican colonization was the Wesleyan chapel.[64] Not only did the colonists demand this attention, but the missionaries themselves fought for their interests.[65]

Arising from this there is also the increasing claim of the town itself, as distinct from the country. The churches became more and more imposing,[66] the institutions more time consuming, the acquisition of suitable land more urgent.[67] Although this is associated with growth of congregations, most (though not all) of it was migration growth. I have cited two commendable references to deployment of missionary staff to open doors, but these are lone references. Anglican stationing also at midcentury was not strategically set for maximum intake of people movements.

Therefore, while it is correct to say of both denominations that the Maori work was not neglected, one feels obliged to qualify the statement. The tremendous people-movement intake from paganism of the 1830s and 40s demanded careful and prolonged follow-up. The movement had to be consummated. At the time that this was vital, much of the attention of the missionaries was claimed by the increasing number of settlers, the growing towns, and the chapel-building programs. The drift was from the itinerating ministry toward sedentary congregations, from the vernacular to English. It is important to see that this trend is apparent in the records before the period of tragic wars we are about to consider.

At the same time the missionaries were deeply concerned by the inroads of Western vice into Maori life. In 1851, Creed wrote of the dangers of a "transition state from heathenism to semi-civilization." He was perturbed about "grog and whalers," who undid some of the glorious triumphs of the gospel.[68] A Maori drift to the town had already commenced.[69] Yet, on the other hand, there are many references to encouraging growth of Christian perspectives among the Maoris, including the missionary sense itself.[70]

Bishop Selwyn drove hard for English standards and patterns. To become a communicant member, a church of England Maori had to demonstrate correct knowledge of doctrine, plus moral conduct, monogamy, domestic faithfulness, and complete renouncement of every form of heathenism. This has been criticized by some.[71] In the 1840s the state of the church was good, but in the early 1850s changes were apparent with the second generation. Those born in the fire were dying. Those coming on were more nominal.[72] Selwyn himself was concerned, but his first decade had been occupied with organizing the Episcopate, founding St. John's College, and planning Melanesian outreach. The Maoris themselves had much less of his time than the land-grabbing foreigners.[73] Because of his pattern he was slow to produce Maori leaders and his church suffered for these things in the

Maori Wars that were to follow. On the whole, however, the Anglican Maoris stood up fairly well to the severe testing of the war period and they emerged with a good body of indigenous clergy "supported by contributions and endowments raised by their own people on the voluntary principle."[74]

The Wesleyan cause did not fare quite so well. Their historian says that due to the scattering of tribes through war, plus decrease in Maori population, the aboriginal department was more circumscribed and church members were fewer.[75] Unintentionally perhaps he has given us the real reason when he describes the Maori work as of a *circumscribed department*. The trend in this direction predates the war period, and its main cause was the process of colonization itself. By 1870 there were seventeen Europeans to every three Maoris in the country.[76]

The current fragmentation of Maori religious statistics, illustrated in this book, stem from the tragic events we are now to examine. We are concerned not so much with the events themselves but rather with the psychoreligious patterns and the resultant state.

At the time when the people-movement work of consummation should have been receiving priority attention, the country was suddenly plunged into a desperate war. The war involved the alienation of the lands of the indigenous people and the matter of foreign laws and authority. Extratribal settlement had always been suspect but Christianity had begun to break down this resistance before the wars began.[77] The history of these wars has been written and we have no need to outline again the events. Our concern is to study the effect of the wars on the growth and development of the church in New Zealand—more particularly the Polynesian church. Some time afterward, looking back over his experiences, Bishop Stuart described the changes in the momentum of what had been an almost universal people movement toward the profession of Christianity as

> a chapter blotted with tears and stained with blood . . . wars which brought no honour to us, and wars which brought terrible devastation. . . . But the end of all that, was that a check came to missionary effort. . . . When I came to New Zealand it was simply a case of holding on to a desperate cause.[78]

Instead of a people movement being consummated, we have here one being arrested—indeed, worse than this, it is undone and being misdirected. All the bitter things the white man had brought were now seen at face value: arms and ammunition, disease, cutthroat competition, license, liquor, land alienation, and authoritarianism.

"A check to missionary effort" was the bishop's appraisal. It is hard to find a good phrase for it. A most informed New Zealander summed it up to me by saying that tensions and wars sprang from land troubles. Issues were confused because certain tribes lined up with the Crown and others for independence— that is, for or against British troops. Personal and tribal rivalries complicated matters. There was no clear pattern.

Vague! There is no appraisal here. A missionary scholar and editor of some standing wrote:

> [These] arose partly from the jealousy of the power and influ-
> ence of the colonists, but chiefly from the endless disputes about
> land sales, which were greatly complicated by the vague tribal
> tenure on which land was held by the natives.[79]

This is an ethnocentric statement. He is writing of Maori lands within a Maori land. The conceptualization of tenure was their own affair. It was the white man's habit to project his own land-sale concepts into situations which had a different frame of reference, and to think himself smart to bargain for another man's inheritance for a string of beads, a red shirt, or a gun—or perhaps a bottle of rum. If by dint of "generosity" he paid more, he seldom sought to discover whether or not the indigenes had such a thing as land-disposal at all, or if the notion of perpetuity was part of the transfer. "Vague tribal tenure" forsooth! One day the traditional lands were theirs. The next day they were not. That is the crux of the matter. From the point of view of our study in the dynamics of church growth (or nongrowth), the alienation of lands and events arising from it terminated the growth of the indigenous church. I am not discussing the prices actually paid for the land. My statement is that the loss of lands (and the accompanying imposition of the foreign will or authority) stopped the growth of the indigenous church. Indeed it set up a group reaction against the church—a negative movement.

Christian anthropology demands that people movements be consummated effectively. The old mana pattern lost its power, but the necessary functional substitute—power of revival—which should have been working through the 1860s, especially on the second generation which had been born in Christian times, was lost. To put this position biblically, the house had been cleansed of the evil spirit and swept clean, but it remained empty so that seven other spirits came and occupied it.

Many Maoris, desiring some of the blessings of Christianity they had tasted, but feeling a void through the losses of the traditional past, and feeling they had lost their land and authority, turned to nativistic movements, strange cults, syncretism, bringing together what they had lost and what they hoped to hold of the white man's new religion. We are suddenly confronted with new names: Pai-marire, Hauhau, Ringatu, Ratana.

This is a miserable end to a chapter that might have told of a glorious triumph. It is charged with the real significance for missions today—for New Guinea, for Papua, for the Solomons. We shall consider one of these movements as a type. We shall study the dynamics of the case, but first let it be noted that a century ago the Maoris were Anglican, Wesleyan, and Roman Catholic. Now they are dramatically fragmented. In the last figures I have, 22,610 Maoris were recorded as belonging to some form of nativism, 1,403 *unable* to state their religion, 14,686 refusing to do so on the census return. Roman Catholics had made good profit from the fragmentation; the Mormons had claimed 8,149 from the churches; and 607 declared boldly they had no religion.[80]

According to Grace, the character of missionary work changed rapidly after the Hauhau wars. The Maoris were scattered throughout the interior. Food was scarce. Old patterns of hospitality were disorganized. The missionary was no longer either a novelty or a fatherly friend, but highly suspect as a spy. The earlier respect for the Lord's Day and morality changed dramatically.[81]

After Hauhauism died down, some Maori communities were ready to return to Christianity but, although they admitted pride and the devil as partly responsible, they did not exonerate the missionaries and preserved their hatred for all Europeans.[82] Time after time the missionary Grace recorded such comments as, "The Maoris will not come back to your Church because the ministers forsook them in the war"[83] and "They still complained that we went with the soldiers."[84] The main two complaints were the missionary chaplaincy in the settlers' army and their involvement in land alienation.

Later on when Grace observed a modified form of Hauhau (which we are about to examine) he urged the appointment of Maori bishops. He wrote in one of his most important letters to the Society in London:

> The tone of mind of the Natives, especially of the Kingites, is improved. They seem to be fast arriving at the position when they will either return to us in a body, or permanently set up a religion of their own.
>
> Now, if we could arrest their attention by some sort of a general effort convincing them that we are in earnest and anxious for their salvation, bringing the Gospel strikingly and practically before them, I think we might expect a great amount of blessing. What we seem to want is a kind of Moody and Sankey revival.[85]

This was a good insight. It is a pity his colleagues did not see it. The subsequent fragmentation of Maori religion shows he was right.

Grace had suggested two things: the appointment of Maori bishops and the need for revival. He also felt that Hauhau had demonstrated a competence at indigenous form and liturgy, which ought to have been more developed by the church. He comments on this in his journal:

> I could not help feeling, so far as forms go, that they are much more competent to frame a service for themselves than we are to do it for them. There is no doubt that, if they survive, they will do it sooner or later.[86]

References in Grace's journals and letters in 1877 show his mind was much exercised on the matter. He felt that Hauhauism was an attempt "to adapt Christianity to their changed circumstances, and to have their worship apart from us"; that "we ought to give Native Churches Native Bishops," which was both "Apostolic practice and common sense," and that "if a revival took place among them" they were quite capable of taking "the Constitution of their Church into their own hands."[87]

In that November the Napier synod met without one Maori clergyman, though they numbered half the clergy of the diocese. A new bishop was nominated without reference to the Maoris, though they contributed to the bishop's fund. Grace recorded his reaction:

Instead of following such an unfair and exclusive course as this, which, sooner or later, will rouse the Natives into opposition, I think that the more prominently we can bring them forward, and the more responsibility we can lay upon them, the better!

In the matter of nominating a Bishop we have lost a splendid opportunity. I cannot help thinking the European Clergy should have declined to nominate till their Native brethren were consulted.

With reference, more especially to the Kingites and others who have, and are, seceding from us, I wish we could copy a leaf from them and announce an itinerating Mission amongst them, to be conducted by men outside our own body, but I confess I do not see much hope of this. There is no doubt very much yet [remains] to be learned as to the management of Missions![88]

Grace then had twenty-eight years of missionary service. We now turn to the kind of situation he anticipated, which has much to say to the current Oceanic situation.

A Breakaway Movement Emerges as a Syncretistic Church

In our study of the web of Maori church growth we now take one of these segregated units as a type for analysis. I was tempted to deal with Hauhauism because of the abundance of data, but I have preferred a movement which actually claims to have become a church. This raises a question of prime importance to missionaries confronted with similar phenomena in other lands today. It is also an aspect of the dynamics of church growth.

A Seventh-Day Adventist graduate student took the Ringatu church as his thesis theme.[89] He claimed, probably correctly, that the Maoris observed the differences between Anglican, Wesleyan, and Roman Catholic missions, and that none of them held much influence over the majority of white settlers. The greatest gift they had brought was the sacred Book, yet each mission had its own interpretation. Why then should not the Maoris interpret it in their own way?[90] This writer drew heavily from Greenwood, whom we cite on this point:

> If the angel of the Lord spoke to the prophets of Israel, he would do so again, but this time to the prophets of another Israel in bondage, the Maori. Thus was established a line of Maori prophets, extending even down to the present time.[91]

Out of this came Hauhauism. We are told that

a pair of mad or crafty *priests* set the tribe in wild commotion, by declaring that the *Angel Gabriel* had told them *in a vision* that at the end of the year 1864 *all white men would be driven out* of New Zealand, and that he himself would defend the Maoris, and that the *Virgin Mary* would be always with them; that the religion of the white man was false, and that *legions of angels* would come and teach the Maoris a better religion.*,[92]

The prophet of the movement known as Hauhauism was Te Ua Horopapera-Haumene. *Horopapera* was a biblical addition (Zerubbabel) to link this leader with the return passages of biblical prophecy. He performed miraculous escapes, had numerous visitations and visions of Gabriel, and used ventriloquism and hypnotism. He had been in the Wesleyan church, having entered that movement from the Tohunga craft priesthood.[93] He established a cult, which featured a *niu* pole, flags, chanting, and a gift of tongues. The chants, though composed of meaningful words and phrases, had no coherent totality. The symbol of the movement was the upraised hand, called *ringatu*. This would protect them from the bullets of white soldiers. They used to call "Hau!" like the evangelical "Amen!"[94] and much of their ritual form and liturgy was borrowed from or patterned on the Christian prayer book and the Roman missal.[95]

In open revolt in 1864 they killed Captain Lloyd and seven of his men with the loss of four of their own, proving to them the effectiveness of Hauhauism as a religion. The heads of Lloyd and the other victims were smoked-dried and used as spirit mediums. Lloyd's head told them to exterminate the whites, for New Zealand was Maoriland. Five prophets were appointed. They traveled from tribe to tribe, appointing cult priests among the *tohunga*.[96] The events which followed make a grim narrative, but the conceptualization of the movement evolved with the course of events. They saw the cause as sacred. Those who died did so through lack of faith. They worked themselves into a state of frenzy round the pole, with their hands uplifted to the heavens. It was quite infectious, even for observers.[97] Considerable military effort was required to arrest the movement, and this only after great loss of life. Some hundreds of Maori prisoners were exiled to the Chatham Islands, among them some other troublesome persons who had really nothing to do with Hauhauism. The au-

*The italics are mine. These are the points which indicate the character of the original movement.

thorities took opportunity in this way to remove one—Te Kooti, according to Tolhurst and others[98]—without a fair trial. This threw Te Kooti and the survivors of Hauhauism together in exile—a natural setting for the growth of messianism.

Te Kooti became a leader in exile. From Hauhauism he borrowed the symbol of *ringatu,* the uplifted hand, and made it an act of worship. The place of bondage and exile was dominant in his preaching. He performed signs and wonders and promised a return. Under this inspiration he and his followers captured the provision ship *Rifleman* and escaped.[99] Running into a severe storm, the story of Jonah was reenacted; the storm subsided, and Te Kooti's prophetic leadership was firmly established.

Back in New Zealand after escape from exile, Te Kooti maintained the prophetic religion, with the *niu* pole and *ringatu.*[100] Hostile to Europeans, he engaged in massacres, raids, and counterraids (1869-72) and escaped justice by flight into the King country, where he preached and engaged in faith healing. The government was never able to apprehend him, and in 1883 he was granted pardon. He lived another ten years and organized his movement into the Ringatu church.

This raises the question of what kind of a church can emerge in this way from a nativistic movement.

The Ringatu church has no buildings, no vestments, no articles of faith, and no paid ministry. The minister (*tohunga*) does not discuss the nature of the church with outsiders, but it is built on the Maori Bible (there being no other written tradition), is Maori-founded, and is Maori-operated. It is sometimes claimed that this is a form of Hauhauism. However, though it arose from Hauhauism, it arose with a determination to be separated from it. Comparison between the 1936 and 1951 census statistics shows that the movement is static. One informant tells me:

> The greater movement of the Maori population is bringing many Ringatu followers out of their isolation into contacts which break the appeal of the movement, which had been strengthened earlier by its separateness and isolation.[101]

The static condition is understandable also by the fact that they do no missionary work, membership being merely by personal wish without ceremony. Apparently nothing more than their cultural entity holds them together.

Te Kooti prophesied that a new generation would follow and revise and settle the true teachings of his church. He appointed a secretary and seven district leaders, but no successor to himself. The executive leadership is elected every two years, but the chosen person may serve two terms. He is known as the *Poutikanga* (Mainstay). The supreme voice of the church is with the general assembly. Some such pattern was required before the government would recognize the body. In church practice they use the love feast as did the early missionaries. At this they take their only church offering, with the one stipulation that it was earned by labor. They celebrate festivals for planting and harvest, but their passover commemorates their escape from the Chatham Islands—their Egyptian bondage. They use infant baptism but have not taken this from Christian ceremonial; it is a survival of the ancient Io cult, in which it was known as *Tua*, and was a foot-washing baptismal ceremony. They also ordain. They believe that in Io, the Maoris had knowledge of the Supreme God before the coming of the white man. They do not believe in the Trinity, but that God operates through the Holy Spirit. Christ is Son of God, Redeemer, and Vindicator. As to the role of Te Kooti himself, he was a prophet, the greatest Maori prophet "involved in predictions and in spiritual leadership for his day."[102] Many of the fantastic aspects of that day have passed away with the passage of time.

Although their doctrinal position is vague and hard to discover because of their exclusiveness, they expect recognition from the churches. They will ask a Presbyterian minister to take part in a funeral or baptismal service. It has become customary for that church to accept such invitations, though there is apparently usually some concern over doctrinal syncretism.[103]

This narrative is significant to those interested in how such churches emerge and develop as they do. This body came away from Anglicanism and Wesleyanism; or perhaps it would be more correct to say the Anglicans and Wesleyans lost what was virtually in their hands because political and social factors denied them the opportunity of consummating their original people movements out of paganism. The syncretism was strongly pagan at first, but the cleansing element has been that the Ringatu has accepted the Maori Bible as its norm. What has changed has been not the norm, but the interpretation of the norm. This study is highly

relevant to those areas of Oceania where traditional Christianity
has suffered losses to nativistic movements since the war.

To pinpoint some of the dynamic factors of the growth of the
church among the Maori people of New Zealand we note several
things.

1. The situation in the 1850s was generally healthy. The people
movement to Christ was almost complete, was effective, and
should have led to the emergence of a strong church.

2. The forces of acculturation—commercial, imperialistic, foreign authoritarian, and conceptual—and especially the alienation
of land, increasing as it did with the colonial period, led to the
Maori wars. These wars represented a loss of faith in Christianity
for allying herself with foreign forces and sought to recover the
mana of the old religion.

3. The revelation of Maori nativistic movements aimed at showing (1) how to worship correctly, (2) how to stop the decline of
the Maori race, and (3) how to drive the white man out of the
land.[104]

4. A large part of the Maori church remained true, though many
groups were scattered and lived a catycombs kind of existence.[105]

5. Te Kooti and his followers, after a fight for existence, came
into their own rights through (1) good leadership on a basis of
prophetism, (2) an indomitable spirit to maintain their own entity, and (3) the acceptance of the vernacular Bible as their sacred
book and norm. They survived by retaining the right to rein-
terpret it for each generation.

6. The missionary factor was from the first also strongly acculturative. The most telling factors were the translation of
Scripture, teaching of reading, provision of worship forms, and
most of all the impact of the gospel itself. These brought about
the people movement from paganism to Christianity, but they
were obstructed by other acculturative factors listed above under
point 2.

7. Obstructed and not consummated, the people movement gave
way to nativism in the second generation of Christians, as we
have witnessed in many parts of Melanesia in our own days.
The consummation of a people movement requires also the train-

ing of an indigenous agency for leadership. Both missions were doing this, but were a little slow.

8. Consummation of the people movement and the training of the indigenous leaders were hindered by the dichotomy of the missionary task. The load of serving both Maoris and colonists was heavy enough, but because their interests were so often in conflict, the Maoris were in two minds as to whose pastors the missionaries were. This applied particularly to Bishop Selwyn himself.[106]

The narrative of the conversion of the Maori people and the losses in the second generation is full of warnings for missionaries in other areas of Oceania today. Once again we see the importance of consummating people movements and the vulnerability of a church that fails to attend to this.

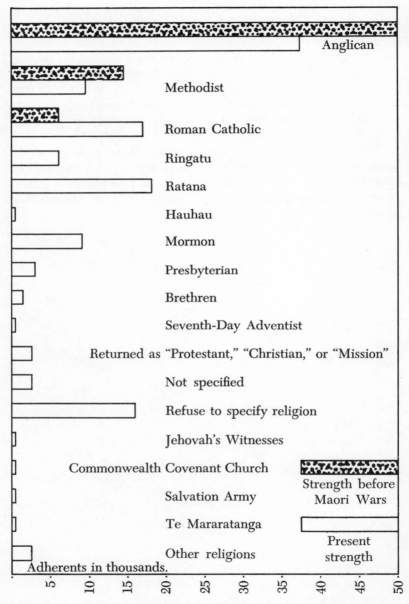

Pl. 6. Current fragmentation of Maori Christianity (based on Maori census figures, 1951).

This war flag was taken from Peka Makarini, the leader of Te Kooti's rearguard at Rotorua (1870), when he was shot by Captain Mair, who made a sketch from which the above has been copied (after Jas. Cowan, *The New Zealand Wars* . . . , 2:545).

This was a long pennant of bright red silk, with the emblems in white. Te Kooti called it the Whip and flew it to indicate a fighting expedition was being prepared.

The whole pennant is highly symbolic. Its length was 52 feet, representing the number of weeks in the year, and had been made by Roman Catholic nuns at their Hawkes Bay school for the friendly chiefs of the Ngati-Kahungunu tribe, but it fell into Te Kooti's hands in 1868 and he wove his own interpretations into the figures. The mountain was said to represent Aotearoa or New Zealand, and the bleeding heart to indicate the suffering of the Maori people. Whatever these symbols meant to the nuns, Te Kooti used it as a whip to stir up enthusiasm for war. The first symbol, thought to be a young moon, is like the bow of the Hauhau flags, which also had used a cross. This is a good example of the manner in which Christian symbolism was used in nativistic movements.

Pl. 7. Te Kooti's war flag "Te Wepu": symbolic syncretism.

3

THE TONGAN WEB

CAPTAIN COOK called them the Friendly Islands—a sad misnomer.[1]
Three of the missionaries left by the *Duff* in 1797[2] were murdered
before the end of the century. The others escaped with no more
than their lives, to tell sad experiences in Australia when they
landed in their rescue ship, *Betsey,* in 1800.[3] The crew of the
Duke of Portland suffered similar circumstances in 1802. Two
years later an American vessel, *Union,* shared the same grim fate.
Two American ships left Port Jackson (New South Wales) set on
reprisal.[4] Shortly afterward the crew of a British vessel, *Port au
Prince,* was massacred.[5] From this a Tongan chief equipped himself with ammunition and eight cannons for a new type of warfare.[6] Quite apart from these attacks on foreign ships, the century opened for Tonga with two decades of civil war among the
islands.[7]

After the fortunes of Napoleon had been determined at Water-
loo, a British ship, *Arrow,* cruised the Pacific, exploring and
making observations. Much of this information of Tongan destruction of shipping was collected and published on return to
England.[8] Mariner's famous *Tonga Islands* appeared in print in
1817 and elaborated further on these events. This two-volume
work was reviewed in length in a journal with wide circulation.[9]
Public opinion in Britain agreed with the captain of the *Arrow,*
who advocated changing the misnomer Friendly Islands to
Tonga.[10] These publications and reviews influenced the opinion
of British secular and economic circles and caused much concern
for British shipping in the Pacific. The L.M.S. mission to Tahiti,
which began with some popular support, had passed into its
second decade with no sign of success and public opinion turned
against it. Then suddenly Tahiti became Christian, and the missionaries were now praised for their patience. Within a year or so

public interest switched from Tahiti to Tonga, and the *Quarterly Review*, an influential journal, after a gruesome description, recommended that Mariner "be read with deep interest . . . by those good men who direct the Protestant missions."[11] The reviewer ended:

> Meantime, as the Missionary Societies extend their views, we hope the Tonga Islands will not be overlooked. A translation of the Gospels might be accomplished in this country, by means of these volumes, with Mr. Mariner's aid.[12]

British secular forces were ready now to support missions and Scripture translation if they could make the islands safe for commerce. They apparently did not realize that the Tahiti missionaries, with a vastly superior knowledge of the language of that group, had yet attempted virtually no Scripture translation at all.

So the second decade of the century, both in England and Australia, saw Tonga become an object of public interest. The widow of one of the L.M.S. survivors from Tonga settled at Parramatta, near Port Jackson. The Tongan people were still on her heart. She transmitted this interest to Walter Lawry, who pressed the British Wesleyan Conference to appoint him to Tonga. He was designated for this task in 1820 and another nominated to accompany him.[13] Lawry had tremendous zeal for the spread of the gospel, but he was an aggressive and impatient character. Feeling the lines of communication between the authorities in London and the men on the field were too long, and that slow ships meant lost opportunities, his impatience became manifest. The Wesleyan church in Australia now had considerable numerical strength and was in a general mood for expansion. The wide Pacific lay before them. Whalers, bêche-de-mer traders, and sandalwooders and all kinds of adventurers roved at their own sweet will, and brought a medley of tales to Port Jackson, The Pacific was literally dotted with islands and the field for evangelization seemed unlimited. Reports from Tahiti showed it could be done. John Williams was still at Raiatéa and had not yet burst the bonds of the reef than contained him.

At the same time that Williams was pressing his Committee to widen its vision and change its policy,[14] the impatient Lawry was straining under the delays that hindered his journey to Tonga.

Though the appointment had been approved, the Society was not in the financial position to launch the scheme. His colleague, Samuel Leigh, had got away to New Zealand under his own efforts by inaugurating a special type of appeal on his visit to England,[15] but the man expected from England to accompany Lawry to Tonga failed to arrive. The impetuous Lawry whipped up enthusiasm in Australia and obtained the approval of his brethren for his own venture of faith.[16] He chartered a vessel, equipped it, paying for most of it out of his own pocket, and, taking a few craftsmen, set out to explore the missionary possibilities of Tonga, in August 1822.[17] We note in passing that Walter Lawry, Samuel Leigh, and John Williams were all men with initiative and courage to act ahead of their London Committees. In one sense they were three impatient rebels—but theirs was a sanctified rebellion.

Lawry, a great evangelist within the pattern of his day, and a splendid organizer among his fellow countrymen, was prevented by his impatience from achieving much as a communicator across cultural barriers. Later on he found his natural role as the General Secretary of the Wesleyan missions on the field, but his Tongan venture failed. He returned after fourteen months, somewhat disillusioned, and with his wife's health seriously impaired. He had no converts and all that can be said is that he established a station and left the craftsmen there in Tonga after his own departure.[18] Of the L.M.S. mission of a quarter of a century earlier, not a trace remained. Yet, despite his disappointment and disillusionment, he did not lose his pan-Pacific vision or his love for Tonga. He kept pressing the British Conference for action in this direction. Thus Thomas and Hutchinson were appointed in 1825, and arrived at Hihifo in 1826, setting to work with a will to learn the language. By 1829 they had seven baptisms.[19]

Two months before the arrival of Thomas, two Tahitians had been dropped at Nukualofa. They had intended going to Fiji but their ship sprung a leak. They were permitted to build a chapel and their teaching received a hearing. Some two hundred and forty persons had attended the chapel but none had been converted to Christianity.[20] When more Wesleyans arrived, as planned, to take up their post at Nukualofa, they discovered the Tahiti men there. The latter were pleased, however, and the two parties set down to work together. That was in 1828. In 1830, when the L.M.S. missionaries Williams and Barff called, they discussed the relationships of the two bodies and agreed that Samoa be considered an L.M.S. area and that Tonga and Fiji be left to the Wesleyans. The two committees in London stood by this agreement.[21]

Prior to this meeting Thomas had removed to Lifuka, in the Haabai group of islands. It was here and at Vavau that the real spiritual people movement into Christianity began, although there had been a few earlier converts at Nukualofa, where the labors of William Cross and Nathaniel Turner bore first fruit in 1829, built on the foundation of the Tahiti teachers.[22] The conditioning at Lifuka was quite different. Thomas had met with a strong resistance at Hihifo and that field did not seem ripe unto harvest. His three and a half years there had nevertheless provided him with a good knowledge of the language and customs, so that when he removed to Lifuka he was able to commence immediately with direct preaching.[23] Furthermore the Lifuka chief was disposed to be interested in Christianity. He had seen the teaching program at Nukualofa and was impressed.[24] Under the influence of the first Tongan preacher, Peter Vi, the chief experienced a dynamic conversion,[25] although he was not brought forward for baptism for nearly two years. This wait was apparently because of his own conviction that he should wait until a group of converts could be received as a body.[26] The sympathy and support of this chief from the start greatly aided Thomas. He was permitted to set up a school and acquire a fine chapel at an early date. This meant facilities for public worship. Thomas's removal from an unripe to a ripening field was good strategy, which should be observed by many modern missionaries in other lands today. The people did not follow en masse, or by compulsion, but the conditioning was certainly such as to make conversion acceptable. The heathen showed a great interest in the changes and were permitted to attend worship services if they so desired. On one such occasion Thomas preached to fifteen hundred people.

Available reports permit the reconstruction of the pattern of mission methods and the dynamics of the resultant conversions. I have already mentioned the principle of strategic stationing. Thomas and Hutchinson did not continue with Lawry's station, though much time and effort had gone into this. Hihifo remained resistant. Lifuka had open doors and Thomas transferred in January 1830.

Again, when both Vavau and Haabai appeared to be opening, and Tongatabu seemed to be moving toward response, and the mission had not enough men to attend to the openings, they were prepared to bring the most promising of their own Tongan converts into frontline action. Thus, after the chief concerned had swallowed his pride and was ready to accept the Tongan preacher, Peter Vi came into action as a missionary to his own people.

Later on, when this system was more widely established both in Tonga and Fiji, seven books were reviewed in one long article in a British journal.

> In one respect the Wesleyan system accommodates itself remarkably well to the tendencies of Polynesian converts; namely in the ready provision which makes for receiving them into the active service of the Church. These islands swarm with "local preachers."[27]

This was written about twenty years afterward. Peter Vi was the first of a long line of tremendous personalities for whom conversion was an experience of dynamism, or a dynamic encounter with the powers of animism.

In the records of Tonga (and also of Fiji) we are fortunate in having indigenous documentation of these dynamic experiences.[28] In view of the modern criticisms of iconoclasm it is well to let those who took part in them speak for themselves where possible.[29]

POWER-ENCOUNTER CONVERSION

Peter Vi was a convert of Nathaniel Turner, whom he had assisted in translating the gospel of Matthew. Undoubtedly the Spirit of God worked through that exercise in preparing him for conversion, as he did through Turner's preaching, which brought conviction of sin and the discovery of forgiveness. Vi traveled round the small villages that encircled Nukualofa trying to communicate his new experience to others, until he was chosen to go to Haabai.

Despite the mind of the paramount chief there to receive him, this transfer involved considerable risk, for public opinion was still against the acceptance of any Christian preacher. The heathen chiefs who were commissioned to take him there were so fearful that they had a mind to sail for Fiji and escape the unpleasant task. Vi had difficulty in persuading them to do otherwise. They performed special protective magical rites before going on shore at Lifuka. In the face of mocking from the women, plus misrepresentation and much trial, Peter Vi worked with the chief, teaching him the gospel. Eventually the chief, Taufa'ahau, reached the point where he felt he must begin to worship God. This demanded a dynamic encounter or confrontation with his old god, Haehaetahi.

The priestess who served this god was much feared because she herself became the shrine of the deity under possession. Taufa'ahau pulled a young banana tree and cut a club from the soft stalk. "I will strike the devil-god with this," he declared. On Vi's advice he removed the harder part of the root lest he kill the woman when he smote her under possession. At the moment when the priestess, under possession, was drinking the ceremonial kava, the chief struck her a blow on the forehead, which sent her rolling on the floor. Then before the drinking god had time to recover the chief struck again, and shouted a cry of victory that the god had been clubbed while drinking kava.

This symbolic act was against the gods of Haabai, not the people. No one was forced to become a Christian, but the whole fraternity of gods were now afraid to possess their respective shrines lest they be similarly treated by the chief. They found their authority greatly undermined. In a power-orientated society, change of faith had to be power-demonstrated.

This accounts for the plotting to seize the chief and murder the few who had now become Christians, while they were yet few in number. But the plot was discovered and the chief made his open declaration of faith. However, instead of killing those who had plotted to take his own life, he gave vent to his anger by destroying the idols and idol-houses about Lifuka. It was at this stage that Thomas removed from resistant Hihifo to Lifuka, where this door seemed to be opening.[30]

Now there are three ways of viewing this kind of behaviour. There is the attitude of the "salvage" anthropologists, who may blame the missionaries; or (better informed) say that, while some missionaries preserved valuable records, native converts and pastors ruthlessly destroyed all material objects of religious significance.[31] To all who think it important to preserve knowledge this has some justification. Then, secondly, there is the attitude of some Western or foreign missionaries, who see this "breaking

down idols and treating priests and priestesses with a violence
that their ignorance of the spirit of Christianity can barely excuse."[32] This, in terms of Western ethics, has its justification also.
But there is another view, which springs from the indigenous
religious forces active within the situation itself. Here are a
people in a mana-orientated society, for whom there can be no
possible change of faith without a change of mana. There must
be a demonstration, physical or symbolic, but at least ocular—
a power-encounter. This is a picture of dynamics, in the primary
meaning of the word. This is how the islanders saw themselves
situated. If we see these demonstrations within the cultural
matrix and philosophy of life of the island people, we must
admit their behavior was quite meaningful.

Taufa'ahau well knew that his enemies would use every available mechanism to achieve his death. God had to give him victory over them all. Indeed, as soon as the priests saw the teeth
of their gods had been drawn they employed foreign (Fijian)
sorcery to their ends. While Thomas and Cross were administering emetics to make him vomit away the poison that had been
given him, the little Christian group spent the whole night in
prayer, even until the dawn. "And the Lord heard our prayer,"
Vi recorded. "Our king lived, and therefore we rejoiced in the
Lord. From that time Christianity spread and increased in
strength, while the kingdom of the devil became weaker and
weaker."[33] It is good to have that statement from the mouth of
the Tongan. Though the missionaries did not organize iconoclasm, they were content to see it do its work. The Wesleyans
demanded a definite break with paganism. To them it was
Christ or Belial: "Resist the Evil One and he will flee from you;
negotiate and make terms with him and he is your master for-
ever."[34] The view has much biblical support.

Basil Thomson, a British Colonial Servant who went along
more with civilizing than with holiness preachers, regarded the
Wesleyan pioneers as ignorant and narrow, though he did give
them credit for effecting a marvelous change. He was yet prepared to admit that their success was due to the very narrowness
of their vision, which view he also held of the apostles, their great
prototypes.[35] With some degree of insight Thomson saw the
Tongans did "not understand half measures. If their gods were
false gods then every custom connected with their worship was . . .

fit only for the most rigid prohibition. . . . Their own creeds were hedged about with tabus . . . so they made their new code as uncompromising as that they were displacing."[36] I think I am right in my interpretation of Thomson when I say that he saw natural psychological factors within island conversion that belonged to the island mental configurations themselves, and that the forms of conversion and postconversion behavior were indigenous, not imposed from the West. This was a good insight. Yet the superiority with which he relished sitting in judgment on the missionaries is so prominent that the real insights are submerged.[37] However, he is an important witness and cannot be bypassed.

He cited the episode of Taufa'ahau thrashing the possessed priestess, hanging the idols, and burning the god-houses, to "convince the people by ocular demonstration."[38] He also narrated Finau's precipitation of a similar dynamic encounter at a time of decision. I cite Thomson's account of it:

> Being, before all things, practical, Finau determined to give his fathers' gods one last chance before finally breaking with them. He had seven of the principal idols placed in a row, and addressed them as follows:
>
>> I have brought you here to prove you, I will tell you beforehand what I am going to do, so that you may have no excuse. I am going to burn you. If you be gods, escape!
>
> But as the gods made no attempt to escape, he gave orders that the spirit-houses should be set on fire. Eighteen were thus destroyed; but the weather being damp, they took four days to consume, and the people sat by terrified, waiting for the retribution that must follow such iniquity.[39]

Although Thomson was adept at omitting isolated facts in his data which did not support his general thesis, things like this were not isolated facts. It is a whole body of solid evidence that holds together and refuses to disintegrate. Conversions were dynamic encounters in which onetime worshipers confronted their old deities, and their life-orientations were dramatically reversed. Evidence is equally cohesive that soon afterward there followed consummation experiences of spiritual power. They were spiritual experiences, not merely educative processes, which fit remarkably that experience which Wesley himself described as *sanctification*.

Theologically this was too much for Thomson, but he could not escape the mass of data or evidence. He interpreted it thus:

> They [the Vavauans, with whom the movement really began] may be violent partisans or bitter enemies—they cannot be neutral. They are, in short, the Irish of Tonga. It was not long before the missionaries, by awakening this curious quality of hysterical enthusiasm, had established over them a clerical despotism.[40]

Thomson saw the revivals (i.e., the consummating movement as distinct from the original converting movement) as hysterical enthusiasm and admitted the phenomena to have been historic, whatever the explanation. He fittted it into his general purpose of showing how a clerical despotism developed. It would have been more correct to have shown how a situation developed that permitted the coup d'etat of one despot, who used the church as a ladder to power; for Baker was an opportunist and in no sense a typical missionary. What Thomson fails to allow for—and for church growth dynamics this is important—is that this "hysterical enthusiasm" was not confined to Vavau. If he dismisses these people as the "Irish of Tonga" he must still account for other "Irish" in all parts of Tonga, in Samoa, in Fiji, New Britain, Papua, and the Solomons, to name a few areas I have myself studied and can document. Furthermore, be it noted, these "Irish" were not all Wesleyans. The Wesleyans' interpretation was to see these consummation experiences as a second work of grace, what Paul called *deuteran charin* (second grace) and immediately after conversion they strove for the sanctifying experience. But whatever name we give it, and whatever way we explain it we cannot escape two clear facts: the experience was real and widespread; and it had a remarkable aftereffect on the lives it touched. Because of the anthropological dimensions of this book, I usually speak of it as a *consummating* movement.

It was not merely the religious orientation of the Tongans which determined the character of the people movements we are about to examine. Social factors were also involved. We can never escape the fact that the diffusion of the gospel by people movement invariably follows along lines of social structure or organization. This indicates that the movement is indigenous and not imposed or foreign. Let me cite two examples: the kinship pattern, and the organization of social functions.

When a chief was converted, he usually set about zealously to win his relations farther afield. Thus, for instance, Taufa'ahau was keen to win Finau and went to great trouble to gain this end. Behind his evangelical zeal lay the social structure itself, the realization of the need to maintain the solidarity and cohesion of the kin group. The wars that were yet to come were part of a series of struggles that lasted for over fifty years. Until Tonga was entirely Christian, kin solidarity was a matter of physical survival. This is one good reason why all people coming out of tribal war-orientated societies tend to move into Christianity in people movements rather than as individuals.

The organization of social functions was also involved. How could Taufa'ahau best present the new faith to Finau with some hope of his accepting it? Finau's attitude fluctuated. In individualistic society this might have been presented as a reasoned argument; but Taufa'ahau, though he had never heard of group dynamics, knew a great deal about them. Acting within the pattern of intergroup intercourse and festivity he and his people organized a great gift-exchange. Some three thousand Haabaians, a great number of Christians among them, visited Vavau with twenty-four of their giant canoes. As the chief of Haabai strove to win his relative, the Christians of his party were backing up his efforts in the houses of the other members of Finau's group. Taufa'ahau had even secured a letter from his missionary to support his case, and agreed to stay at Vavau over the weekend. The Sunday worship of the Christian party had its own effect, and that night the Haabai Christians sat up till dawn telling all they knew (little enough as it was) of the gospel. The people of Vavau were impressed, but divided in their response. However, the Vavau chief made his decision and burned his godhouses, and the best part of a thousand Vavauans were prepared to act with him. These people were brought under instruction— they had far to go before being received as members. Even so there was a real change in them, as there always is when men bring themselves to destroy their ancient deities. This is evangelism within a pattern of social organization, which works through its cultural mechanisms rather than against them. It also shows something of the multi-individual character of these people movements and group decisions.[42]

Against this backdrop we are now ready to examine the distribution and character of the great people movement of Tonga, which became the nucleus of a web that was to reach out into Melanesia. It is the best case of a total movement we have in Southern Polynesia, because it offers scope for the study of both the initial conversions from paganism and the consummation phase, plus subsequent missionary outreach beyond its own geographical limits. This is not to deny the political features; but the documents do permit the clear delineation of the dynamic character of conversion.

THE PEOPLE MOVEMENT

One is obliged to make it clear that except for any divine connection with respect to the fullness of His time, the Tonga movement and those movements already discussed in Tahiti and New Zealand have no relation whatever. Little if anything was injected into the Tongan situation by the Tahitians, and it was not from their locality that this movement sprang. The Maori movement was not consummated; neither did it develop any missionary outreach. Even to this day New Zealand missions in Oceania have been unable to enlist Maori evangelists and have had to seek them from Tonga and Fiji.

There were many ways in which the Tongan movement differed from its contemporaries. We have seen it differed in its wholeness. It differed also in its theological dimensions. True, culture change was going on in Tonga as in other places, but the country was free from many of the problems of colonization which we met in the New Zealand story. Tonga was a small compact group of islands with close-knit cultural ties, not attractive to colonists, with no wide plains for cultivating temperate zone crops and herding, and off the main shipping routes which began to develop in the last century. Tonga was almost a conditioned situation for experiment or research, and this is why it is so important in our study.

But there is another, and even more important difference. The pioneer missionaries who witnessed this people movement had no illusions about their missionary policy. They had no dreams of civilizing first in order to evangelize. Although the secular world of Britain would have desired this, the men themselves believed in dynamic encounter. They sought evidence of dramatic encounter of the pagan with his gods in the name of Christ. They sought to bring sinners to the penitent-form. Having seen this they received them and put them in classes that encouraged testimony, the sharing of the fellowship, and sought to bring them back to the cross again for a second work of grace and a state of sanctified living.[43] They were holiness preachers, pure and simple. They were not colonizers or civilizers, and were extremely critical of any of their own number who showed any desire to acquire native lands for himself.

It may be that they represented a reaction against the colonizing pattern, departing from England in a day when the church was reacting against the policy; or it may have been that Wesleyanism naturally worked out this way when it had a field to itself without being "conditioned" by cooperation with another Society. This was a positive gospel—not what had to be given up, so much as the experience that was offered in the name of Christ. Although they did not avoid the doctrine of hell, they emphasized much more the glory of heaven.[44] Many a Tongan and a Fijiian came from paganism with a vision of heaven. (Half a century later this was reversed by missionary preaching.) The early converts developed a strong Methodist doctrine of assurance. The missionaries planned no preliminaries in bringing pagans to conversion. Every act, every prayer, every word, was aimed at getting a verdict either for conversion or for sanctification. The islanders were left in no doubt whatever about where the missionaries' priorities lay. They were men of a single business. Their one priority was to bring men to Christ—to repentance, to forgiveness, to sanctification. True, Tonga, like the other areas, ran into her problems later on, but the pioneering period is as clear a case study as one could ever hope to find. Tahiti and Tonga represent the poles of the theoretical axis of missionary methodology as they stand at the opposite frontiers of Southern Polynesia. The Wesleyan work in Maoriland differed from that in Tonga, not only because it was shared with that of the C.M.S. and possibly influenced by Marsden, but also because the people movements were not brought to consummation because the time and labor of the missionaries were turned aside so often to work among the colonists, which cost the missionaries their rapport with the Maoris.[45]

We now return to Vavau to examine the physical statistics of the movement that was fired by these holiness preachers.

We saw that baptisms began early in 1829. By the end of that year thirty-one had been advanced to full membership: that is, their experiences had been considered adequate to advance them a stage beyond baptism. They could now meet in the class meeting and testify and share the experiences of others. It was here the quality growth of the fellowship was cultivated. The physical statistics of full membership show remarkable growth of approved experience over the next five years, as the following table shows:

1829	31
1830	72
1831	516
1832	1,422
1833	3,456
1834	7,451[46]

These are not conversions from paganism, but fully tested and proved members, who had been brought out of paganism, instructed in belief for baptism, brought to a personal experience of sin forgiven, and proved themselves by a period of membership on trial and received (confirmed). These figures do not include members on trial, or adherents (those who had turned from their pagan gods and were in the instruction groups). Thus, for example, when Woon reported the *total membership* strength as 1,044 in 1831[47] it should be broken down thus:

Full members	516
Members on trial	528
Total Membership	1,044

This actually shows the position better than West's table above, because the growing in experience is reflected in those "on trial." In this type of Wesleyan statistical pattern the on-trial figure tells the story of the current year. It also reflects the continuity and effectiveness of the follow-up work being done in the congregations.

The total membership of 1830 was 466, with 394 of them on trial. This shows the 1829 movement had gained momentum immediately and was effectively followed up from the start.

To clarify one more point on Tongan statistics: references like "Thomas preached to 1500 on one occasion" mean nothing statistically. Factually this means that the gospel was getting a hearing from the pagans, maybe a merely curious hearing, but certainly not hostile. The Tahitian teachers in Tonga and in Fiji never had any other type of response beyond this.* When men were convinced that their old way was wrong and were prepared to commit themselves to Christ in faith, demonstrating their stand in some specific manner, and turn to the church for organized instruction, they were recorded as adherents. These were people whose lives had been changed. They were instructed for baptism. They aimed at providing every candidate for baptism with a knowledge appropriate to his faith.

Baptism could be delayed through polygamy; and where Christian marriage was delayed (as it sometimes was) for social security reasons baptism would also be delayed, but none could become full members without first being baptized. To become a member one was required to have a deeper spiritual experience and to undertake the highest type of life and standards of holiness. Usually this came in a revival experience, as a result of which he was led to ask to be put on trial. Further manifestations of grace led men on to become class leaders or local preachers. Every step was supposed to be accompanied or stimulated by a "fresh manifestation of grace." This statistical pattern has a theological foundation.

With these explanations in mind, we return to the situation in December, 1830: 72 full members plus 394 on trial, making a total membership of 466. Another 1,034, having come out of the pagan world by an act of faith, were under instruction and being prepared for intelligently understood baptism. A large number of those on trial had already been admitted to communion. Nathaniel Turner administered this to two hundred on January 2, 1831. It had been a year of good growth and good follow-up. On January 20 Turner baptized another seventy adults and married twenty couples, and the expectant tone of his letter on the subject showed his awareness of the signs of the times. We meet such phrases as, "In event of all Tonga turning. . . ."[48]

Woon, a dedicated man, whose call was to print and circulate the Scriptures in Tongan in Tonga, was at work at the beginning of 1831. He produced readers, scripture portions, lesson books on the Old and New Testaments, hymnbooks, and catechisms.

*A principle of mission statistics is involved here. The street preacher missionary, who has no ecclesia, or congregation called out of the world, should not record his audiences statistically. They are merely pagan hearers. To record them as statistics invalidates the compounded figures in world mission handbooks.

By April he reported his press already producing scripture portions.[49] He wrote of the Tongans as "an inquiring people" and of the gospel as "spreading from island to island and from group to group." By September he had increased his momentum. A twelve-page scripture book had been printed (3,000 copies) and a hymnbook of sixty-four pages (1,500 copies), and he was at work on another scripture book of thirty-four pages. Commenting on the life of the church he said that he believed that most of the six hundred attending worship did so "in spirit and in truth." He added:

> Almost every week we have new converts; persons of all classes are leaving the enemy's camp and joining the ranks of Immanuel.[50]

Five months later he reported that he had printed four different readers, books on the Old and New Testaments, more hymnsbooks and more catechisms, so that full facilities for organized worship were being provided in the vernacular from the outset. Then he added that requests for preachers were coming to hand from as far as Samoa and Fiji (where there was a strong Polynesian fringe in the Lau group).[51] One cannot help contrasting this aspect of missioning in the pioneering days of Tahiti and Tonga.

Woon was certainly a man for the hour in Tonga, but his contribution was possible only because he was part of a team. His colleagues did the translation work. They all recognized the importance of vernacular material, and their attitudes were alert to the possibility of "all Tonga turning." They realized that Scripture and aids for worship would be required in increasing numbers, and that catechisms and other material for follow-up would be essential.

Woon was a layman, like the craftsmen of Tahiti and New Zealand. However, his craft was not directed toward the process of civilizing. It was wholly devoted to providing for the needs of the evangelists and converts. The islanders, who saw Woon at his craft, saw that it was not used for profit or trade but as equipment in the great work of bringing men to Christ. One wonders what would have happened to Woon had he been sent to Tahiti, where the ministerial members felt the Word of God too sacred for them to run the risk of mistranslation, where progress was expected to be slow, and where Puritan and legal perfection was expected for advance in the church, rather than spiritual experience. It is not enough to have a printer in the missionary team: it is the whole orientation of the total group that counts. To read the records of the pioneering periods of the Tahiti and Tonga missions asking oneself the question, did this mission expect and prepare for slow or rapid growth? is to discover them charged with meaning, even for us at this present day. Quite regardless of the theological position of the two societies,[52] we are concerned here with two basically opposite attitudes. One expected it to take time, the other anticipated "all Tonga turning." This of course is not the whole complex, but it is a most important element in it. Furthermore, in this respect the men on the field reflected the attitudes of their respective directors. One body sent the men to civilize and expected them to earn their own living at their crafts; the other supported the printer as one of the costs of the mission in order to strengthen the evangelistic thrust and the efficiency of its follow-up.

By April 1831 some hundreds more had renounced idolatry. Comments from the Chairman's letter, like, "Idolatry bows and expires at Jesus' name," reveal his awareness of the power-encounter character of conversion in the Tongan scene. A large building seated two thousand at worship. Thomas saw there many chiefs to whom he had often spoken personally about turning to God. In an important paragraph he described the follow-up or consummation growth. He had one hundred fifty "in the society," indicating an increase of forty-five in that congregation on the full membership level in three months.[53] This was still less than a decade from Lawry's hasty commencement of the mission. We are not surprised that a speaker presenting a promotional resolution at the annual meeting of the W.M.S. in London should throw out to the large gathering the following oratorical question and its answer:

Is the door closed against us in the Friendly Islands?

Let the spectacle which is there presented, of the accomplishment of the prophetic announcement that "A nation shall be born in a day . . . and the isles shall await for His law" answer the question.[54]

The fact that this approach was presented to a large gathering of the supporters of the mission and subsequently printed for circulation among them suggests that the missionary attitudes reflected the attitudes of the church which sent them. Meantime their London Committee had already included Fiji on their station sheet, and had entered two names, sending the designated men to Tonga for experience in people-movement intake prior to their transfer to Fiji.[55]

Throughout 1831 and 1832 letters and reports had this atmosphere of expectancy. Actual progress was steady and encouraging. J. Egan Moulton, Jr., writing in 1914 (after long experience in Tonga), said, "While Christianity was said to have been 'embraced' true conversion was wanting. And this was a matter of concern to the missionaries. In 1834 the 'baptism from above' came."[56] This is stated as it would be by a missionary of a later day, writing for a missionary reader of a later day. It is true that the great Tongan Pentecost came in 1834; but the missionary correspondence prior to that date vibrated with exciting expectancy—an awareness of opportunity, expectation of response, and praise to God for the wonder of it all. The concern of the missionaries was the normal Wesleyan concern that conversion should not be the goal but the gate of life, that there should be a growth, "grace upon grace," or as they put it themselves, that their converts should move on to sanctification.

We must not allow the later period of great intellectual growth in Tonga in the 1860s and 1870s, which became more and more Western in character, to hide the real character of the original encounter. True, the missionaries were concerned! But they believed in two experiences, both real, both sincere, both intensely dynamic. Without the first there could be no second; without the second the first was never consummated. When we see that nine thousand came into full membership in six years we are dealing with the record at the second level: the consummating experience.

In the former, people came in groups, some of them large social segments, households, and sometimes loosely held sodalities with some cultural base. Missionaries of a later day were disposed to decry these conversions as "mass movement"; but those who saw them take place were never in doubt. They saw, for example, that a single individual could not alone destroy a family deity:

it had to be a family act. Sometimes such group action was delayed by the resistance of a single member. Sometimes one member might steal some sacred object and hide it for himself. The group might destroy the group god; but he, being not fully participant, would then take the deity, with the stolen sacred object as its shrine, as his personal deity. Thus a family god could become a personal fetish.[57] This is currently met in parts of New Guinea. If such a person did this secretly, while making a show of standing with the group in the destruction of the family god, one of two things inevitably happened before long. Either under the threat of persecution he would fall away; or, coming into a real experience later, he would make a public confession and personally demonstrate his rejection of the fetish he had taken as his own. This would be a public act of setting himself at one again with the fellowship. Secret insincerity was a cardinal sin in communal society. As long as a member held out against a group decision in the communal discussions, his individualism was respected; but an insincere show as described above was a form of falsehood that threatened the cohesion of the group. It was for this reason that some incidents in the record of the apostolic church are more meaningful to these people than to us in the West (e.g., the narrative of Ananias and Sapphira). It is in this kind of atmosphere that missions to animist people begin to grow. However we might wish to do so we cannot Westernize it. We must, like Ezekiel, "sit where they sit."

Sometimes a group was ready for decision and it was the leader alone who held up the demonstration. Then when he was ready to "bow the knee to the Lord" a great crowd would follow. To one looking back years later it might seem a mass movement. Studying the primary sources in the historic sense, one discovers the operations of individualism within communalism. Finau's conversion opened the way to a large group that had been awaiting such an act. In 1834, Tamaha, a female chief (and regarded as a deity by some), became a Christian and thereby rejected her own entity as a deity. This threw her worshipers into a state of confusion. Group deliberation was held and as a result about a hundred of them (but not all the group) determined to make further enquiries about Christianity.[58] Here was a case of a religious sodality being split through the loss of its deity.

As we look back over records like this we see that the steadily increasing momentum of conversions from paganism from 1829 to 1833 represented an important and essential stage in a whole series of events. In that period of four years the Spirit of God was certainly at work. This permitted the young mission to organize itself for the big event that was about to burst upon them. They established their system, developed techniques for testing religious experience, provided opportunity for new converts to testify to "what the Lord had done unto them." They established schools, taught reading and especially Scripture reading, printed hymnbooks, catechisms, and Scripture portions in great quantities beyond their immediate needs. They fixed a pattern of follow-up to transform conversion growth into quality growth, and they had brought some of their earliest converts into the roles of class leaders, preachers, and teachers. Only two things can account for all this: on the divine side, the approval of God and the presence of His Spirit; and on the human side, the attitude of expectancy on the part of the missionaries.

In those years thousands were gathered in as adherents (not to mention the many pagan listeners), their patterns for growth were formulated, and the encounter between the power of the old gods and the power of Christ was specific. The process toward spiritual maturity is reflected in the full membership figures: 31; 72; 516; 1,422; 3,456. Then came the great year 1834 when the full membership jumped to 7,451. The missionaries could never possibly have handled the spiritual intake on either the conversion or sanctification levels had it not been for the steady increase of the five preceding years plus their awareness of the opportunity and their excited expectation. Those who had been received into full membership prior to 1834 had not been lightly received and they were to play an important part in prayer and witness and teaching. They were "as it were" fully with the missionaries in the upper room when the fire of Pentecost fell again.

This new movement began at Vavau in July 1834. It spread spontaneously to Haabai and to a lesser degree to Tongatabu. At Vavau 2,262 persons shared deep personal experiences in six weeks and almost as many in a fortnight at Haabai. A great many of these had been among the more nominal adherents for a year or so.[59]

Basil Thomson, we have seen, called it "hysterical enthusiasm" (though he lived much later and did not witness the events personally).[60] Whatever term is used, the records show it grew out of intense prayer. The missionaries and Tongan converts met daily for prayer at noon. There were prayer groups in the villages. In one village, folk cried for mercy all night, refusing to leave the building until the day had come. The whole island was moved. It was in this movement that Taufa'ahau took the step of complete dedication in the Wesleyan pattern. He had been soundly transformed in his conversion experience, but had not yet sought membership for fear he could not maintain the standards.[61]

The vigor of the movement completely disorganized the life of the community. People laid aside their regular daily work, while they wept their way through to divine peace.* The wave of spiritual power swept from island to island. How it crossed the water, none could say. It transformed life and manners. Polygamy disappeared overnight; a high value was set on all the means of grace; morning and evening devotions became radiant with praise; men known to hate each other made public confessions and became reconciled.[62] Even West (who came a little later and was naturally skeptical of statistics) avowed that "the moral aspect of the Vavauans was wholly changed" and that when he arrived the area had been "completely purged of its former heathenism."[63] Perhaps the picture should be painted not by historians but by the men who lived through the experience. The passages to be cited now not only record what they actually saw happen, but also show what kind of missionaries they were— how they thought, believed, and acted.

Peter Turner, at Vavau, wrote on July 27, 1834, when the movement was in full force, but had not yet run its course:

> We believe that not fewer than a thousand souls were converted; not now from dumb idols only, but from the power of Satan to God.

> We had prayer meetings six times a day. We could not speak five minutes before all were in tears . . . absorbed in deep concern about salvation.[64]

---

*The terminology of the primary sources themselves has been retained throughout this paragraph. In fact this has been a general practice throughout the whole book. This seems to be the most accurate way of showing the difference between the civilizing and holiness missionaries.

Tucker at Haabai, after having conducted four services one day, wrote:

> As soon as the service began the cries of the people com-
> menced—what a solemn but joyful sight to behold. One thou-
> sand or more have bowed before the Lord, weeping at the feet
> of Jesus, and praying in agony of soul. I never saw such distress,
> never heard such cries for mercy, or such confessions of sin
> before.
>
> We have not yet received an account from all the islands [of
> the Haabai Group] of those who have obtained peace with God
> during this revival, but from the numbers already brought in by
> the leaders, we believe that upwards of two thousand were con-
> verted to God in the course of a fortnight.[65]

Perhaps for a moment, in passing, we may focus on Taufa'ahau, who abandoned heathenism as a system in January 1830 and began there and then to live a changed life, attended worship, was instructed in the faith, contributed much to Christian stewardship, witnessed for Christ, and persuaded others to join their fellowship. He had satisfied the missionaries of his sincerity and was baptized by Thomas with the first group at Lifuka in March or April 1830. When he had been forced, in his chiefly capacity, to take military action on one occasion, he did so *without blood-shed*—an unheard-of experience. This is what Peter Turner called "conversion from dumb idols" and its real practical outworking in a changed life.

But then we have another record of Taufa'ahau having been soundly converted in Christ through the outpouring of the Holy Spirit beyond the salvation from sin past, and now over the temptations of sin in the midst; what Toplady's hymn speaks of as "the *double cure*" that saves from "the *guilt* and *power*" of sin. In other words, the missionary records indicate more than one work of divine grace in the life of Taufa'ahau. After his second experience Taufa'ahau went "from grace to grace," or as those Wesleyans used to put it, "to fresh manifestations of grace," or as John put it, "of his fulness have all we received, and grace for grace" (Jn 1:16). Taufa'ahau became a class leader and then a local preacher. Prior to this he had manumitted all his slaves. He had also built a fine church, working his prized military heirlooms of the family into the communion rail and pulpit steps. This he did so that the symbol of the greatest of all pagan values might be brought low before the true God and transformed into

the physical instruments for bringing people to communion and
to hear the preaching of the Word. This was a cultural demonstration and a perfectly meaningful witness to his contemporaries.[66]

That brief vignette of the chief was reconstructed from missionary statements. These were the men who had watched, prayed
for, and guided this chief along the road. They saw the changes
in his character, baptized him, received him into membership, and
could tell the story.

But there are also Tongan testimonies that have been recorded,
both in English and in the vernacular, that narrate the same type
of spiritual pilgrimage. Some of these men were torn between
being individual Christians without the group, as a Westerner
can hardly understand unless he has immersed himself in communal society. There was Joeli Bulu, who, having heard of the
better land, decided to become a Christian, and, in fear of his
heathen kin, went to a Christian group and sought to live with
them.

> When my father heard what I had done, he was very angry;
> and called together our kinsfolk. He sent for the heathen priest,
> and told him. . . . The priest became inspired . . . and uttered a
> lamentable cry. . . . Then were my friends mad against me, for
> when a priest was inspired we thought it was the god who spoke.
> They sprang to their feet in heated wrath, and said, "Let him
> be clubbed! He shall die today. . . ."

By this Joeli was intimidated. All the same, he knew that by
giving up his intention of becoming Christian, he had also lost
his hope of the beautiful land.

> Stealing away into the forest I kneeled down and prayed to
> God—"I have cast away the *lotu* [Christian religion], because I
> fear the anger of my friends; but I lied to them. I wish to hold
> it still." Day after day I hid myself in the forest and prayed.

Then the Christian with whom he had taken shelter interceded
on his behalf. Joeli's own family made a feast to their heathen
god and called the priest. On their account the priest sought the
god's clemency as they made Joeli over to the *lotu* and wrote his
name off the family roll. By ritually disinheriting Joeli, the family
thought they had protected themselves from the anger of their
family god.

Joeli had been little more than a pagan *hearer*, a desirer of the better land, and an honest seeker.

> All this time I knew little of Christianity—my soul was dark: I tried to be good because I was looking for the beautiful land and I thought I could get there by my own strength alone. When Mr. Thomas came to Vavau, and standing under the tree in the public square, preached from the parable of the tares among the wheat, it pierced my soul. I had thought I was wheat. I found myself among the tares. It seemed the spirits awaited me behind the trees of the square. . . . The sermon over, I sat quaking in fear, and weeping in great anguish, the strength gone from my body, unable to rise, till friends led me away staggering like a drunken man. At the house I fell down and wept. The people thought some evil disease had taken me. . . . I said, "Pray for me!" They knelt and prayed, first one and then the other until they were tired. . . . I went to an empty house, knelt down, wept and prayed before the Lord, for I knew myself as a sinner. But I did not then know that this sorrow and fear of mine were marks of repentance. This continued for a long time. I often hid myself in the forest to pray. . . . The Christian people had compassion and taught me what they knew of the way of life. The missionary too. I began to know more and more of that way, but still found no rest for my soul.

As a result of his sincerity, his seeking, his diligence in prayer, his readiness to accept instruction, his knowledge of the correct answers to the catechism questions, and his reformed life, Joeli had passed on through baptism to membership. The missionaries were pleased with his statements of Christian truth and he was now appointed to exhort others. Joeli himself was far from satisfied. "I, who was exhorting, needed exhorting," he said. This was his status and state at the beginning of 1834. He was not an accredited local preacher, but he could testify when no preacher was available.

Then, with others of his status, he attended a love feast, at which Nathaniel Turner, the missionary, gave his testimony. Joeli subsequently recorded:

> My heart burned within me as I listened to his words; in speaking of himself he told what I felt. I said to myself—we are like two canoes sailing bow for bow, neither swifter, neither slower than the other. [He was telling of his repentance.] When he went on to speak of faith in Christ and forgiveness of sins, and then further to a state of peace and joy, I said—My mast is

broken and my sail is blown away, and he is going far ahead out of my sight, and I drift helplessly. But as I listened to him tell of Christ my eyes were opened. I saw the way to believe and live. I was like a man fleeing for his life from the enemy, groping along the wall of a house in the dark, seeking the door. Suddenly it is opened before him and with one bound he leaps within. The tears streamed down my cheeks. Often had I wept before, tears of sorrow and fear, but these were of joy and gladness. Mr. Turner, seeing my tears, called on me to speak—Stand up Joeli, and tell us how it is with you. I stood up, my soul seemed to part from my body, I remembered no more till I found myself lying on the mats and Mrs. Cargill ministering to me. "What ails you, Joeli?" they asked.

"I live!" I cried, "I live! Let me tell the mercies of God." And even as I spoke, there was a cry in our midst, and weeping, and hearts were moved. Mr. Turner, himself weeping, said we should all go to prayer.

Oh! What a day! I can never forget it—prayers, praises and tears. There were many, like myself, who had been long seeking the Lord, who found Him that day. Nor did we break up our meeting till night came over the land, and even then we were loath to part. Before we left, Mr. Turner said, "Blessed be God for the thing He hath wrought this day. But this is only the beginning. Let us now go, each man to his own house, and pray that the heavenly rain, which has watered our souls, may fall on the land, for the land is athirst."

This is an important testimony from a Tongan, not merely as a record of his own experience (though that in itself is important), but because it shows how the missionaries acted in these circumstances—what they said and did. It also shows their spirit of expectancy and how they transmitted this to the Tongans.

Joeli went on:

And this word of his came to pass; for when a teacher named Isaiah, who was with us, went to preach in another town, the same great work broke out there also. So it went from place to place till it reached the town of the Chief, whither we all went.

(He narrated at length the conversation with the Chief and ends this part of his testimony.)

The work went on from house to house, and from town to town. Strangers also, who had come sailing from other islands, carried it home with them. . . . As for me I lived in great peace and joy.

He has now passed on to the great revival. His own experience came just before it. The records mostly state that the 1834 revival

18245

started in the town of Utui, but surely that meeting of exhorters, which Joeli described, was the upper room experience. However the work had been going on in a less conspicuous way all through the preceding five years.

By this testimony we are warned that despite the care and caution with which persons were admitted to membership, people who were pious seekers could slip through without the required experience, so that at best statistics are only roughly indicative of the real position. The record also shows the roles of missionary and Tongan convert in the drama, and the place of prayer and of testimony. The redeemed of the Lord were expected to say so.[67]

In Haabai, as in Vavau, the movement spread with personal testimony. One, Jone Mafileo, was much used by God in that group. In February 1835 Peter Turner went to Keppel's Island (now Niuatobutabu), one hundred and seventy miles away in the direction of Samoa, and farther still to Niuafo'ou, whence had come a call for help. Though no missionary had ever been to these places, they were fields ripe unto harvest. Turner married two hundred and forty couples and stayed until he was able to prepare the most advanced of them for baptism, leaving Tongan preachers there to carry on with the work of follow-up. Subsequently Thomas visited these islands and baptized those whom the preachers had instructed. The two islands had become Christian and by 1841, 877 of the 1,292 adults had been admitted into full membership, as a result of clear revival experiences.[68]

By 1836 auxiliary missionary societies had been established and Tonga was launched on its own missionary record. The societies were at Vavau and Haabai. Tongatabu felt some of the impact, but was not nearly as ripe for harvesting because of bitter sectional rivalries. The societies of Haabai and Vavau developed rapidly also on the level of stewardship, new members being eager to contribute to the program of the church, including its missionary ventures. Offerings were made, not in coin, but in mats, tapa cloth, baskets, root crops, oil, turtle-shell, artifacts, and pigs.[69]

GROWTH AND OBSTRUCTION IN TONGA-TABU

The church grew also in Tonga-tabu, but it had nothing like the same power. The very name Tonga-tabu ("Sacred Tonga")

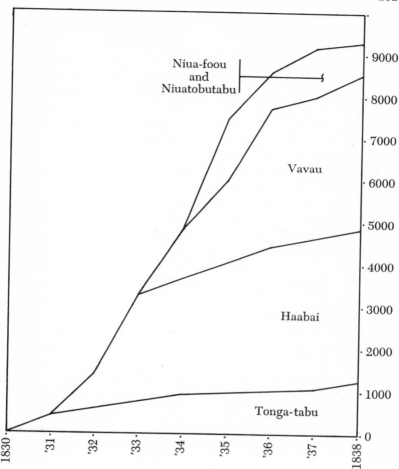

This illustrates the structure of the people movement over its period of greatest activity. It shows the intake from paganism was much slower in Tonga-tabu. A vertical section taken from any point in the base (year) will show the composition of adult baptized persons in all segments at that point of time. The top line of the graph shows the baptisms for all Tonga.

Note how the people movement spread. Starting in Tonga-tabu, it spread to Haabai (1831), Vavau (1833), Niua-foou and Niuatobutabu (1834).

Pl. 8. Cumulative pictograph showing the number of adults baptized during the Tongan people movements: 1830–1838.

singles it out as the stronghold of the ancient religion. Thousands
clung to their god-houses and set their faces vindictively against
the growing faith, the *lotu* as it was called. Were this a *history*
of the Tongan church, one would need to devote a large amount
of time to the documentation of this period and evaluate reports
that conflict, but my theme is the dynamics of church growth and
obstruction to growth. Our concern is why the Tongatabu
responses differed from those in Haabai and Vavau. When
W. Butler prepared his survey of the Christian mission in Tonga
at midcentury, based on the correspondence of Nathaniel Turner,
Charles Tucker, John Thomas, and others, together with material
published by the London Committee, he devoted a hundred
lines to the character and spread of the 1834 revival, but he
dismissed the Tongatabu unit with a secondary phrase: "in a less
degree to the Tonga Group." He gives no reason why the revival
was "less" in Tongatabu.[70] Yet Tongatabu had good men and
the strongest missionary staff. What obstructions operated there?

I have already suggested that the suffix *tabu* indicates one
cause. Moulton said that progress there was slowed because of
a "strong reaction amongst the aged chiefs and priests." The
opposition was centered in Bea and Houma. When the new faith
was accepted by the chief, Tu'ivakano, matters came to a head.
He was deposed in a thoroughly pagan manner "which moved
all Tonga" and led to war. Finau, the Christian chief mentioned
earlier, was confronted with hostile forces determined to uproot
all Christianity. He was obliged to call in his relation, Taufa'ahau,
to help. The latter came and crushed the rebellion in a manner
surprisingly Christian, but the growth of the church was retarded.

Upon his departure the peace agreement was broken by the
rebels. A plot to murder the Christian chief was discovered.
Small Christian work parties were attacked without cause from
time to time. Taufa'ahau was called in again. He made no
effort to strike but urged the rebels to lay down their arms.
They refused. Then Taufa'ahau surprised them one morning at
dawn and five hundred of them found themselves prisoners. He
pardoned them and did not follow up his victory. Guerrilla war
continued for six months. Two naval commanders became involved and tried to effect a reconciliation, without success. Eventually it was achieved by missionaries Tucker and Thomas going

personally to the rebel fort as peacemakers. Bea remained hostile.[71]

Superficially these appear to be wars against Christianity. Underneath they were political and followed the long-standing social cleavages. The chief's profession of Christianity was merely an excuse for working off old scores that had run hot for forty years. When Tubou died in 1845, he had at the end nominated Taufa'ahau as his successor, according to Tongan custom. The latter moved to Tongatabu and the heathen party was now faced with a different proposition. Two heathen chiefs refused to pay the traditional respects, thereby making themselves rebels again. They determined to fight to the bitter end. They sought to overthrow the government altogether and fortified themselves. The chief now had to defend his authority and confronted the rebels with a force of ten thousand loyalists. Houma yielded and received pardon. After a five-week siege Bea was sacked and again the chief (now called king) was merciful. The war ended in 1852. It was the last of its kind, and the kingship did not again have to defend its authority.[72]

But the war had a serious effect on the growth of the church, and the membership statistics actually showed a decline. Tungi's conversion in 1850 brought in a segment of about two hundred—an important segment. However, though the number of adherents increased, the full members dropped; there was a growth at the nominal fringe but a drop in quality at the core.

There was another factor responsible for the obstruction to growth on Tongatabu: the entry of the Roman Catholics into the scene. They had failed to effect an entrance into Haabai and Vavau and threw in their lot with the enemy stronghold at Bea. They argued that by surrendering now the rebels would not be surrendering to the Tongan king but to the English missionaries who had become his ministers of state.[73] This matter of French-English, Catholic-Protestant, relations of the 1840s and 50s is a subject in itself which grew largely from the Tahiti affair. Here again much would have to be written at this point in a history of Tonga, but for our purposes it will suffice to say that this intrusion gave an unpleasant aspect of Western religion to the struggle and left a permanent scar on Tonga. The defected segment, represented by Tui Tonga (the sacred chief), found a denominational face-saver when it was apparent that the old religion had to go. Rather than being converted to the Christianity that had fought for Tonga from the start, he chose to become a Roman Catholic, and to this church he remained faithful to his death in 1865. More tragic even than the presence of rival Christian groups was the fact that their very rivalry was now established on bases of local Tongan political and social rivalry on the one hand and the international rivalry of their white spiritual advisors on the other. This was permanently unhealthy.

The fortunes of war had fluctuated during the period and interfered with the state of the missionary work. At one stage the missionaries had to leave Nukualofa and the local Christians had to take refuge in a fort. It was at this period that the French priests ministered to the needs of the rebels, in those years following the death of the British Captain Crocker, who became involved in the situation. It was also at this time that the heathen were most aggressive against Christian work parties for whom they lay in wait. It was also a period, let it be frankly admitted, when the missionary policy of "revival unto sanctification" lost its priority and was subordinated to a policy of "hostility to French Roman Catholicism." The men themselves would probably have denied this; but the fact remains that their correspondence reflects the shift in their major concern. Their evangelical aggression had temporarily become defense against their own religious rivals from the west.

On bringing together a great deal of somewhat imperfect data and impressions from the documents, I am inclined to estimate that about two thousand Christians perished in that war over the twelve years it dragged on, and the greater portion of this number fell between 1841 and 1846. Clearly the heathen gangs that fell on work parties directed their attention to Christians at the core of the church—hence the fall in members. In spite of this, conversions were still taking place and when the Wesleyan commissioners visited Tonga soon after midcentury, they figured that all Tonga had turned to one form of Christianity, save for about fifty heathen "diehards."[74] Setting this against the pagan state of two decades earlier the commissioners were satisfied, but the membership figures do show that the war and denominationalism had brought about a quality decline, at least in Tongatabu.[75]

Where figures are available one discovers now a poor score in statistics of members on trial—that is, fewer coming on into full membership. This is vital in the Wesleyan pattern. It shows that in the second decade the follow-up of conversion was not as effective.[76] Yet Robert Young reported the church in a healthy state as far as family devotions were concerned.[77] I think it probable that to some extent this may be accounted for by the fact that adolescents (who would normally come on for membership if their experience was right) who should have been responding were infants at the worst period of the wars, the children of the Christian victims, or perhaps there were large casualties among the Christian children also. Unfortunately we have no total population figures of the period. The war could have meant a lost generation. Apart from the 1846–47 revival, the figures did not improve greatly until 1859.

THE 1846–47 REVIVAL

There is another side to the picture. Set off against the decline were two points of growth. One of these, 1846–47, fell in the middle of the period of decline at a time when things were at a low ebb in Tongatabu; and the other marked the end of the decline when postwar growth recommenced in 1859. These were real revivals. Thus in each of the three formative decades in the emergence of the Tongan church the people experienced a revival. Undoubtedly these carried them through the years of trial and gave the church its distinctive character and missionary vision. While these revivals were admittedly the work of the Holy Spirit, it is clear that the people worked, prayed, and prepared for revival. In other words, they planned regular missions to bring each generation to the penitent form for itself. What the great revival of 1834 stamped indelibly on the mind of early Christian Tonga was that a dynamic encounter was required to give man victory over his pagan gods, and that for this demonstration to be truly effective there had to be a subsequent consummating experience. The structure and theology of the Wesleyan church suited these experiences and permitted the emergence of a thoroughly indigenous church in Tonga.

In biblical terms these people learned to wait in the upper room for Pentecost, and to wait expectantly. They never saw themselves as "converters," but were alert to open doors, were quick to detect the signs of ripening harvests, and increased their prayer pressure in their upper rooms. I mix these metaphors deliberately because they were used by the people themselves. Missionaries and Tongan leaders alike would meet for prayer and contract with each other to pray for specific blessing at specifically nominated prayer times (usually midday). Then, sooner or later, it would come. In the middle of a prayer or a sermon, the congregation would suddenly melt into tears, and with no new doctrine, a spiritual work would spread from village to village, from island to island. Truly, the Acts of the apostles was to these people an unfinished book. It was the same with each revival. The 1834 and 1846 revivals began in the same way and in the same village.[78] On a tiny island, thirty miles from Vavau, the captain of an English vessel sent men ashore for firewood. One got separated from the others and found himself in a weeping, praying village. He knew nothing of their language, but discovered himself a sinner, sought grace, and found it (cf. Ac 2:6, 8, 17, 21, 37-42).[79]

Young, the Wesleyan commissioner, cited with approval personal letters from Turner and Wilson concerning the 1834 and 1846 movements. Turner wrote:

> The results of this revival were, religion was realized and enjoyed, the Church was saved from a dead formality. The people now understand the Gospel, look for its blessings, and many have lived and died in the possession of entire sanctification. The churches in the Friendly Islands will bear comparison with any churches in the world for simplicity, zeal and holiness.

On the 1846 movement he cites this important statement, which shows again the upper room aspect of the revival:

> For some time previous, our local preachers, leaders and some of our members, had been manifestly growing in grace. The spirit of piety had been deepening and spreading for two or three months. . . . This was particularly the case at a prayer-meeting held with the local preachers and leaders once a week. At one of these meetings the presence of God was signally manifested. . . . [He goes on to describe how folk from here went to Vavau and there the revival began. On their return to Hihifo in Tonga it commenced there also in a normal service.]
> The most solemn awe pervaded the place, and then in a few moments the crowded chapel became filled with suppressed sighs and groans. . . .

> When a number of chiefs met together for the transaction of business, they were unable to proceed, and were obliged by an influence from above to change the meeting for business into a meeting for prayer. The results of the revival were glorious . . . sinners . . . were converted; . . . church-members, who had been living in a low state of grace, were quickened and saved; others were sanctified wholly. The revival produced a change in many of the ruling chiefs . . . exerted a blessed moral influence . . . improved all classes. . . . Such have been the results of all the revivals I have seen or heard of in the Friendly Islands.[80]

Farmer also agrees that the 1834 revival began with "a deepening of piety of the church members."

From among the men born in these movements came the indigenous Tongan ministry and also that splendid band of pioneers who took the gospel to Fiji: Joeli Bulu, Sailasi Faone, James Havea, Paula Vea, and many others (Lk 24:49 and Ac 1:8 over again). The period following the wars saw the consolidation of the island nation, the development of Nukualofa as the capital,[81] and the establishment of the monarchy and the government.[82] Impetus of these revivals made available men for special training. Settled government and men for training made possible the growth of educational institutions in Tonga which were, for many years the finest in the Pacific.[83] The people-movement phase of Tongan church growth was effectively consummated and the principle of each generation needing its own revival was established.[84] The problems of modern Tonga have arisen from the institutional phase of her church history, not from the pioneering period.

THE SEQUEL

The purpose of this study has been to examine evidence relevant to the character of early Tongan people movements. This has been done. There is a sequel however. The problems of the present-day church in Tonga cannot be understood without knowledge of the second phase of Tongan church history. This is so well documented that it requires a volume in itself. I can give it no more than a two-page summary. The relevance of Tonga to the general theme of this book is to show that her people movements represent the nucleus of a great web that broke through the frontiers of Polynesia into Melanesia at Fiji, and after winning that land reached out to New Britain, New Ireland,

Papua, the Solomon Islands, and even to the aborigines of North Australia. This also is another story for another volume, but let it not be overlooked, as we examine the sequel in Tonga itself, that the church that emerged from these people movements never lost its missionary passion.

Immediately after its conversion to Christianity Tonga introduced its own form of civilization. The missionaries were instruments and agents bringing it about, but they did not initiate it. The driving force throughout was the Tongan chief who had acquired a kingship in a very real way. By the time his authority was established he had acquired a great respect for European institutions. The names of Louis Napoleon, Frederick William, and Queen Victoria circulated round the Pacific like spirit presences. When the Tonga war ended Napoleon III was working on his new constitution. The experiences of the Protestants in Tahiti was much in the mind of George of Tonga, who, with his followers, felt that his kingdom had a right to its place in the sun, and that the only way of dealing with foreign Westerners was by using their own methods of treaties and agreements. The missionaries approved. They certainly influenced the legal code that was formulated, but they did not initiate or formulate it— nor were they completely satisfied with it. The Tongan laws and constitution were modified from time to time. The king had surrendered his slaves and his "absolutism" to be a constitutional monarch. Each of the three groups of islands had its governor, resident in a foreign house suitable for a colonial officer of rank "up to a viceroy." They kept supplies of soda and champagne, and went to church only once on Sunday, because "this is what English gentlemen did." Some critics have spoken of a "Gilbert and Sullivan kingdom" with full uniform and regalia. Others, like H. Stonehewer Cooper, were impressed with Tongan civilization, feeling the laws were strict but just, printed and understood, road planning was effective, and there were comfort and education and religious toleration.[85] He was impressed by the manner in which they determined things for themselves. The historian will have to decide between these opposite conclusions of observers. The one point I make firmly is that if the missionaries *aided* this, they did not *initiate* it. It was all the desire of the Tongan people, and of the king in particular.

Henceforth missionary involvement was mainly in religion and education. The king longed for an institution like the British public schools, of which he had heard. His select young men, the Tongan nobility, should be trained for the Civil Service and the church. In the senior Moulton he found the person for this task. Moulton had a free hand and full support, and produced the best institution of its kind in the Pacific. A brilliant scholar, he raised the standards of education and provided the opportunities for making young islanders into Europeans. This meant a well-educated ministry. Following the English Kingswood School pattern, he maintained discipline by means of a monitor's meeting. In itself this had the capacity for developing indigenous leadership. In many ways the school was a great success. Moulton himself left a wonderful legacy in Tongan hymnology, literature, and language study, a debt which Tonga still recognizes. On the practical side he developed agriculture, printing, carpentry, and weather study, which helped the Public Service. On the impractical side he established proficiency in Euclid, in algebra, in astronomy, and chemistry—impractical because Tonga had no openings for the use of such knowledge, and they tended to become a symbol of superior education.

All this changed Tonga, *but* Moulton could have done little of it had not the drive of the king been behind it all.

The vulnerability of such a system lay at two points. (1) It opened too much for missionaries the involvement in the training of civil servants, and influence over them and eventually over the political office itself. (2) Such a system was moving more rapidly toward Tongan independence than the Wesleyan Conference at home was prepared to permit.

Sooner or later trouble was bound to come. It did. Moulton was absent in England from 1877 to 1879, putting his revision of the Tongan Bible through the press. Tonga fell the victim of one unscrupulous missionary who took this opportunity for so pressing the claims of independence (to his own advantage) that a large segment of the church broke away as a Free church. The claim for independence was just and the church was ready for it. The request had been sent up in a constitutional manner. The home conference that rejected this is largely to blame for what followed. But the activities of the missionary Shirley Baker, who had assumed the political office of premier, and took advantage of Moulton's absence in England to press the claims for independence to his own personal advantage, make very unpleasant reading—except to cynics who like telling the story in the style of Voltaire, as Basil Thomson has done. Baker caused a split in the church, a large segment breaking away and establishing itself as a Free church. The split has been perpetuated unto this day, so that Tonga has, alas, two Wesleyan causes with no difference of doctrine. How much good can be undone because of a vulnerable spot and one man taking advantage of it! And again how much damage can also be done when a home church holds up independence when a young church is ready for it.

It seems a pity to end this study on this note, however, because the character given the Tongan church by its original people movements has persisted throughout all these vicissitudes. It is still, together with Fiji, its own mission field, the greatest missionary island church of the Pacific, and has remained true to its doctrinal position.

4

TWO WEBS MEET

Two webs of church growth were spreading across the South Pacific. Wesleyanism had strong roots in the west in Australia, New Zealand, and Tonga. Calvinism was rooted in Tahiti and spreading through the Polynesian Islands. Both were moving toward the south central Pacific. Somewhere they had to meet.

Both expansions had been foreseen by men of insight and action. John Williams had intended working through Tonga into Fiji and the New Hebrides, although he was not unaware of the cultural differences between what is now differentiated as Polynesia and Melanesia.[1]

While Williams was operating in the east, preparing his vessel, *Messenger of Peace*, to sail westward, Walter Lawry (as we have already seen) was looking eastward from Australia, planning to move through Maoriland into Tonga and back into Melanesia through the Tonga-Fiji cultural bridge.

These two men had much in common. Both were dynamic personalities, both zealous for the spread of the gospel, with pan-Pacific outreach, both believed that God Himself was their source of inspiration, and both were prepared to be "obedient to the heavenly vision," even in the face of delay by their respective administrations. One built his own ship and sailed from east to west from a nucleus at 150° west. The other chartered a ship at about 150° east and sailed from west to east. The resultant webs of church growth, like East and West themselves as the geographers conceive them, met somewhere near the international date line. An important meeting took place when Williams and Barff (L.M.S.) called on Nathaniel Turner and William Cross (W.M.S.) at Tonga, and found them fruitfully working a plot which did have some L.M.S. origins. There might well have been a disagreement, but wisdom ruled. Much historian's ink has been

111

spilt about this conference, which has usually been appraised in the light of subsequent events rather than in the historic context.[2] Present also was a Christian trader, Samuel Henry, son of one of the earlier missionaries to Tahiti, and with him a Fijian petty chief, Takai. The latter had made a voyage to Tonga with the specific intention of seeking teachers to take the gospel to Fiji, and he was an advocate who would not be put off. Also present in Tonga at the time was a Samoan chief, Fauea, who had been converted in Tonga and was now anxious to return to his own land with his Christian family and the gospel. He too was an effective advocate.

The context of the conference was therefore one of wide-open doors for evangelism. All four missionaries were disposed to expand, despite shortages of staff. The indigenous advocates were both men of standing, each with a key to high places in his own land. Takai and Fauea both promised to escort teachers and sponsor their cause. In the face of this something had to be decided. The missionaries could not avoid discussing spheres of activity. Both the L.M.S. and W.M.S. records and published writings show that Williams changed his mind at this conference in 1830, and deliberately turned from Fiji to Samoa.[3] Both records are clear that Takai was to take the Tahiti teachers designated for Fiji, but that they would serve for the Wesleyans and the results of their labor would be subsequently incorporated into their church.[4] Significantly enough it was Cross, one of the participants of the conference, who effected the incorporation.[5]

THE LONDON MISSIONARY SOCIETY NARRATIVE

Williams' heart had been set on winning Samoa for Christ since 1824.[6] The presence of Fauea and his family in Tonga with their desire to return home was too good an opportunity to miss. It suited his overall purpose to take Fauea himself, making use of him enroute to explore something of the Samoan customs and language. We note that in this agreement both societies drew on the labors of the other, for Fauea was a Wesleyan convert, though he became the agent for introducing the L.M.S. into Samoa, in the same way that the Tahiti teachers served the W.M.S. in Fiji. It had been a clear comity agreement.[7]

In 1824 Williams had no vessel nor the sympathy of his wife for such a venture;[8] but certain events led her to change her mind, and Williams became a shipbuilder. By 1830 he was on his way.[9] On the voyage Fauea warned Williams of the most likely obstructions to their church-planting program. Foremost of these was the man Tamafainga, who controlled the religious opposition they would meet.[10] However, upon their arrival at Sapapalii, they heard the astonishing news that less than two weeks before their arrival Tamafainga had been killed, and no successor had yet been able to establish himself.[11] The door was certainly open.

Fauea moved from house to house, conversing on the effects of Christianity on Tonga. As a traveled man, he had a good hearing, as did his wife among the women. They told of the Polynesian church spreading across the Pacific. He reasoned simply:

> Can the religion of these strangers be anything but wise and good? Look at them and look at ourselves: their heads are covered, ours are exposed; their bodies are clothed, we have a bandage of leaves; they have clothes on their feet, ours are like dogs; look at their axes and their scissors.[12]

Fortunately we have evidence that Fauea's religion was deeper than this, but it shows the type of argument he presented to his unconverted relations when his Christian appraisals were questioned.

The important facts that emerge from the records may be summed up in the following manner:

1. The arrival of a white man's ship, built in the islands by those who sailed her and could tell the story

2. The arrival at the psychological moment soon after the death of the most likely opponent of Christianity, and before the appointment of his successor

3. The emergence of a mediator, in the person of the chief, Fauea, who had committed himself to Christ and had the right family connections, again at the psychological moment[13]

4. Fauea's experience in travel and religion, his family prosperity and good standing with the men on the *praying-ship* (his own term),[14] together with his argument that the comforts and prestige of civilization came in the wake of Christianity

Here is an ideal battlefield for the materialistic and theocratic historian. Undoubtedly the acceptance of Christianity was because of a concentrated focus of relevant facts at a specific time and place. Was it fortuitous, or God acting in history—what the Bible calls "the fulness of time"? Throughout the whole story of the planting and growth of the church in the Pacific, the missionaries of all societies recognized a divine element in their successes—it was God's work rather than their own. In their writing, when they recognized a human effort (Fauea's, for example), they invariably added a phrase like "under God." The missionaries accepted the biblical view of history. Thus Williams wrote:

> We were constrained to admire the goodness of God, in providentially bringing us to an individual, whose character and connections so admirably fitted him to advance the objects we had in view.[15]

And again—

> Much of this success was attributable, under God, to Fauea, with whom we met so providentially.[16]

Not only did Fauea know the right people to approach, but his own chiefly connections were with the family of Malietoa, the paramount chief at the time, who was engaged in a war of revenge and honor, according to the requirements of custom, on account of the death of the unloved Tamafainga. Malietoa himself was fairly receptive in spite of his war responsibilities. The visitors were ceremonially received and an exchange of goods was made. Fauea saw that the rapport of custom was properly established. Another chief, Matetau, came from the island of Manono and sought teachers for his community. Williams left the men he had with Malietoa, but assured Matetau he would return in about a year with teachers for Manono. That was in 1830, but two years passed before he could honor his promise.[17] The effective witness of Fauea, his accounts of people movements into Christianity in various parts of Polynesia, his customary rapport,[18] and the testimony of his wife[19] all impressed Malietoa, who, in spite of his temporary engagement in war, readily offered protection to Christian teachers and facilities for evangelism. For the duration of his absence on the war campaign he gave the Christian teachers the use of the public assembly house, the largest building in his settlement.[20]

Having established his teachers, Williams faced the open ocean again on his homeward way, with the thought he recorded at the time:

It may neither be uninteresting nor unprofitable to pause, and erect an Ebenezer of praise to that God, who protected our lives, directed our course, and opened before us so "great and effectual a door."[21]

After a paean of praise on the work of Fauea he ended one of the most significant chapters of his historic work with these words:

In first going to Tongatabu, we were led by an unerring hand. . . . Our meeting unexpectedly with such an efficient assistant as Fauea, was a remarkable and interesting intimation of Providence that the set time for God to accomplish His purposes of mercy to the Samoa islanders was come.[22]

Malietoa had demanded four teachers.[23] These were stationed in his area of control. Church-planting for the L.M.S. in Samoa had begun.[24]

Williams returned in 1832. The teachers had established themselves and built a church on Savaii. Malietoa, his family, and many chiefs and people had embraced Christianity, at least nominally. In other islands village groups desired to have the gospel preached to them.[25] At Manua they asked for a missionary or teacher whom they promised to house and give a hearing.[26] In the district of Leone some fifty persons had declared themselves Christian and were awaiting a teacher.[27] They had heard of the movement from Savaii, and they had sent their representatives to learn what they could of it and then return and teach it. They testified to their being Christian by means of a symbol: a piece of white cloth tied round the arm. They had built a chapel. The chief who was their leader made regular visits to the chapel in Savaii and upon his return home transmitted to his own group what he had learned. When they found Williams had teachers only for Manono they broke down and wept.

At his next port of call Williams found the same kind of situation— the chief passing on what he had heard. He had learned a chapter of a Tahiti primer and the Lord's Prayer. At Upolu the next day, Samoans came from various parts with similar stories. Only at Tutuila had things been different; there, Williams was asked for powder and muskets.[28] At Manono the teacher was stationed amid great rejoicing.

Thus in village after village Williams met groups of people who already called themselves "Sons of the Word." Even without knowing who he was they explained that some twenty moons before a white chief named Williams left some "workers of religion" at Savaii. Some of their people had been there, seen the new religion at work, and returned home to their own villages to start the movement there. It meant changes of life patterns, a sacred day, building a chapel, and waiting for a teacher. There was something almost messianic about it all—multitudes ready, believing, waiting![29]

Faced with this situation, Williams visited England in 1834 to appeal for more missionaries, though it was 1836 before they arrived.[30] Even then they were inexperienced, without knowledge of the language and customs, and confronted with the leadership and instruction of twenty thousand would-be converts.[31] There were fresh outbursts of people movement in 1840, 1841, and 1842,[32] so that the missionary Gill wrote, "All the islands in this group appeared ripe unto harvest, but the labourers are few," and bemoaned the fact that the eagerness for baptism would drive the Samoans to any white man, even escaped convicts. He cites the case of one such person who openly made good profit by baptizing pagans in return for the priestly offering he demanded for the service.[33] The arrival of a team of missionaries in 1836 permitted the establishment of organization. With a will they attacked the task of learning the language and assigned portions for Scripture translation to each man (Tahiti Scriptures were used first). By 1839 a printing press was in operation; from this a gospel of John appeared in 1841, then Mark, Luke, Acts, and the other New Testament books. The Old Testament, translated by 1855, was printed and in the hands of the people by 1860.[34] They had learned from their Tahiti mistakes.

By 1844 they had a theological seminary at Malua. It had a good record afterward and a missionary vision.[35] Captain Erskine found two missionaries established there with well built homes a few years later. They were working on a chapel, a schoolhouse, and accommodation for sixty students.[36]

THE WESLEYAN MISSIONARY SOCIETY NARRATIVE

Quite independent from the growth and expansion of the church in Tahiti, news of the new religion drifted through to Samoa from Tonga, via the isolated islands that lie between the two groups. The picture is difficult to reconstruct because data of the configurations of Samoan growth are buried in Tongan

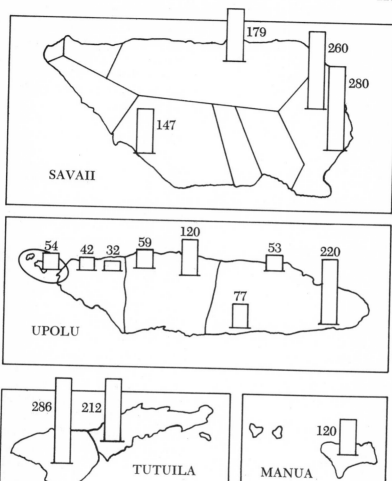

This depicts two decades of growth at the membership level. It only represents a small percentage of those received from paganism as converts. The segments most noted for rivalry and war at the time show slower rate of membership growth. The growth (indicated by the height of the columns) took place in the parts of the country which experienced the charismatic movements rather than those noted for war and rivalry.

Pl. 9. L.M.S. communicant growth in Samoa by midcentury.

records. Changes in control from the British Wesleyan Conference to the Australian took place in the 1850s, and data relevant
to this present segment of our study have to be sought for in more
than one archival repository. But it has to be attempted.[37]

Before the people movement swept over Tonga, when missionary John Thomas had some two hundred and forty attending
worship but few real converts, Saivaaia, a Samoan from Savaii,
visited Tonga. That was in 1828, when the Tongan field was
ripening and some thirty Tongans came into the church. Saivaaia
was caught up with this movement and, returning to Samoa, he
proclaimed himself as of the Tonga Religion. He established
small Christian causes among his friends and family at Tafua
and Salelologa in Savaii. Some other Samoans, influenced by the
witness of these groups, renounced their heathenism, but the
cause lacked organization.[38] So, when Williams and Fauea arrived
in 1830, Christianity was not unknown.

Early correspondence from Tonga reveals an awareness that
the church could expand into both Fiji and Samoa from Tonga,[39]
but the absence of references to Samoa in 1830 and 1831 suggest
the conference decision was taken seriously. Tonga's full membership had jumped to 1,422, and exhorters were available for
any expansion project. Williams had promised to return to Samoa
in ten months, but "twenty moons" passed before they saw him
again, and in the interim the Samoans had commenced petition-
ing Tonga for aid. Furthermore these requests had been presented within the traditional interinsular patterns of political
request: the Samoan chief, Tuinaulu, appealed through the Tongan chief, Tubou. If custom had any significance at all this had
to be taken seriously. They had requested a missionary.[40] The
Wesleyans referred the matter to their London Committee and
set about preparing a book for Samoan instruction.[41] I take this
to mean that some of the Wesleyan men had come to the conclusion that the Samoan open doors should not be allowed to close,
and Williams' failure to return had made them disposed to by-
pass the earlier conference.

Meantime, inspired by the state of Christianity in Tonga,
Tuinaulu returned to Samoa and became himself a keen evan-
gelist, so that within three years forty villages and hamlets on
Savaii and twenty-five on Upolu declared themselves to be Tonga
Religion.[42] This growth would appear to have occurred during

1833, 1834, and 1835.[43] A glance back at the segmented graph of growth in the Tonga study (pl. ix) will reveal that this was contemporaneous with the movements in Vavau, Niuafoou, and Niuatobutabu. Another glance at the map which accompanies this study of Samoa will show the location flow of the 1834–35 Tongan movement, northward through these islands; two of which, though politically Tongan, are nearer to Samoa. The flow of the people movement had moved into Samoa *before* the Wesleyans had sent any missionary or Tongan teacher to that group. It was a spontaneous expansion, but of the Tongan, not the Tahitian, movement. If a comity agreement was broken as a result of this, the movement was rather of the Holy Spirit than of the missionaries.

By 1834 under the force of the charismatic movement the Tongan Wesleyans were expansionists—certainly both Peter Turner and John Thomas (the Chairman of the Mission), neither of whom had been involved in the 1830 conference. John Williams visited Samoa and Tonga at the end of 1832 and was astonished at the power of religious developments in both groups. He says nothing of any further discussions on comity, but may well have disclosed in Tonga his concern that he had insufficient teachers and no missionaries.[44] He certainly could make no promises and knew that the L.M.S. system was so structured as to demand missionaries when a church began to grow. The situation in Samoa was out of hand, and in 1832 he knew the danger of thousands of unshepherded converts—syncretistic Christianity did, in point of fact, grow worse and worse during 1833 and 1834. It was this which drove him home to England for more missionaries in 1834. In the same year the Wesleyans acted. The men in Tonga determined to send one of their own number to bring the Samoan people movement under control and organization. Thus the Wesleyans were established in both Fiji and Samoa before the L.M.S. men who responded to Williams' appeal arrived in the Pacific.[45]

On his arrival in Samoa, the Wesleyan Peter Turner (not the same man who was involved in the earlier conference) found some two thousand persons who called themselves Tonga Religion. After his first itinerancy another two thousand had been gathered. Danks says of this:

a great spiritual work, self-originated, self-propagated, and self-sustained, had spread from place to place, despite fierce local jealousies. Congregations had been formed, churches built and societies instituted without a farthing of expense to the Methodist Church.*[46]

Applications for teachers came from everywhere to Turner, who had soon established himself at Satupaitea. Before long his initial two thousand had increased to thirteen thousand, which was described in the following manner by Dyson:

> This marvellous work was accomplished in the short space of twenty months. During this time eighty churches were built in as many villages. Four thousand persons were distributed into three hundred classes; and a thousand teachers, who had themselves been newly taught to read, were busy as bees in the midst of six thousand scholars, teaching them the wonderful "Pi" [lesson card] and the art of reading.[47]

Danks says that the first intimation Peter Turner had of the 1830 comity discussion was from the new L.M.S. missionaries.[48] I find this difficult to reconcile with the records, but be this as it may, it must have been as great a shock to him to be told by the new L.M.S. team to withdraw from the situation as it was to them to find such a highly organized Wesleyan cause on their arrival. Turner decided to fight back, and did so for three solid years, generating heat all the time. Dyson admitted that Turner had linked Methodism with powerful chiefly factions opposed to Malietoa and that these affiliations still applied in his own time (1865).[49] In the heat of the dispute Turner had considered resigning from the Wesleyan Society and refusing to leave Samoa at all.[50]

With the team of new men it was a matter of honor and agreement—whoever had made that agreement. With Turner it was a case of withdrawing from a half-finished task, which had terrific momentum, for the handling of which he had a superior capacity. A series of communications passed between the London Committee and the men on the field. The final statements from the Wesleyan leaders in London were dogmatic and in terms of severe rebuke.[51] They were circulated to every missionary in the Tonga,

*The Wesleyan Church was incorporated into the Methodist Church in Australasia at the beginning of the century. Danks was writing in 1914. As a Mission Board secretary his writing had a promotional orientation, for which allowance must always be made. His motives were mission policy at 1914.

Samoa, and Fiji locality, and left everybody smarting. Turner withdrew in bad grace in 1839, destroying all the Wesleyan records, supposedly to assure the discontinuation of Wesleyanism in Samoa. I cannot see why the records could not have been handed over to the other Society, which was to carry on the work. This would have been the correct archival procedure today.[52] It had been a strong church and it was a tragedy that its origins were bathed in such bitter controversy, because this was itself transmitted to the young converts and led to the crystallization of a whole network of rivalries, instead of guiding energy into the consummation of the people-movement experience, which Turner had natural gifts to have accomplished.

The thirteen thousand Samoan Wesleyans were left in a serious dilemma. There were operational and theological differences quite apart from the personal rivalry that had been generated. Those who went over to their rivals had to "eat humble pie," and especially was it so where there were political antagonisms with the family of Malietoa.[53] The patterns of growth within the two churches differed. One delayed baptism and reception into membership for an inordinately long time on a basis of Western perfectionism; the other brought them faster through a more refined gradation of status, each step based on a spiritual experience or work of grace, so that perfection was seen as charismatic rather than performance. When Wesleyan experiences were met in L.M.S. congregations the latter missionaries were quite at a loss in how to deal with them.

However, the Wesleyan people-movement intake patterns demanded a drive for the consummating experiences. As things worked out in Samoa, the long period of waiting for reception left a void, and the psychological ripening for the second experience was often lost so that many Christians settled down to a formal nominalism, and often the last state was worse than the first. Left alone, after the missionary withdrawal, with houses swept, many now found them possessed by mere "Christianized" forms of the evil spirits they had thought exorcised. To the pre-Christian rivalries and jealousies were now added some theological and organizational twists.

Even so, a large part of the Wesleyan movement was absorbed by the other. This is set off against a determined core which positively *refused* to be absorbed. Unity movements in the West frequently have similar adamant cores that will not give way. In Samoa this core was not really theologically Wesleyan; the factors responsible were political and social.

The Australasian Conference of the Wesleyan church was given independent entity in the 1850s, with the Pacific Islands districts as its mission field. This greatly reduced the long lines of communication from Britain, and likewise the costs. It brought the administrative center closer to the field and autonomy into the Australian colonies. Immediately upon this shift of authority the Samoans and the Tonga district reopened the question of Wesleyanism in Samoa. They presented the case that Wesleyanism in Samoa simply refused to disintegrate and was in a pitiable state for the want of shepherding. The colonial conference, feeling itself to be a new body, untied by past British decisions, reentered the field. Peter Turner had withdrawn in June 1839. Martin Dyson landed in September, 1857. A brief examination of that interim of two decades is called for.

The bitterness of the withdrawal may be seen by the Samoan efforts to prevent it: a refusal to join the other branch of the church, a plot to prevent Turner's departure by force, an offer to maintain the entire work without cost to the parent Society. On another level they pressed Tongan political relations:

> Tongans and Samoans are one people. We were one people before the *Lotu* came. What do we know of Tahiti? What communications had Tahiti with us? We only heard of Tahiti last night?[54]

Though it all failed they continued to maintain their church and worship patterns. In 1840 they met at Manono and elected three influential chiefs[55] to appeal to King George (Taufa'ahau) of Tonga and the missionaries there. They made a pathetic appeal for teachers and sent further appeals to England. The Tongan king sent a band of men with canoes and provisions under Benjamin Latusele, Barnabus Ahogalu, and other teachers and three chiefs, instructing them to try to persuade the Wesleyan Samoans to join the other group. He added the rider that if the appeal failed, Latusele was to stay and teach them.[56] They arrived in Samoa in 1841 and restored the work on the Tongan Wesleyan model. I cannot say whether or not they seriously tried to press the policy of assimilation first: it was of course *assimilation* not *integration* and this is what caused much of the trouble—prestige was involved.

The visit revived Samoan hopes and satisfied those of Atau and Tuamasaga. A further appeal now came from Wesleyans at Savaii and Manono. Again the leaders were political figures, and a deputation led by Pau of Safotalafai, Talo of Manono, Aufai of Saleaula, and Piliai of Leulumoega headed for Tonga.[57] King George now determined to visit Samoa himself and his intentions may be implied by the fact that he took another ten Tongan teachers. A great gathering was held at Manono, quite beyond any missionary influence, and the people determined to continue the Wesleyan church in Samoa. An important principle is involved here, namely, the right of indigenous self-determination contrary to mission society comity agreements. I only wish we had the documentary evidence to show if this was the Tongan king's own initiative or inspired by the Wesleyan chairman, Thomas, in Tonga.

George of Tonga wrote to the London Committee, again without avail. The missionaries kept out of the picture after Turner's withdrawal, but George of Tonga kept Latusele in Samoa. In 1847 Latusele returned to Tonga for ordination and went back to Samoa again. That ordination implies the complicity of at least the Tongan Chairman. It also marks a point from which we might say that all attempts at reconciliation were abandoned.[58]

Latusele pulled things together until his flock numbered about three thousand five hundred, some four hundred of them full members, when the Wesleyans reentered the field in 1857.[59] The figures would have been better had it not been for his interference in Samoan politics. His church was static.[60]

By having lost their missionary in 1839 the cause lost prestige. With the reappointment in 1857, this was regained to some extent and is reflected in the statistics. The procedures of the period of abandonment were at least irregular, and were clearly aimed at circumventing the motives of the London Committee and the original Tonga agreement. Comity never had a chance in Samoa. When the Australian Conference became an autonomous body it was Thomas, the Tonga Chairman, who pressed the claims of the Wesleyan church in Samoa. He prepared the evidence and it was a one-sided case he presented.[61] The Conference would have been wiser to have opened a new mission field than to have reopened an old mission scar.[62]

After many years of studying this situation I posit the following as a reasonable interpretation that fits the facts presented in the documents:

1. The Tonga Conference of 1830 was a sincere agreement in the light of the situation at the time. The roles of Takai and Fauea cannot be explained in any other way.

2. The comity agreement, though it dealt with the 1830 situation in a sound and realistic manner, did not anticipate the terrific charismatic force of the Tonga people movement and its spontaneous flow across the comity boundary.

3. The changed attitude of some of the Tonga missionaries seems to be dated to the second half of 1832, when they were confronted with (a) repeated requests from Samoa through lines of cultural rapport that were difficult to ignore, (b) the long delay in Williams' return to Samoa with the teachers he had promised, and no real guarantee that he would return (They must have known Williams' policy was not exactly the same as that of his principals.), and (c) the real dangers of an unshepherded people-movement in Samoa.

4. When Williams did return he was short of Polynesian teachers and had no assurances of any missionaries for Samoa. The big question during 1833 and 1834, then, was, Is the open door in Samoa to be made use of by *anyone?*

5. In the face of this situation two parties acted independently. Williams went to London to present an appeal for new missionaries on a basis of (a) the Tonga Conference agreement, and (b) his dilemma in Samoa. The Wesleyans on the field acted and appointed one of their number to follow up the movement which was an overflow from their own Tonga revival. The Wesleyans both in Tonga and Fiji were masters at strategic deployment. It was a major factor in their growth pattern. They had occupied both Fiji and Samoa by 1835, not with men from faraway England, but by deployment of field staff. The new L.M.S. men did not arrive until mid-1836.

6. With a Wesleyan movement of thirteen thousand confronting them, the new L.M.S. missionaries saw the situation as comity or coexistence. Was the gentlemen's agreement to be honored?

The Wesleyans involved (mainly Turner and Thomas) were inclined to argue that the opportunity was ripe and the L.M.S. had no resources to handle it. The waiting had extended into some years. The argument that two men could not make a comity agreement for the whole will not stand, because they did and the London Committee ratified it.

7. For the two committees in London the whole question of intermission relations was involved (a world issue, not of Samoa alone). Some field missionaries and the London Committee disagreed strongly, but the men in Fiji (including Cross, one of the 1830 discussion group) acted on that side of the agreement, assimilating the Tahitians in Oneata, Lau.

8. Two missionaries in particular smarted under the rebukes of the London Committee and would not let the matter rest. By the circumvention of the Society authority, either the Tongan king, or Chairman, or both, preserved a Wesleyan entity in Samoa. (I am not justifying or otherwise, merely sorting facts.)

9. By 1857 the situation in the unconstitutional Wesleyan communion in Samoa was met by action from the new Australasian Wesleyan Conference. This was a new mission with a new parent body, no longer under the London Committee. This was the A.W.M.S. The W.M.S. never dishonored the comity agreement, ratified in London in 1834.[63]

10. Dyson, who reopened Wesleyan work under new auspices, has argued the case at length. He justified the entry as *honorable,* but was strongly of the opinion that it was *inexpedient* and *impolitic.*[64] It was largely done on the determination and advocacy of Latusele and Thomas. The latter as chairman and prime actor must be held responsible.

I am sorry to have been forced to inflict so critical a historical reconstruction on the reader, but it is essential to our general purpose. In this study in which two webs of church growth meet, we are led to see the kind of problem a people movement can cause for comity agreements. Furthermore the historical reconstruction is, as it were, a frame of reference in which an anthropological analysis is to be made. We are to see how denominationalism tends to affiliate itself with social and political rivalries and tensions within the culture complex itself. I cannot do this accurately unless I first assure myself that the historical framework is accurately reconstructed and documented.* Up to this point we have seen how the two webs reached out into Samoa and met; then how one of the missionary societies involved withdrew only to find the movement it had established refused to disintegrate or become assimilated in the other, so that, in a round about way it had to reenter the field. We must now investigate how the other body fared when it had the field to itself.

L.M.S. Activity in the Interim of Sole Occupancy

It must be fairly admitted that the L.M.S. work after the withdrawal of the W.M.S. was sufficiently elastic to receive the Wesleyans, although there was certainly undue delay about receiving them into membership. Nevertheless, after Turner's removal things did begin to happen in the L.M.S. communities, even as far as Tutuila. It is my considered opinion that this was a direct result of Wesleyan intake, for the movement was certainly of the Wesleyan Tongan type, and was not publicised, as far as I know, in L.M.S. promotional material. On Tutuila it spread from Pagopago to Nuuli and Vaitogi and to the district of Leone, traditionally rival to Pagopago. Outpourings of the Holy Spirit were reported on November 2 and 4, a fortnight later, December 1 and 7, and on into 1840, February 3 and 9, March 1 and 8, with a real climax at Pagopago in mid-June—a movement of considerable power.[65]

It is true that similar movements were being experienced among the Presbyterians in Scotland at the time, but they were already at work in Samoa before any Scottish reports reached them.[66] But the movements of this kind were far more common in Wesleyan than Calvinistic atmospheres and in the present case I believe they were stimulated by the influx of Wesleyans. There is some evidence for this contention. First, the L.M.S. missionary Murray reported, in his own way, what is very like the Wesleyan "second work of grace":

> The members of the church seemed as if they had undergone a *re*-conversion, and had risen all at once to a higher life.[67] (Italics in orig.)

*Actually this has never been objectively reconstructed by any historian. All reconstructions have been partisan and conditioned by later situations and interests. Because I know many supporters of Samoan missionary work will disagree with me I have felt obligated to document at length.

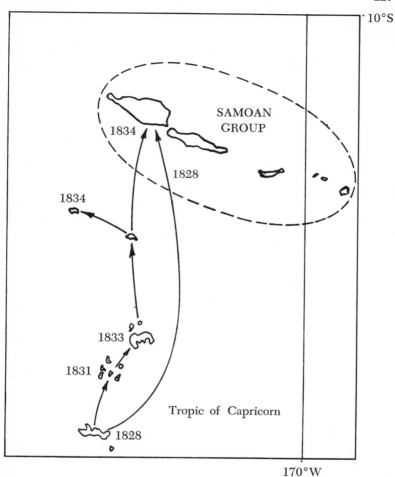

This is a good example of how people movements into Christianity can interfere with comity plans and agreements. Two streams of Wesleyan influence had reached Samoa before any English missionaries of any denomination were established there.

1828: Spontaneous expansion from Tongatabu
1833-34: Spontaneous expansion from Vavau, via the chain of islands

Pl. 10. Flow map showing diffusion of Wesleyan Christianity from Tonga to Samoa before 1835.

Second, Murray indicates that they had experiences that were normally not within their pattern:

> . . . The feeling swelled higher and higher, till, like a pent-up flood, it burst forth, and there was such a scene as I had not before witnessed. Very many were quite prostrated and others were seized with violent convulsions. This was a *new feature* of our awakening. The afternoon service was very similar to that of the morning.[68] (Italics mine)

Murray describes many such incidents but also admits the great caution on the part of the missionaries, who did not seem to know what to make of it.[69] Yet they recognized that many conversions led to real life transformations.[70]

The converted units took to a pattern of family prayer. Though both missionary societies pressed for this, it was culturally acceptable because of the role of the father of the household as family priest in the pre-Christian society. We will return to this in our anthropological analysis. At present we are merely noting features that can be historically documented:

> There was again an astonishing commotion during the meeting, and at night every family seemed to be mourning apart. . . . "The land shall mourn, every family apart."[71]

and again—

> Soon after sundown I took a walk around the village. . . . It was the hour of family prayer, and the different households were gathered round their domestic altars. All can be heard that is going on in native houses. . . .* It was most affecting to go from house to house and listen to the simple, fervent pleadings.[72]

This was all possible because of the large number of men, who were among the first to break down under conviction of sin.[73] Here we are dealing with something that cannot be explained in terms of political, social, or material advantages. Many actual cases can be documented, and some of the most remarkable show that the convert lost materially by his experience, or lost prestige through having to surrender his known values, as in the case of the haughty Maunga.[74]

The actual course of the movement can be traced and dated throughout Tutuila, where the movement was concentrated from 1838 to 1840 and observable by a missionary, and where the

*Samoan houses have not true walls, but blinds that may be up or down.

two divisions centered at Pagopago and Leone were socially and politically rival segments. In Pagopago the heathen had been won by a series of experiences, and by twos and threes they came into Christianity. Except for a few of the most distant villages, which held out for years, the last of them were won in the meetings of June 15, 1840.[75] Over two-thirds of the whole island had "anxious concern" for religion. The experiences were shown to have been permanent. From the three persons who partook of the first holy communion in 1838 there had been growth by the addition of over a hundred tested and approved new communicant members by 1840. A decade later there were five hundred communicants,[76] and this part of Samoa was relatively the strongest part of the church for some considerable time. Yet even here the membership figures were far too small a percentage of the number of adherents who had made clear breaks with paganism.

By 1844 people should have been coming into membership in hundreds if there had been effective follow-up to the original movement from paganism. Membership was approved for islanders with extreme caution and anything but Western Puritanism exposed an approved member to possible suspension.[77] Admission to membership was apparently competitive and by selection. In Manua, for instance, where there had been only five members when the charismatic movement hit them, some thirty new members were subsequently admitted, but these were "*selected* from three hundred candidates." The congregation of members was thus controlled by the missionaries on a basis of merit, in spite of the fact that revivals were going on all the time and people were professing deep experiences of conviction and forgiveness, and the whole movement had restored peace and brought the social and political hostility and war itself to an end.[78]

One can readily see why the Wesleyans were unhappy about having to be selected competitively for though they were expected to "grow in grace" and to maintain moral standards, and could be disciplined for failure in this, merit was never a demand for admission. A man entered the church on the basis of his own experience, his faith, and his sincerity. The very idea of selecting 10 percent of applicants was a problem to the Wesleyans, for whom entry into the fellowship was the means of follow-up growth from grace to grace. Furthermore, this exclusive character of the fellowship militated against the assimilation of both pagans and Wesleyans. Although I believe the main obstructions to assimilation were political and social rivalry, the different denominational attitudes regarding the nature, function, and growth of the fellowship of members were against assimilation. The L.M.S. missionaries were embarrassed by enthusiasm; Wesleyans welcomed it.

THE AUSTRALIAN WESLEYAN NARRATIVE

Wesleyan operation officially commenced in 1857 with Samoa as part of the Tonga District.[79] Four Tongan teachers were to work under the leadership of Martin Dyson. They were taken to Tonga by the Conference Deputation, Thomas Adams. Dyson found things at Manono, where they landed, *disagreeable* and *wild*, and writing of it later cited Adams' reactions:

> The brilliant reports of the Methodism of Samoa might fit the year 1839, but they were certainly untrue of 1857. We soon discovered that we were illuded and baulked by the natives. . . . Our missionaries are prepared for such indifference among heathen tribes; but it was in our case intolerably galling to find ourselves victims of odious Samoan hypocrisy and guile. The ring leader of them [Leiataualesa] belonged to the L.M.S. and only became a Wesleyan after our arrival.[80]

The statistical strength of the church stood at three thousand five hundred adherents, some four hundred of them full members, and eighteen local preachers. Some of these must have been Tongans. Their strength was regionally distributed over forty preaching places, so the average congregation would have only 87.5 people, of whom no more than ten would be members. The number of local (or lay) preachers was less than half the number of congregations. The Wesleyan system requires more preachers than congregations to function properly, unless preachers are to be preaching three or four times each on Sunday. A healthy Wesleyan congregation requires a membership of at least a third of its total number of adherents. The genius of this pattern in the islands has been the manner in which it has developed the experience of the members and brought new converts quickly to places of leadership and witness. When such converts witness to pagans, they are judged not by their perfection but by their transformation. The figures Dyson was confronted with on his arrival in Samoa are just not like Wesleyan statistics. They reveal the lack of any spiritual follow-up after the people movement of the 1830s. The vital decade—the 1840s—had known rather the sapping of spiritual power, as a vegetable parasite sucks the nourishment from its host.

During the interim of two decades some ten thousand Wesleyans had gone over to the other body and accepted the W.M.S. withdrawal. Half the church buildings had gone with them. In the localities where assimilation was resisted, the Wesleyan communities were divided roughly half and half. Thus, in many villages where Dyson found Wesleyan causes, these groups represented but segments of the total group. Denominational rivalry was strong there and in line with patterns of inherent rivalries that had survived from pre-Christian times. Dyson had a major problem of rehabilitation on his hands. He faced a sociodenominational rivalry-orientated situation with no more than 11 percent of his adherents having the status of full membership, and with more than half his congregations without either pastor or preacher. The figures, though bad, were not nearly as bad as those of the L.M.S.,[81] though for different reasons. In neither case were the people movements consummated by bringing converts on into the full life of the church. The majority of converts remained on the fringe.

Erskine, who approved the L.M.S. work, and currently considered their statistics reliable, summed up the form of Christianity manifested by their adherents as "softening manners and purifying morals."[82] He also suggests why they were not being led on to responsibility. They had developed a fine style of handwriting by copying out sermons of the missionaries, because the "missionaries insisted they are not to teach anything of their own."[83] This is the very opposite of the Wesleyan policy of encouraging converts to testify to their own experiences.[84] Yet our analysis shows quite clearly that the member-adherent ratio in *both* denominations is lower than their own figures in other parts of the Pacific. Neither church developed at its normal rate in Samoa. I believe this can only be explained by the heat and rivalry generated during the two disturbing decades, when "Christian" rivalries attached themselves to inherent sociomilitary rivalries. The sap of the tree, which should have produced fruit, passed into the parasite of discord.

Confronted by this situation, Dyson had to fix his policy. He did not concentrate on winning back the ten thousand Wesleyans who had gone over to the other denomination. He determined to start with the adherent fringe of his flock, to try to bring them into a deeper experience and membership, and then to bring more members into commitment as preachers. In spite of the fact that his own arrival restored some prestige to the Wesleyan cause, and in spite of the other fact that many who had transferred to the L.M.S. after Peter Turner's departure now returned, after six years of work, Dyson had not brought his number of adherents beyond five thousand,[85] an increase of only fifteen hundred, and was not at all worried about it. The old people-movement "door" had long since closed and had never permitted the consummation of the movement.

The Wesleyan statistics of Dyson's first few years are revealing. In 1858 the number of adherents (in spite of prestige and transfer intake) dropped from 3,500 to 2,445.[86] This could have indicated disciplining and/or correcting standards, but it most likely means that Dyson himself prepared more accurate figures than those given to him when he arrived. However, if he had a thousand or more fewer adherents, he had brought his number of local preachers up to 80 (an improvement of 62) and had improved his member-adherent ratio by bring 160 adherents through the instruction classes into membership and had another 104 on trial. By raising the ratio from 11 to 20 percent he had physical evidence of quality growth within. By 1859 he had his class leaders at work within a true Wesleyan pattern.

There were 78 of them, though the number of congregations remained the same. This means that classes had been introduced in all the smaller congregations by means of local leaders.[87] At the same time the more alert members were reaching out to win back the lost or indifferent fringe. It appears that this was concentrated on specific groups and localities, because not only did the number of adherents rise from 2,445 to 3,814 in the year and continue to 4,863 the following year, but in 1860–61 a few new preaching places were opened. There were now 43 regular congregations with church buildings and another five, without buildings, but with regular services for worship.[88]

The major concentration, however, was still on those within the church, organizing the new congregations and improving the member-adherent ratio. Thus although the increase of adherents for 1861 was only 20 the total membership of 900 (649 full, 251 on trial) in 1860 rose to 1,148 (873 full, 275 on trial) in 1861. I have shown that in the Wesleyan pattern the number on trial is the key to the quality growth in the congregation. In 1862 Dyson was able to report 458 on trial and had his member-adherent ratio at about 27 percent. This was much more like a Wesleyan statistical figure, and far more healthy than what he had found five years earlier.[89]

It is good to have this fine statistical vignette of a highly critical half decade. It might have been lost because it comes from Tongan sources (Samoa having been under the jurisdiction of Tonga for the first few years), but it shows how physical records can reflect growth on a spiritual level. If records are carefully and honestly kept they reflect theological levels, and quantity can reveal quality. In the interim they did not do this, because they were unreliable. This particular bunch of figures reveals church growth on the level that McGavran calls *perfecting*,[90] and should be a suitable rejoinder to any who use the quality-quantity dichotomy as a critical cliché against the physical or statistical approach to church growth research. This method depends on the accuracy of the figures supplied. It begins by testing their accuracy. If the quantity does not reflect the quality then the fault is not in the method of research but the unreliability of the statistician.

Dyson, forced by his conference appointment (but somewhat against his own personal judgment) to a policy of coexistence, was concentrating on quality growth within rather than external expansion. As leader of a minority group beside a larger denomination, what procedure could he follow with respect to their relationships? In the first place he sought uniformity on any points they had in common. He sought the standardization of Scripture translation and orthography, but found it tended to become a matter for contention. Everywhere he felt the tension of denominational differences. He was the recipient of a letter from his own Samoans on account of his attempts to fraternize with the others at all. Significantly enough the shadow of Turner's belligerence was as a cloud over him:

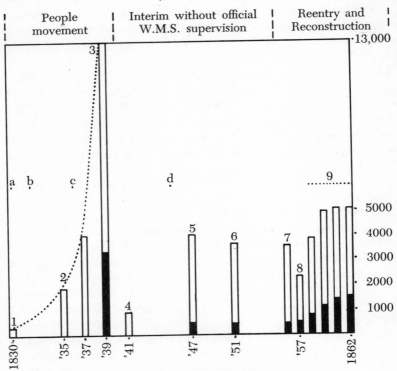

1. Effects of Tongan movement recorded prior to 1830
2. Tonga District sends Peter Turner to Samoa
3. W.M.S. highest figure (13,000) as at the time of withdrawal (1839)
4. Units refusing to be absorbed into L.M.S.
5. Reorganization under Latusele
6. Drop due to Tongan political activities
7. Statistical strength on Dyson's arrival
8. Purging rolls, etc.
9. Statistical evidence of quality growth

a. Williams' first visit
b. Williams' second visit
c. Arrival of L.M.S. missionaries
d. Roman Catholic entry

    Columns indicate total number of converts at worship (i.e., adherents). Shaded parts of columns indicate the number of converts received into full-status membership.

Pl. 11. Statistical analysis of Wesleyan strength in Samoa: 1830—1862.

> We have no sympathy with the *Ituaiga* (L.M.S.), whose customs
> you are introducing. We hold to the customs formerly practised
> by Mr. Turner. Our reason for this is that if we discontinue
> them the missionaries of the London Society will write to Britain
> saying that there is nothing left of Methodism in Samoa. . . . We
> are troubled on account of your associating with the missionaries
> of the London Society. Mr. Turner did not so associate with
> them formerly; but everyone held fast to the customs of his own
> *lotu*. These are our views about it.[91]

This valuable statement from an indigenous body after deliberation shows not only their own mind, but Dyson's sincerity at
making the best of a policy of coexistence. It shows the depth
of the personal issues in the case, the personality tensions that
had taken root in the rivalry structure inherited from pre-Christian Samoan society, and an unhappy loss of the concept of
encounter that might have been used for good. The spirit of
encounter in Samoan thinking should have been captured for
Christ—encounter with sin, Christ versus Satan, the power of
Christ's authority over that of demons, and so on. Instead of
purging society and making it holy, which was the Wesleyan
aim everywhere, the holy warfare was lost sight of and the
spirit of encounter was sublimated in denominationalism on a
basis of existing sociopolitical contention.

It was a tragedy that Turner had his hand on the helm in this
particular storm (in spite of his fine capacity to captivate a
people movement). A helmsman must know when to "give" to
the wave, lest he wreck the boat. Twenty years later, we see
from the above letter, it was Turner's personal method of handling matters, and not the Lord and Saviour whom he preached,
that lived in the minds of those who remembered him. Nothing
would have been further from Turner's desire. All the records
show him as a great evangelist but an unbending personality.[92]
"Our reason is . . ." the letter reads and shows a distrust of the
other denomination, and a fear of losing their own prestige.
Churches are not built on this kind of thing. Dyson knew it and
set out to correct it. It was a thankless task and he made a noble
effort, but something of the shadow still hangs over Samoa.

Feeling the Wesleyan cause should not have been reestablished
at all, Dyson tried to effect a reconciliation. When he became
acquainted with the true facts of the situation he would gladly
have withdrawn; but John Thomas, the chairman in Tonga,

"would hear of no relinquishment of our mission."[93] Dyson tried
to avoid proselytism and has left a good lot of data on this matter,
but admitted quite frankly he could not control his Tongan
teachers, who "drove furiously along . . . observed scarcely any
order, had no church government, but were merely a kind of
flying column of preachers."[94] Splendid as they were for encounter with paganism, Dyson found them a problem when religious
affiliations were supposedly fixed. After one year of this he began
reorganizing the church life, as we have seen. By this time also
he realized the chairman was adamant, and something more stable
had to be provided. In the meantime he had become more
acquainted with the place and people and had come on well
with the language. But he still met trouble.

The *Rules of the Society* he presented for acceptance included
the responsibility of members contributing to the church. This
was normal Wesleyan procedure but again he met with obstruction: "It was not so when Mr. Turner was among us!" It is to his
great credit that he did get matters organized and eventually a
great gathering was held and communion celebrated. It was not
until after the reform of the church was effected that Dyson had
any evidence whatever of the Holy Spirit working in the hearts
of the people, but once the core of the church got spiritually right
with God, then the times of the "showers of blessings" began
again.

When he subsequently reconstructed his impressions of the
period, Dyson agreed that in the reopening of the mission they
had been "carried away with an excess of zeal that should have
been directed elsewhere" (meaning New Guinea, where there
were some open doors at the time).[95] From Samoan informants
he himself came to believe that it was "the hope of gifts and
secular gain, which led the chiefs in 1855 to clamour for Wesleyan
missionaries" and that this did not come from the common people,
who were not accustomed to getting presents from missionaries.
The hope for presents had been stimulated by Roman Catholic
policy.[96] Dyson saw Samoan unreadiness to heal sectarian division because it involved personal chiefly interests and prejudices.[97]
Even so when a spiritual foundation was restored to their movement, blessings returned in abundance.

Part Two

THEORETICAL DIMENSIONS

5

CULTURAL DETERMINANTS AND THE ACCEPTANCE OF CHRISTIANITY

An Anthropological Analysis of the Case of Samoa

WITH THE HISTORICAL STUDY of the conversion of Samoa as a backdrop for our stage, we must reenact the drama of cultural change of that period when Samoa became Christian. We are confronted by such questions as these: What were the form and function of the pre-Christian religion? What processes were at work in the changes brought about by the missionaries? What were the sociopolitical factors influencing and being influenced by the new religion?

In the historical reconstruction of the period we saw how events converged on a single point of space and time, in the domain of Malietoa in Savaii in 1830. Things seemed to be ripe for the gospel. While both missionary and convert recognized the divine element in the pattern of events, the church-growth viewpoint insists that the culture pattern also is important, because God has been pleased to work through it. We must investigate the bearing of this pattern on the responses to the gospel; and because culture patterns vary in different localities responses vary correspondingly. Patterns provide at least part of the answer.

Pre-Christian Samoan religion was certainly Polynesian, even though it showed differences from other Polynesian forms. These were differences of *weighting*, to use the term employed by

Lowie for distinguishing between the various Polynesian cultures themselves, which he described as

> not so much set off from one another by distinctive traits as by the weighting and the organization of these traits into a distinctive whole.[1]

We have already seen that in Tahiti and New Zealand, Polynesian religion comprised two levels: (1) a superstructure of Io worship, an esoteric cult, with an extensive oral tradition known to and understood only by an elect minority that dominated the whole society; and (2) a substructure of popular animism. There are traces of the superstructure in other parts of Polynesia, but absence of evidence does not necessarily mean it did not exist in any given area. It required certain environmental features and political situations to bring it to fruition, and considerable good fortune to ensure the preservation of its oral traditions after the initial clash with Western acculturative forces.

There is no extant evidence of the esoteric cult in Samoa, but the psychic dynamism of Polynesian animism is true to the general pattern. I find no justification for Benedict's claim that supernaturalism was (or is) at a minimum in Samoa.[2] She made her observation at what Linton described as "a point of time" without any allowance for the flow of change and a series of specific historical events responsible for the situation she appraised. Had she made a prior historical reconstruction she would have seen that those elements she was observing were *results* of specific events. She contrasted Maori supernaturalism with the Samoan lack of it. In both cases she was examining results of historical events. They were not different traits, but different historical events that gave them *different weighting*. Supernaturalism was found among Maoris and Samoans, both before and after their respective conversions; but in one case it was latent and in the other manifest, as the result of historical events, or *accidents*, as Nadel called them. Events in Maoriland had led to new manifestations of hitherto latent supernaturalism. Events in Samoa kept it submerged, because the old manifest trait of rivalry was reinforced by the denominationalism of the new supernaturalism, among other things. This is an important distinction, which can be substantiated by historical documentation.[3]

The distinction is important because it explains so much of the change which took place in Samoa with conversion to Christianity—why, for example, the resistance to the new religion was so slight. The supernatural dynamic encounters between the old and new Gods were there, as everywhere else in Oceania; but instead of a physical clash between the social organization and Christianity, with perhaps a wave of persecution, Christianity was merely assimilated into the existing system. The missionary assumed an indigenous role which can be equated with that of the pre-Christian priest. Fathers of families retained their lesser priestly functions. Old emotional attitudes were retained and made manifest in new forms of rivalry. Social dislocation was slight despite the dramatic changes in basic theology. Keesing put it thus:

> The chiefs and orators merely rejected one set of interpretations and functions and took over the other without any vital blow being struck at the fundamentals of the existing order. The *tala aitu* [class of priests (not organized)] was replaced by the white missionary and the *faife'au* [indigenous pastor], the old theology by the new. The *matai* [head of a household], from being the family mediator with the gods, became a deacon in the church and conducted the regular evening service, which has become an essential part of Samoan household life; his authority was bulwarked by Biblical injunctions—indeed, from the first there could not have been much basic difference between the patriarchal system of the Old Testament and the *matai* organization.[4]

Both Malietoa of Samoa and Pomare II of Tahiti saw in Christianity an instrument with potential for maintaining and reinforcing the existing social organization, yet the systems were very differently weighted.

1. Samoa had a class of priests with limited power. Tahiti had a strongly entrenched priesthood with more actual power than the chieftaincy itself.

2. From the priest class in Samoa, one individual had assumed a dominant position of considerable power. His assassination immediately prior to the arrival of the missionary ship left the post vacant. The class from which the new official would have been selected had become subservient and was able to present no organized opposition to the new religion as had been possible in Tahiti.

3. A tendency to accept the Tongan religion and its strong supernaturalism had been manifest before the visit of any missionary to Samoa. Growth of the new religion was spontaneous. In Tahiti Christian beginnings were slow. There was no tendency toward acceptance for a decade and a half. In church growth and biblical terminology we have here a *ripe* and an *unripe* field.

4. The paramountcy of Pomare II was by no means as firmly established in Tahiti as that of Malietoa in Samoa, though the latter also had rivals. The influence of chiefly conversion was thus quite different in the two cases.

5. In Tahiti there was a direct face-to-face encounter between paganism and *a single form* of Christianity. In Samoa *rival forms* of Christianity were presented from the start, and the rivalry, as we have seen, was assimilated into existing segmental rivalries. Samoan indigenous competition was thus a determinant in the breakdown of mission comity. The rivalry latent in comity itself became manifest.

This list of contrasts shows how two Polynesian communities can have political, psychological, and structural similarities and yet present strong local differences—not variant traits, but weightings caused by historic events. Those resultant variations can have important consequences for any major innovation, as, for example, the acceptance or rejection of Christianity.

Both historical and anthropological dimensions are important. Our study becomes ethnohistorical. Communities, like the people who comprise them, are living things, not static. Change is going on all the time.* Every existing pattern has a past from which it has emerged, and is proceeding in some specific direction. Knowledge of that past and awareness of that direction should have practical value to any advocate of innovation—and that means to an evangelist. The advocate is concerned with the response he gets: acceptance or rejection, or perhaps acceptance in a modified form as a result of local weighting and motivation. Exploring this complex of past states and current direction may

*This is why church growth research uses instruments like the long-range line graph as an indicator of specific forces at work. The record of the first century's growth of a church in a particular society is always revealing. Like a thermometer, it asks Why? Graphs of two Christian communities from localities with cultural affinity but local differences may reveal different patterns of growth (e.g., spontaneous growth in one, initial delay of two decades in another).

well explain the different patterns of response one gets in a single culture area. Failure to investigate historical depths may lead to wrong conclusions. But history also is open to error. A study of a community (and this includes an emerging church) has to be ethnohistorical.

We now focus this ethnohistorical methodology on an actual situation of church planting, namely, that of Samoa in its formative years. To discover the relationship between the personal roles, individual experiences, and group responses we must first outline the nature of the social system, the pattern of family control, the Samoan value system, and the cardinal features of that religion from which the Samoans were converted.

THE NATURE OF THE SOCIAL STRUCTURE

The unit of basic structure in political affairs was the village; in social affairs, the family. As a rule the two were closely related, but families were seldom confined to one village, and a village might not be confined to one family.[5] In local matters the village was reasonably autonomous, and jurisdiction might well be segmented because of the scatter of habitations along the coast into self-contained pockets. The confines of a village (*nu'u*) were originally definable by the use of the oratorical greeting in traditional rituals (*fa'alupenga*).[6] Apparently these villages were much larger a century ago than they are today.[7]

The family (*aiga*), the unit of social life, is an extended family, not merely biological—blood, marriage, and adoption being involved. Its leadership is vested in an individual known as *matai*, who is appointed to office but can be dismissed. He has considerable authority but not absolute. He performs both social and priestly functions. In Samoan customary relationships, membership in a family may be claimed either through the male or female line and thus a person may belong to more than one family,[8] a fact which had some significance in the spread of the new religion. We shall return to the family shortly.

Larger than the villages were village combinations (*itu*) originally comprising villages with kin ties, once again each distinguished by its oratorical greeting. Later, Keesing says, the bond of unity was the need for defense. Today they are districts and subdistricts, though not quite regionally identical with the old leagues.[9] They are relevant to our present study in that they

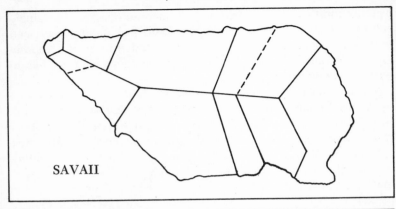

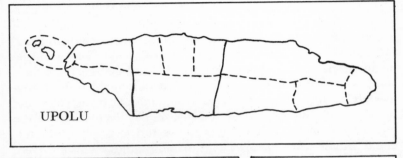

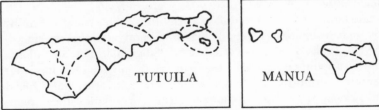

Political divisions (———) and subdivisions (————) partly account for the intense rivalry. Margaret Mead says rivalry between districts was "firmly entrenched in ceremonial usage" and at certain festivities it was stimulated in clubbing contests. Within the districts, standardized competitive situations were often set up and recognized ceremonially. Wars was part of that ceremonial rivalry. (Margaret Mead, "Samoa," in *Co-operation and Competition Among Primitive People*, pp. 299, 302).

Pl. 12. Political segmentation of Samoa at the time of the arrival of Christianity.

explain how, with a little regrouping, the more recent administration was able to substitute a political structure that met the needs of the changing conditions and was culturally meaningful to the people obliged to live under it. The organization of the church was a substitute of the same category. The pattern provided for small autonomous units (in local affairs) with a larger loyalty for the sake of security, prestige, and military action. They must have been very similar in the early days to the Philistine league of the Old Testament. They held within their structure the embryo of the federation principle and permitted an easy establishment of church organization.

Quite apart from family, village, and league, Samoan social structure had its class divisions. Lowie considered that "in the whole range of human history no people probably ever attached greater significance to distinctions of rank than the Polynesians."[10] He divided their society into noble and commoner, which "basic dichotomy rested in theory on the divine lineage of the aristocrats" and the gradations of status depended on the position of the ancestor in the scale of divinities. Practical problems frequently arose, however, over succession through rival claims of precedence, which were often "proved" by magical or military means. Thus it was possible in the case of Samoa for a subgroup of the upper caste (though a low group in that class) to hold more power and prestige than the titular sovereign.[11]

The priestly class usually came from this group, but it should be remembered than a person could hold a multiplicity of offices on different levels of prestige. Lips tells of a Samoan king who held four titles, acquired by conquest after the wars with Tonga.[12] A man could be head of a household on the family level and a warrior chief of a league. The patriarchal head of a family would also be its priest.[13] An orator who was also a chief carried the double title orator-chief (*tulafale ali'i*).[14] At the same time a man might be appointed to office one day and find it taken away by the same authority the next day,[15] so that the positions and their accompanying prestige were by no means permanent.

Often these men of rank were conceptualized collectively, that is, officials taken to be of equal rank. The *tu'ua* would select the storyteller for the moment from a group of orators.[16] A group of chiefs, united by ties of kinship, under a *sa'o* was known as *usoali'i*. There was also a priestly class, *taulaitu*. These are

examples of conceptualized collectivity or egalitarianism, which
served as a break on the intense rivalry and desire for prestige.
Within the priest class, although Samoa had no organized priesthood as in Tahiti, the class was subdivided into functional
groups: war priests, family priests, and so on.[17]

The absence of a strongly entrenched priestly cult and hierarchy provided opportunity for aggressive individuals to assume
the priestly role, which brought rich rewards and often extended
and elevated the worship of one's family gods and spirits. Both
the deity and the priest gained prestige thereby. This office could
be transmitted to the son of the priest, but this did not establish
a hereditary line of priests or a hierarchy. Thus, Margaret Mead
claims, an individual with psychic gifts could gain prestige and
wealth by exercising the gift in such ways as ascertaining or
divining the cause of calamities or in exorcising evil spirits.[18]

Mead has other things also to say on the gaining of prestige
in Samoa. The social organization was understood only by a
limited group of village elders, who had prestige from the fact
of that knowledge itself. The talking chiefs, having no say in the
appointment of chiefs, manipulated their formal status. The
ambitious new-rich exploited the orator's desire for prestige.
Villages, like individuals, sought prestige in unique patterns,
such as by varying the social structure and creating new officials.
Mead cites the case of a village with seventeen high-ranking
chiefs, whose names all had to be mentioned with every formal
speech, and another which had three different ways of arranging
its *fono* (council) seating for prestige purposes.[19]

In spite of the conservative traditional background, a free
hand is given the individual within the social organization and
great personal rewards are offered because of this structural
flexibility. Mead's figure of speech is "pliable to bend without
breaking." She goes further to describe it as "so minutely adapted
to manipulation, that it is possible to change the appearance of
the *fono* in twenty years."[20]

This pattern suited the new religion. It permitted the introduction of such groups as elders, deacons, lay preachers, class leaders,
catechists, and indigenous pastors. It virutally gave free play
in determining specific roles and discipline, rites and taboos. The
missionary himself found he could be incorporated into the system, and both the L.M.S. and the W.M.S. discovered their church

organization and practice were assimilated by the Samoan social structure with ease.

I have also implied, if I have not stated it directly, that all persons with prestige and status were not necessarily born with it in them. Society provided ways and means for outstanding individuals to build up prestige by personal achievement, and mechanisms existed whereby such persons could be elected to office. A family head of humble birth might find himself received into a higher group, where normally kin requirements determined membership. In matters of succession, when qualifications were equal, election would probably be on a basis of birth, but there were times when individual achievement determined the issue.[21] Sometimes a chief would make a nomination before his death.[22] One of the social functions of rivalry was to provide a way for dealing with the weakling in the line of succession, thus permitting a stronger personality to establish himself for the general security of all. Social inferiors feeling dissatisfaction with insecure conditions could withdraw their support, and if they represented a group opinion, that group might transfer its support to some different organizational unit.[23]

Two observations of importance to church growth need to be made at this point. We have seen that early Samoan society gave scope for any outstanding individual.[24] Thus it was possible for the church to select likely men for special training as preachers, teachers, and leaders, according to requirement and on a basis of spiritual experience. The church had a free hand in specifying requirements for office, for they were new posts. It also accounts for the prestige and status open to indigenous leaders of the church.

It is also worth noting the manner in which a whole segment of a village or tribe could sever itself from its parent body and assume another loyalty in the heat of a quarrel. This explains how, after the French coup in Tahiti, when the new form of Christianity (Roman Catholic) entered the field at the psychological moment, it could win immediate response in what was nominally a discipled area. In 1845 the L.M.S. supporters and the shepherdless Wesleyans were still at loggerheads when the Roman Catholics arrived.[25] Some social segments, determined against joining the L.M.S. as urged by the withdrawing Wesleyans, "joined the Roman Catholics from feelings of despair and anger," as an official record states it.[26] Dyson described a case of a disgruntled chief and his following changing from one church to another, through a domestic quarrel that had nothing at all to do with church matters.[27] In both these cases a traditional escape mechanism was used as a face-saver.

It is not my intention to deal with Roman Catholic and Protestant rivalries in Samoa, because the subject has pan-Pacific ramifications. It must suffice to say that any form of Western rivalry—Protestant-Catholic or French-British—could affiliate itself with Samoan rivalries and quest for prestige. Any foreign group could capitalize on the Samoan situation itself and gain a hearing. The French priests were adept at winning this type of social segment.[28]

In this unit of our analysis we have examined the Samoan social structure and organization—the structural concepts and the people operating them in society. We have seen that they are significant for innovation. However the reception and acceptance of foreign ideas (including the concept of Christianity itself) was conditioned by local cultural structure and organization. We do not blame the Samoan converts for moving into Christian groups which seemed to offer them the best advantage, and for employing their own cultural group mechanisms; for this was their approved pattern of decision-making. But we must be critical of the church's failure to follow up these decisions to spiritual maturity. Many of these would-be Christians were never brought into the real *fellowship* but remained on the fringe for the sake of any prestige advantages.[29] Rather, in one sense, the rivalry-orientated community incorporated the church into itself. Yet it would not be fair to leave the matter there, because there were many great spiritual achievements, even in the same three decades we have examined. The picture is one of light and shade, of both success and failure. But the Samoan way of life lay open to Christianity and structurally the passage from paganism to Christianity was simple. The missionaries were able to establish their organization and discipline as they desired. Yet a dark cloud of denominationalism casts its shadow over the scene. This feature was highly significant because the Samoan himself lived in an atmosphere of bitter rivalry and equated it with denominationalism, even to the prestige motivation. A study of social structure thus reveals features that influence the conditioning of the acceptance of new ideas. In the case of the church in Samoa it had bearing on the type of church which emerged. The reader will remember that when Dyson tried to cooperate with the missionaries of the other society after 1857, his own followers collectively rebuked him, stating their motivation in terms of losing prestige.[30]

THE PATTERN OF FAMILY CONTROL

We turn now from the wider political unit to the basic social unit, the family household. Because space demands our limiting the subject this unit will be slanted toward the elements of authority and control.

The family (*aiga*) is under the leadership of the *matai*. He is a titled person, a chief (*ali'i*) or an orator (*tulafale*), and has the responsibility of caring for and leading the group. In return for his effort he may expect cooperation and services. The family may extend beyond one house or village, but can be assembled at the house of the *matai* if desired.[31]

The family is a unit of persons bound together by ties of everyday living and activity and is constituted, as Mead points out, by three principles: blood, marriage, and adoption.[32] This permits a wide range in the personnel involved in family affairs—much bigger than the household, which comes under the daily control of the *matai*. Marriage and adoption permit the acquisition of skills and perhaps prestige.

"An ideal *matai*," wrote Schultz, "will control his regiment in patriarchal style, and in important family affairs will undertake nothing without first consulting with his family or his own branch of it. A legal limitation of his power (*pule*) exists with respect to his authority over the land (*fanua lau'ele'ele*) which belongs to the family."[33] This important legal statement raises three significant matters: family lands, family council, and family authority. Let us look at them one by one.

1. *Land.* Land is owned by the family but administered by the *matai* on behalf of the whole group. It is his duty to divide it out for use to the members of the family according to their respective needs, and for this service he is entitled to some return from those who use it.[34]

Work on the land is also determined by the *matai* and the various assignments are allocated by him. He distributes the produce harvested, including any cash income.[35]

2. *Council.* As lands are corporately owned, there is also a corporate voice in matters of public concern. This is heard in the assembly or council of the household or the village. The household *matai* gather in the village *fono*. At any level matters are debated until unanimity is reached.[36]

3. *Authority.* The authority of family and village heads is considerable, but it is confined within specific limits. Beyond this the *matai* must have the agreement of the group, the family. No *matai* dare act against the unanimous vote of the *fono*; so although he has much scope for individual decision at domestic levels, there are two checks on his authority, the family group and the village *fono*.[37]

Prior to the discussion in the *fono*, "private consultations (*taupulega*) will have been going on among the groups in which the heads of different families exchange ideas, seeking to convince one another."[38] The purpose of this is to reach unanimity without violent disputes, which might always end in the exodus of a segment from the political unit. The system of checks and balances seeks to maintain security and perpetuity. It may appear that one or two dominate affairs, but the voices of the others are ready to make themselves heard at any time. In olden times division came most frequently in matters of war or succession, because these were the issues that most involved prestige.

Sometimes when the leadership of a family involved a choice between two equally matched contestants the title could be split by compromise and the family divided into two.[39] The multiplication of titles caused no difficulties, especially if the group was large. This had benefits for the works program. There was a process of slow democratization at work. However, such divided families would show full respect for each other's wishes in all matters which involved both segments. The splitting of *matai* titles in this present century has become a mechanism for recognizing the competence of the younger men in the families and providing them with opportunity.[40] Thus individualism and democratization increase in modern Samoa,[41] but the process had begun before Christian times. Christianity has accelerated it.

Schultz's picture of the ideal *matai* has been subject to change under the processes of acculturation. The most important of his roles in old Samoa was that as priest of the household gods. This was the tie which held everything else together. In society the *matai* functioned as provider. He planned and organized planting, harvesting, and the distribution of food; he cared for distant members, who were beyond the physical grasp of his hands; he protected the family lands and their use; and he kept the members of the family contented (or might well lose his post if he failed to do so). All this required something of powers beyond his own. It was therefore natural that he should also serve as the priest or mediator with the household gods. This meant knowing the mode of access, the incantations and rites, the taboos to be avoided, and the seasons to be remembered, that the goodwill of the gods might be with them all. Each evening the family priest took control of the situation as the family gathered for the evening meal. He poured out the libation of 'ava, gave thanks, and set things right with the gods. He was indeed the patriarch of his family. It was this service he rendered which held the whole family complex together.[42]

What then was the significance of this ancient pattern of family control for the planting of the church in Samoa? The conceptual structures had many similarities. The advocates of Christianity made good use of the family concept. All that was best in Samoan society was found in the pattern of the ideal *matai*, and it was but a step from the ideal family to the family of God: the idea of a corporate body in which individuals had roles, responsibilities, and privileges, both as individuals and as members of the group. There were no obstacles here for the church. The stories of the Old Testament patriarchs had a ring of acceptability for the Samoan; and likewise the Jewish concept of land, as God's gift to them for their use and cultivation.

The concepts of group discussion and the institution of the *fono* provided the old Samoans with the mental wherewithal for conceiving church organization of the democratic type as used by both the L.M.S. and W.M.S. It was not necessary to explain what a synod or a quarterly or congregational meeting might be. There was a direct appropriation of the term for application to church as distinct from civil affairs.

In their conceptualization of authority also there was a direct take-over, as the Wesleyan missionaries in particular were to discover. Turner's departure was against the will of the *fono*, so they plotted to forcefully intercept his embarkation.[43] Dyson's fraternization with the L.M.S. men was also against the desire of the *fono,* and he received an official letter about it. The capacity of the system for splitting offices for the purpose of sharing responsibility and avoiding jealousies created no obstacles. Above all, the insistence of the missionaries that each Christian father should lead his family in "table" devotions in the home was thoroughly appreciated. They simply expected that it would be so. In other words, in the network of family controls, the system presented no evident obstructions to the gospel—that is, provided the people could be persuaded to change from their domestic and regional gods to the one true God.

I finish this unit on family controls with two descriptions, which I set together for comparative purposes, leaving them to make their own impressions.

> The father of the family . . . offered a short prayer at the evening meal that they might all be kept from fines, sickness, war and death. Occasionally too he would direct that they have a family feast in honour of their household gods, and . . . a cup of . . . *'ava* draught was poured out as a drink-offering. They did this in their family house, where they were all assembled, supposing that their gods had a spiritual presence there.[44]

I merely ask the reader if this picture of a pagan household suggests a people with a capacity to receive the gospel or not?

Against that passage, which describes things as they existed in Samoa when the church was first planted there, I set the following, written in English by an educated Samoan woman (Mrs. Willis Laulii) some thirty years after the end of the period covered by this article:

> . . . ney [the Samoans, her people] differ somewhat from the inhabitants of more civilized countries. After rising in the morning their first act is prayer, which is always accompanied by the singing of a hymn; no meal or even the slightest refreshment at any time, is partaken of until preceded by a prayer or blessing. Upon all of their labors, enterprises or undertakings, a blessing is invoked, and a true Samoan would feel guilty of a flagrant violation of divine law should he begin his day or end it without thanks to the God who created him.[45]

The passage continues in the same style. I am not offering it as missionary promotion but as anthropological appraisal for comparative purposes. Within the limitations of a pagan religion one finds its own forms of devout behavior; which, if sanctified by Him who is Himself the truth, becomes devotion of a high order. I am not unaware of all the faults of the pre-Christian Samoan; but I am convinced that he had his own natural capacity for receiving and responding to Christ. The patterns of his animistic family worship did provide him with a natural stepping-stone into Christianity.

Their daily life began and ended there. They built houses, made fish nets and fishhooks, plaited cords, wove mats, and made bark cloth. Every task began with an offering and a prayer for skill in workmanship, and ended with thanks to some guiding household god, whom they thought to watch over their interests. The cooking, the gardening, the drudgery—they did it all in the name of the god. "The Samoans are a religious people," Laulii truly said. If they retained their rivalry, they also retained their intense devotion.

The Samoan Value System

We have now assembled enough historical and cultural data to permit an attempt at structuralizing a tentative schema of the value system of the Samoan way of life as it was when Christianity imposed itself on those islands. It has to be reconstructed, of course, from primary sources of the period.

1. The supreme positive value was *prestige*. This was achieved in at least four ways: (a) through *status* in honorific language, terms of address, ceremonial, authority, and so forth; (b) through *ostentation* and *generosity* in providing feasts, approving big requests, and so on; (c) through *power demonstration*, especially in war, but also in magic for some persons; (d) through *proficiency* in production, craftwork, administrative controls, oratory, and so forth. (Note that though war and magic gave the greatest prestige, one could achieve it in any area of choice.)

2. The negative value at the opposite pole was *shame*. This sprang from failure in any of the above aspects or from slight or offense at any of these points.

3. The value set on the achievement of prestige, and the negative value of shame through nonachievement or offense, stimulated both latent and manifest responses which were recognized as normal. The latent response was *jealousy*; the manifest response was *rivalry*. The manifest rivalry might take the form of active war; overt competition in, say, ostentation, oratory or craftsmanship; or magical encounter, and so forth.

4. In spite of dependence on communal solidarity for security, balance or equilibrium was maintained by means of *individualism*. Outstanding individuals could rise in prestige in their status group, or achieve new status. The authority of those at the top was restricted by the *multi-individual* group, which watched the corporate interest. Individualism led for progress, and growing democratization prevented it becoming too radical. The supreme corporate value then was *solidarity* with strong leaders and a strong council in equilibruim. The social group could demonstrate its prestige or shame in the same way as persons and react with manifest demonstrations of rivalry.

5. The supreme religious value was *piety* or *devotion*, which was expected to be attended to with regularity by the approved persons in the approved manner. Proficiency and protection were due to piety. Although this aspect was left to select individuals, the group was identified with the act either by sending the priest to perform it, or by being present as a group.

This tentative schema reflects Samoan values brought out in the material collected by G. Turner, Gill, and others a century ago.[46]

The whole narrative of John Williams' 1830 and 1832 visits to Samoa could be rewritten in terms of *prestige* without changing any of the real facts. On his own evidence, Williams himself was acceptable to the Samoans because he arrived as *a big chief*,[47] and Fauea, the convert from Tonga, played his own prestige role in the shadow of the missionary. Had he not come from the land where they had everything? Was he not in command of a ship from the world beyond? Had he not built the ship with his own hands? To this set of ideas argued by Fauea, we may add, Did he not come with a traveled Samoan chief as his orator? Fauea gained prestige and status by his role. It might have been different had Tamafainga, the feared priest, been alive. Rivalry mechanisms would have been brought to bear on the situation.

Tamafainga also has been featured in our primary sources with respect to this supreme value. He had been universally feared in Samoa, but the wide range of his power was an achieved one. Samoan individualism had made it possible, and he had manipulated a good many cultural mechanisms to acquire the titles he held. It was not merely the clearness of his priestly predictions and their effectiveness for military victory; but he had himself usurped the title of the kingship of Samoa.[48]

His death made that kingship vacant again, and sometime after the acceptance of Christianity the five necessary titles came to Malietoa, who thus became the first of his family to attain the kingship. In spite of the presence of the great white chief, however, custom demanded his avenging the death of Tamafainga and thus absenting himself for a time. To have failed to do this would have injured his prestige and brought shame upon him. So he magnanimously gave the missionary the use of the largest building in the settlement and went his way.

Prestige became manifest in more than mere attitudes. It was symbolized in overt behavior: in a special language used to titled persons, and in symbolic insignia, special ornaments, fans, weapons, or in symbols tattooed on the body.[49] To a limited extent there was something permanent about prestige. Even though the body which elected a man to a title could take that title away from him, he could never be a commoner again. He would, in fact, be given a lower title, and could still sit with his associates when he recovered from his shame.[50] If he felt the shame too badly he could leave the group and move to another locality or join some other group, perhaps one belonging to the other side of his own family. Their individualism gave them the right to do this.[51] Mechanisms of escape from shame were well developed, but once employed, restoration was difficult.

In the case of a *mati*, for example, he could always admit error, but this decreased his prestige and increased his shame. He could retire from public life if the matter was a serious one, and in this event he would shift his place of abode to that of some other branch of the family, until such time as he felt disposed to inquire if his punishment had been sufficient. Custom would then demand from him an apology and a feast before he could return again to his own village. This is one explanation of the mobility of family segments. Once the head of a family allowed his individualism to evade the shame in the village the demands for shame outside the village were strengthened, and his individualism led him into a prolonged period of ostracism, bearing out what Grattan says:

> Humble submission to the will of his brothers is the quickest way

to forgiveness and reinstatement, and the wise man adopts that course.[52]

This is an important value complex—the prestige-shame poles of an axis. Individualism, which permits a man to progress toward prestige, also permits withdrawal toward shame, as if self-ostracism was a less hurtful atonement than enforced ostracism.

It was because of the existence of this complex that the severe disciplinary patterns of Protestant Christianity were meaningful to the Samoans and other islanders. The assemblies or groups were Christian structures that were very simple to graft on to this prestige-shame value complex. This was partly due to their membership status that was enclosed by rigid moral standards. It was also due to their patterns of strong discipline of offenders, maintained until the guilty ones were prepared to return humbly for forgiveness and restoration through an approved pattern. Structurally they were perfect for the missionary requirement, though they did cause some motivational problems. However the point to be made at this juncture is that Protestant discipline was not the foreign imposition that is sometimes claimed. The Samoans accepted the disciplinary structure of the church in terms of their own value system.

Even so, it had its dangers. A discontented *matai* who could enlist sufficient support among his friends and family might well cause a schism in the village. Thus it was possible to have a Samoan village organized up to a certain point for cooperation and beyond that for avoidance. Grattan mentions this in recent times.[53] It was a precarious state of affairs and rendered a village vulnerable to hostile dichotomies, just because they were dichotomies and Samoan society was rivalry-orientated at any time. I have seen villages like this in other parts of Oceania. They invariably fall victims to any political, social, or religious rivalry that chances to come along. They open the way for strange sects that have nothing worthwhile to give to island society and seem to be just waiting for some new kind of discord. When Dyson arrived in Samoa in 1857 he was shocked by the number of small villages which were fractured in this manner.[54]

The indigenous pattern of prolonged discipline before restoration was employed to the extreme after the withdrawal of the Wesleyans. Quite often the Wesleyan units that were ready to move into the other denomination as requested were denied admission into membership and kept waiting as adherents only for a unduly long period of time. It was as if they were classified as offenders for having been Wesleyans—and six years without status was a long punishment for such an offence.[55] Viewing the matter from their own cultural orientation, one does not wonder that many of them, feeling deserted by the Wesleyans and despised by the Calvinists, should turn to the Roman Catholics or, as some did, return to paganism. It is the prestige-shame complex that explains their behavior.

Status, titles, and military conquest, however, were not the only stepping-stones to prestige. There was also the wide area of craft specialization and the prestige won by fine workmanship. There was the skill of the competent administrator of group activity and the superior orator. These things provided the missionaries with opportunity for developing Christian expression work. Rivalry was thus often sublimated into competitive exercises like reading and penmanship. To write a fine hand meant prestige.

The prestige of fine words, which meant so much to the Samoan orator, was developed even more by the church, with its new roles of preacher and teacher and opportunity for individual testimony. Capacity for oral tradition was retained in Scripture and catechism memory work. Craft proficiency was developed in church-building programs. In all these aspects Christianity found no obstacles in her way.

Prestige was also achieved by means of superior demonstrations, feasting, generous giving, and display.[56] Life crises remained occasions for distribution and festivities. Although some entertainments were drastically reduced, the church did offer in its Christian year a number of festival occasions, when folk gathered in great numbers, with lavish feasting and friendly reunions. Families responsible for these services gained much prestige—the prestige of a job generously and well done—and this passed on into the new day. Even rivalry itself has acquired a dimension of stewardship—competition to outdo one another in generosity to God. With the passage of time the motivation became higher: fear of being shamed became desire to express one's thankfulness to God, but it came first from the pre-Christian psychological orientation of the people. With the change from subsistence to money economy the very generosity threatens to become a problem in many island communities.[57]

A Samoan coming out of paganism would see himself as an individual free to express himself, but within certain limits. He would gain a good name and approval for certain behavior. He would be disciplined and shamed for other types of behavior. One would give him status in the church; the other would deny him that status. He would have new skills placed before him—reading, writing, catechism memory work. He would learn new forms of devotional expression—personal prayer and hymn-singing. He would learn to choose between the things which satisfy and those which do not—to "abhore that which is evil and to cleave to that which is good." In time the prestige-shame complex, modified by divine grace, did help him to see the difference between the worthy and unworthy in Christian moral values. What began as something rather earthy acquired a higher dimension under Christian instruction which probed motivation and spirituality. It would seem, then, that the old Samoan value system did provide something of a meaningful bridge from the old life into the new; but it was not until one came across that bridge and stood on the Christian side that he really saw things in their true perspective. The tragedy of the early decades was that denominational rivalry prevented a great number of early Samoan converts from rising above denominationalism. The small number brought into full membership indicates that quality growth was injured for a generation.

Yet, in fairness, let it be pointed out that we are discussing the passage of people from a pagan to a Christian value system. We are not speaking of conversion, which was an act of faith, a stepping over the line, a dynamic encounter like eating one's forbidden totem fish. We are examining the problems of converts moving from pagan to Christian standards, their difficulties in conceptualizing Christian motivation and their natural misunderstanding of Western denominational rivalry in terms of their own old value system.

Knowledge of pagan value systems is relevant for church growth at two points. First, with respect to the initial acceptance or rejection of Christianity, the value system determines the natural disposition of a people to Christianity, as hostile, congenial, or syncretistic. It may be ready to borrow ideas yet not accept the total Christ, as with the great religions. It may be open for assimilation. Study of value systems helps the missionary, warns him of likely opposition, and indicates points of likely acceptance. Second, it should give him deeper sympathy with those to whom he goes, and indicate stepping-stones along which he can lead his converts to higher ideals and motives that will be both meaningful and acceptable to them as outworkings of the step of faith taken at conversion. Knowledge of the convert's old value system is thus important at the level of follow-up after conversion.

The Theological Encounter

Had the cultic superstructure of Io worship, as I have described in the cases of Tahiti and Maoriland, existed in Samoa, it would probably have been concentrated at Manono. Maybe it was there and died with Tamafainga, but there is no evidence of it. The early observers—and they were good observers—reported fully on the Samoan religion. They found no strongly entrenched priesthood and no esoteric cult with an elaborate cosmogeny. The social role of the priest in Samoa concerned the mediatory office at the family, village, or district level; but usually the work of a priest was confined to one area of service, say, the home, the craftwork, or war. There was a wide scatter of individual roles, not a concentrated central priesthood. The individualism which opened the door to promising young priests, however, did permit an outstanding person to acquire more than one office. These persons automatically graded themselves on a basis of achievement and acquired prestige thereby, but it remained a matter for individual competition and was against the formation of a central priesthood. This is reasoning from known and verified facts, though we cannot be sure all the facts are known.

I agree with Handy that there was another pattern in Polynesia, side by side with Io worship. He calls it the Tangaloa cult.[58] This appears to have been stronger in those parts of Polynesia where worship patterns were more domestic and simple than philosophical and esoteric. The cult concerned the fate of souls and had a strong leaning toward what is popularly known as totemism. It provided a means by which family, personal, and ancestral spirits could manifest themselves in animate or inanimate forms. They did not carve their gods but did make sacred objects and symbols. Animal movements were often taken as omens from protective spirits. They had a strong demonology. The master of ceremonies at public gatherings was the orator, at family meetings the *matai*. Kava was used at all such ceremonials.

This religion offered scope also for the prophet. If a god had no prophet the chief place was left vacant. The patron god was consulted through the prophet. He cared for the god-house but had no ritual function. This aspect of Polynesian religion was highly developed in Tonga and Samoa and had a specific language of its own. It was present in a lesser degree in the Society Islands, where the Supreme Being and First Cause was spoken of as *Tangaloa*; but the complex is almost absent from marginal Polynesia—Hawaii, the Marquesas, and New Zealand—according to Handy, who also sees some similarities between this and the Chinese *Tankalo* and Melanesian *Tangalo*. Again there are linguistic and conceptual similarities.[59]

Attempts at structuring a frame of reference for the classification of Samoan deities have not been particularly effective, although they have led to the preservation of much valuable information. George Turner provided a list of about a hundred and twenty Samoan deities, to whom he could ascribe a name and a shrine. By the term *shrine* I mean an animal, bird, fish, plant, or inanimate object into which a god could enter to present himself to man for purposes of communication or revelation. This is an important Oceanic concept. All the deities in Turner's list involved the two essentials, which were Turner's criteria for religion—something to be believed, and something to be done.[60] For his schema he conceptualized the deities on two levels—superior and inferior—the former being involved with village and district affairs and war; the latter, household and personal gods. These gods (to which he devoted some fifty pages of description) all manifested themselves on earth, each having his shrine: owl, mullet, dog, conch shell, or stone pillar, as the case may be.[61] Some fell from heaven, some appeared as omens, some were foreign and introduced, some agricultural, some associated with festivals and others with healing. The functions and range of power varied, but superior or inferior, they all had shrines.

In examining Turner's data one is confronted by an apparent indiscriminate selection of shrines. A certain animal may represent a superior god in one place and an inferior in another.

The same deity may have different shrines in different localities. For instance, Faamalu was known in a conch shell in one place, a cloud in another, and elsewhere a fish. Fe'e could be a cuttle-fish in one area, but elsewhere a white cowrie or a wooden bowl.

The same thing applies to function. I take the same two cases. Faamalu was at one time and place a war god, but at another he was concerned with agriculture. Fe'e was in one place a village deity, but elsewhere a war god. Turner's lists show scores of examples of this kind of thing.[62] He arranged his material alphabetically and made his comments under each name. He seems to have regarded his task as purely descriptive.

Another list arranged by Stair and cited by Grattan has a four-fold classification:

1. The original gods who dwelt in the heavens (*atua*)
2. The deified spirits of chiefs (*tupua*)
3. Commonest and widest class: war, family, village gods, and so forth (*aitu*)
4. Inferior spirits (mischievous, and having no priests to serve them) (*sauali'i*)[63]

The categories are not altogether satisfactory. Under Number 1 he places Tangaloa, whom Turner compares with Jupiter, though he has earthly shrines—here the moon, there a wooden bowl, and elsewhere a snipe. In one place he is a fishing god, but in another his business is healing, and elsewhere it is war.[64] Deified chiefs (no. 2) also had their shrines; they were either sun-dried gods (embalmed bodies)[65] or natural rocks supposed to be petrified persons.[66] Although the above categories are not exclusive the same common feature is evident: all gods had shrines.

Now, sooner or later all church-planters have to face the question, Where does the Christian gospel actually come to grips with heathen belief? We have seen many ways within the forms and structure of society that permitted the organization of an indigenous church, but ultimately this is of no avail unless somewhere there is an encounter that is evidence of a change of faith. To answer the question I have posed, I shall take three subsidiary questions. What was the capacity of the pagan Samoan for theological conceptualization? Where was the power focus in Samoan pre-Christian religion? What is the historical evidence of Christian encounter having taken place at this point? Let us take these one by one.

1. *What was the capacity of the pagan Samoan for theological conceptualization adequate for acceptance of the gospel?* It is commonly supposed that "primitive" people are not capable of deep theological conceptualization. This is an error. Their ideas of what constitutes sin may differ from those of the Westerner, because their culturally-based ethical values differ. However, all people have concepts of right and wrong, that doing wrong (however they conceive it) leads to trouble either for the individual or the group. In one way or another, all fear the consequences of sin; and in the face of this sin or fear, religion is usually salvation-orientated. Again, what we mean by *salvation* varies, but in its simplest form it is escape from sin or fear. All through the South Pacific, religion could be legitimately described in terms of salvation.

Some Pacific languages are so rich in terms of *sacrifice* that translators of the Bible have experienced trouble in selecting the best of many possibilities for the word they sought, the islanders possessing a refinement that was embarrassing to the translators. One island language, known to the writer, can express the idea of *incarnation* with a further refinement that indicates the kind of body involved.[67] The *call* of the prophet, and the *revelation* through him, and many similar theological concepts were natural vocabulary in the Pacific Islands before the coming of Christianity. A religion without these would have been immediately suspect.

In presenting the gospel the missionary advocated a plan of salvation. Much of this his hearers needed no convincing of. Sin and fear were real. They understood the need of salvation. They did not doubt the power of the God about whom the missionaries spoke. They knew that power (mana) to save had to come from outside themselves. If the advocates of Christianity could offer something better than the religion they had followed they were interested. But the superiority of that salvation had to be proved by practical demonstration. Somewhere there had to be an actual encounter between Christ and the old god. To the Pacific islander this was best done by means of his own act of faith—an ocular demonstration of a change of loyalty. This encounter is the key to the first stage of missionary activity, the stage that brings the pagan across the line into the Christian camp. Those historians and other scholars who have scoffed at mission work because of the material accompaniments of conversion have completely missed this key to the missionary situation— the fundamentality of dynamic encounter.

Let us apply this question to Samoa. In a rivalry-orientated society the pagan had no difficulty in conceptualizing an encounter between the divine and human, just as he saw it daily between man and man, and believed it to apply between one god and another. He believed that encounters continued between the gods on spiritual, zoomorphic, and anthropomorphic levels. A scripture text like "I can do all things through Christ" had a very real and practical meaning for him—even at a deeper level than it has for the average Western Christian. To the Samoan there was a continual state of encounter between Tangaloa of the skies,[68] and the land god, Moso.[69] This struggle between heaven and earth opened the way for the Samoan to conceptualize the encounter of Christ and Satan in the personalized form familiar to us all. Turner said that certain families, who worshiped the god Moso and opposed Tangaloa, actually believed that Moso's shrine was a human being. How would a follower of Moso interpret the words of our Lord to Peter, "Get thee behind me, Satan!"? I am not presenting these fragments as identical concepts, or even as stepping-stones from Samoan to New Testament teaching; but I am demonstrating the existence of numerous *encounter concepts* on the religious level, that reveal the natural capacity of the Samoan for this type of conceptualization.

Could a Samoan individual in collective society, which acted collectively in matters of religion, understand a personal encounter, involving him as an individual? We have seen individualistic mechanisms within the rivalry patterns aiding the man of special merit to achieve or become what he desired. Likewise, expressive individuals were able to influence group decisions. Capacity to conceptualize offers no problem. On the contrary there is considerable evidence of processes of Christian conceptualization going on from the very beginning—say, before 1832. Without any aid from John Williams the situation was developing its own terminology, possibly under the influence of the teachers he had left in 1830. The Samoans he met at Manua in 1832 described themselves as "Sons of the Word." They declared, "We are awaiting the religion ship."[70] On the 1830 visit Fauea had spoken of the vessel as a prayer ship.[71] It was to this kind of ship that a pagan Samoan chief learned to apply if he desired Christian teachers.[72] These teachers brought Tahitian Scriptures with them. Here is a fixing of terminology associated with patterns of behavior. The giving of a title is evidence of the fact that the emerging body has developed a consciousness of its own entity.

Williams accepted the terminology they gave him and indeed when at Tutuila, where a chief asked for muskets and powder, he countered in their own new terminology: "Ours is a religion ship!"[73] Thus from island to island the terminology preceded the experience. News of the people movements on Savaii and Upolu spread to other parts, and even the pagans conceptualized the movement as that of the "Sons of the Word' and in terms of "religion ships," which brought teachers, preaching, and Scripture, but not guns and powder.

At Leone, where Williams found some fifty would-be Christians, he picked up the term *tama-fai-lotu*, "workers of religion," so that the "Sons of the Word" had been categorized. Furthermore, together with the title went a symbol—a piece of white cloth tied on the arm indicating commitment or incorporation in the group as it envisaged itself.[74] They had now set themselves apart as a corporate entity, a multi-individual group. These are the regular processes of group emergence.[75] I should also point out that these are not merely Williams' observations. It was a heathen informant who said to him of them, "They are the Sons of the Word, and that cloth is to distinguish them from their heathen countrymen."

In addition to the concept of entity there was conceptualization in the *area of belief*. Another word that was becoming fixed was *lisilisi*, "become a believer";[76] and of course there was the word *lotu* for the Christian religion.[77] The early church confession that "Jesus is Lord" had its Samoan counterpart in "The *lotu* is true."[78] The Lord's Prayer was fixed as a prayer norm, as the Lord gave it as an index prayer within the Hebrew pattern. Williams discovered that the Sons of the Word could often recite the prayer in broken Tahitian.[79] One of the first things Malietoa pressed Williams for was some kind of ethical code so they could distinguish good from bad in Christian standards. The date of all this, be it noted, is 1832.[80] When an individual was personally convinced of the truth of the *lotu* he would declare, "My heart is single!" The dualism of indecision had been solved by the encounter. He was ready to be committed.

Once the Samoan Christians began forming into groups committed to Christ—Sons of the Word, with the symbolic white armbands—there emerged a negative awareness on the part of the pagans that they were *not* Sons of the Word. Demanding entity also, they assumed the term *Sons of the Devil*, and pagan villages were spoken of as devil villages. Possibly the Christians used these terms first, but Williams discovered pagans using them of themselves as "terms of distinction."[81] So the Christian concept of sons of light and sons of darkness had formed itself in pre-Christian Samoa before any missionary was resident there.

With these observations and documentary references I dismiss the first question. Did the pagan Samoan have a capacity for theological conceptualization? He certainly did. These people should never be treated as childish or childlike. We are dealing with competent adults.

2. *When we seek the locus of power in Samoan religion, on what must we focus our attention?* The Westerner would probably seek out the great high god(s). The Samoan *atua* was dimly recognized and remote. There are several well-documented studies of Polynesian religion, with good accounts of the hierarchy of high gods; but the very absence of such data in Samoa is evidence in itself. It is not here that we find the point for encounter.

Neither do the sun-dried (embalmed) gods (*tupua*) demand our attention, because their power was over a limited area only and involved but a couple of families.[82] With those two families, of course, they may have been the locus of power for encounter.

The inferior spirits were not taken sufficiently seriously to warrant the appointment of priests to serve them,[83] so our answer is not here.

If Stair's classification be used we are left, after this process of elimination, with the *aitu* only. These were legion: district gods, family gods, and personal gods; gods of the harvest, of fishing, and of every type of craft. Could there ever be effective encounter with so many gods?

Perhaps we should not be seeking a kind of god at all. We have already noted one point they all had in common: every one had some shrine. Every man knew the *aitu* of his god; treated it with reverence; observed strict taboos, especially eating taboos if it was edible; and feared the dire consequences of breaking these prohibitions. (Even *aitu* like the moon and clouds had their strict taboos.) One writer says the penalty for eating one's *aitu* was to be cooked oneself in the same oven.[84] This may have been a penalty laid down—but people just did not eat their *aitu*.

It would seem then that the natural point for power encounter was the *reverence and taboo of the aitu*. This provided a vital criterion for every Samoan individual and every Samoan corporate group. The strongest taboos, the most terrible fears, and the sacred traditions transmitted from untold ages were concentrated here. Their health, their security, their prosperity, their perpetuity all depended on the reverence and observation of taboos connected with their *aitu*. To desecrate, destroy, or devour one's *aitu* required a real act of faith in some power greater than that of the *aitu*.[85]

3. *What is the historical evidence of power encounter at the point of reverence of, and taboos concerning, the aitu?* In common with other people of Oceania, the Samoans believed that the only real and effective way of proving the power of their new faith was to demonstrate that the old religion had lost its powers and fears. We have already seen this in the case of Tahiti and Tonga. I now cite two cases from Samoa that can be historically documented.

Malietoa had accepted Fauea and the teachers, had cared for them and built them a chapel. The day before its opening he assembled his family, for it was on the family level that he had determined to act. He announced his intention of becoming a follower of the Christian God.[86] The family, after discussion, approved. Socially all was correctly done; but in his own mind he was still not quite certain, and therefore determined to exclude his sons from the experiment. They were to wait and see how things turned out for their father and the members of the family who shared the experiment with him. Again the matter was debated and the family decided on a four-to-six weeks test. If all went well then the sons would follow. It was a communal decision.

The *aitu* of Malietoa was a fish called *anae*, a kind of mullet.[87] On the appointed day the forbidden food was set before Malietoa. The incident created tremendous excitement. Friends and distant relatives had come from afar to witness the daring spectacle. Many expected all who ate to drop dead there and then. Those of the family who were to share the experiment were in some cases so frightened that they dosed themselves with oil and salt water as possible antidotes to the mana of the *aitu*. But Malietoa and a few others with him took no precautions. As a power encounter it had to succeed or fail on its own merits. By partaking as a social unit the encounter involved both Malietoa as an individual and his family as a group. They ate. The excitement subsided. No evil befell them. Thereafter for many the *lotu* was true and the *aitu* was false. Malietoa's sons could endure the separation for no more than three weeks, and then pleaded for the family's permission to take the same step.[88]

This incident led many people to dispense with their personal *aitu* or break the taboos, and to put themselves under the instruction of the Christian teachers. The movement gained momentum. Chiefs took the initiative; and thus it was that when Williams arrived after twenty moons, he found villages all around the coast where large groups had eaten or desecrated their *aitu*, built chapels, and were awaiting the return of Williams with more teachers. Their gods had been discarded, evil spirits had been cast out, and the houses swept—and were empty.

For the second example I have chosen one that concerns an inanimate and inedible *aitu*. It is the case of the war god, Papo, whose considerable power was concentrated in a venerated shrine, a piece of matting that was attached like a battle flag to a war canoe going into action. At the *fono* (council) of this group it was determined that they destroy the shrine and put on the white cloth or armband. The shrine would either have to be burned or drowned in sea water (recognized methods both widely used throughout Oceania). The matter was debated at length by the group, which decided to tie a stone to the matting shrine, and, taking it on a new canoe (i.e., not one dedicated to war, in itself an act of desecration), throw it overboard in the deep sea. Several chiefs, Fauea among them, set off to do this so that the shrine of Papo might be visibly and ceremonially drowned.[89]

These two incidents, in which the deities and persons involved can be identified and documented, demonstrate that the locus of power was regarded as the shrine of the god, and conversion to Christianity had to be an ocular demonstration of encounter at this power point. There were, no doubt, scores of important features in the total complex, but in the final analysis decision to quit paganism and become Christian was a dynamic demonstration on the level of the *aitu*. This was so on the level of the individual, as it was also of the group. In the case of the group there had to be a *fono* discussion and agreement. When we examine these mechanisms at work we see why it is quite wrong to speak of these people movements as mass movements. They were, to use the term I have taken from Dr. Homer Barnett, *multi-individual*. The only difference between the decisions of the Samoan *fono* and those of Western democratic assemblies is that the former continued debate until unanimity was reached, instead of acting on a mere majority.

Laulii, a Christian Samoan who lived nearer to those times than to ours, described conversion in these terms of encounter with the *aitu* by saying that when any Samoan "resolved to declare himself a Christian, he commenced by killing and eating" his *aitu*—grasshopper, centipede, octopus, bat, snake, eel, lizard, or parrot, as the case might be.[90] I note that Laulii conceives this as an individual act. Yet it was a public act and would usually be at the family meal when the taboo creature was served up before the whole family. From evidence in other areas we would expect the family to eat the family *aitu*, and the individual his own personal *aitu*, if this distinction existed as it did in some places.

The question of what pressures might be exerted to achieve unanimity is a serious one in some communities; but in Oceania such pressures operated more against conversion than for it. Sometimes persons who agreed with the common decision were nevertheless quite frightened about the power test, as we have seen in the oil and sea water antidote incident, and this is why the period of Christian instructional follow-up is so important. Perhaps it is true that some would be swept into the movement with the crowd, but this was never exploited by Protestant missionaries and they were most vocal about its undesirability. When a certain chief asked for a Christian teacher and promised that his whole group would accept his teachings, John Williams told him clearly:

> that he must not force them contrary to their own wishes, but having set them an example *himself*, and exhorted them to fol-

low it, then to leave them to their own convictions; but the employment of any kind of co-ercion to induce men to become Christians was contrary to the principles of our religion.[91]

After years of reading the source material I feel the Protestant missionaries of the South Pacific were careful at this point.

Yet it was natural for the people to move in group action. In pre-Christian Samoa the people were conceived as being the property of a village and of its god.[92] One could only break with that by a denial of the god. For an individual to do this would also mean his denial of his village; that is, unless he could induce the whole council to take the step together, by raising the matter frequently in the village council. A village could change from the pagan god to the Christian God and survive. This would be done by a public encounter, which proved the impotence of the old god and marked the beginning of a Christian village. Thereafter the killing and eating of the village *aitu* became a reference point marking off the old times from the new.

SOME CONCLUSIONS

E. B. Tylor visualized an old *matai* at evening prayer:

> In vain in the Samoan house the head of the family would pray to the household deities, when the fire was made upon the hearth before the evening meal—

> > Drive away from us sailing gods, lest
> > they come and cause disease and death.[93]

From this prayer Rowe took the title of his book, *Samoa Under the Sailing Gods*. It is a study of the influences of the white man on Samoa. Yet Tylor realized that "for good or evil, the old order had to change." We have been examining the religious aspect of this change, and particularly at those points of initial clash between Christianity and the old social and religious pattern. Half a century after our period of study, one who knew the Samoans well said of their religion, "Religion is respectability; all are church-goers; in almost every home family worship is conducted."[94] The church which had emerged in this later generation was truly Samoan, respectable within the social pattern, pious in attendance at worship, and built on the basic social unit, the family. That it would work out in this way had not always been apparent in those early days of dynamic encounter and rivalry, which we have been studying; yet often we noted that the social structure was such as opened the way to Christianity, and conversion had on the whole been by means of social units. The type of Christianity which emerged was partly due to the Samoan social determinants themselves.

It seems right to conclude this unit by asking and answering a question: What does this analysis have to show to others interested in church-planting and church growth? I think it says seven things.

1. The account of the Samoan acceptance of Christianity illustrates the significance of social structure and personality characteristics as determinants of the forms of Christianity that may be expected to result. Dominant personality traits tend to persist even through culture change. It therefore follows that evangelistic and educative efforts directed along lines that are natural or characteristic in the culture are more likely to lead us to rapid and permanent acceptance than efforts built on foreign patterns. The features which flourished in the Samoan church, for good or evil, were those which attached themselves to indigenous characteristics and values.

2. The Samoan study has offered scope for observing lines of cleavage within the social structure. This explains the frequent segmentation met in church growth studies. It has significant consequences for comity policies. Comity policy should always be set against a background of social structure and kin distribution, not geographical regions. The overflow of Tongan religion into Samoa reveals the danger of comity agreements which ignore cultural factors. Modern missions have much to learn at this point.

3. This study shows how the projection of foreign theological issues may unexpectedly become attached to indigenous traits with unfortunate results. The projection of denominationalism into an area, for example, can stimulate local rivalries, latent and manifest. While this may not necessarily hinder numerical growth from paganism, it greatly injures the quality of the follow-up. It is doubtful if the unfortunate bitterness stimulated by this combination of Western denominationalism and indigenous political and prestige rivalries of the early period has even yet been really effectively eliminated from Samoan religion.

4. Some institutions and values within pagan cultural con-

figurations, though less than Christian, may yet serve as stepping-stones into the Christian religion. Society must have continuity, whatever changes may occur in its religion; and the emerging church needs a structure that will function within that society. Wise church-planting will retain as much as possible of the old system. The more the manifest continuity, the less the shock of conversion. The preservation of the role of the *matai*, family devotions, the function of the *fono*, the scope for individualism, and the checks against its excess were features aiding the growth of Christianity within rather than against the social structure.

5. At the level of actual conversion from paganism, this study demonstrates that, no matter how many elements may be woven into the conversion complex in communal society, the group action (which is not mass, but multi-individual) must fix itself in encounter at some material locus of power at some specific point of time. There must be a psychological moment or experience when the persons involved actually turn from the old god(s) to the new. There ought to be some ocular demonstration of this encounter, some specific act of faith. Both Christian and pagan alike frequently demand some such act to indicate the bona fide nature of conversion. Where such demonstrations occur churches begin to grow.

6. Emerging from the last point, we note that when one important group or individual fixes such a locus of power encounter (like eating the *aitu*, burning a fetish, burying the ancestral skull, or destroying the sacred grove), this tends to become a reference point for other groups and individuals in the locality or within the social orbit. This is a universal for the South Pacific. Once this begins to happen we may expect a period of people movements of considerable size, for it indicates that the field is ripe unto harvest. This is going on in places like New Guinea at the present time.

7. Last, but perhaps most important of all, this Samoan study demonstrates the importance of such fields ripe unto harvest. The Samoan field was certainly ripe unto harvest between 1830 and 1832. If Williams had been ready with fifty Tahitian teachers and perhaps a missionary or two, the conversion of all Samoa could have been accomplished within a few years. The Wesleyans in Tonga saw what was happening and moved in because the field was ripe and no harvesting was being undertaken. Socially,

religiously, intellectually, Samoa was ripe and remained ripe through 1830, 1831, 1832, 1833, and 1834. In 1835 the Wesleyans moved in under pressure because their own people movement had crossed the waters. In the twelve months they were in Samoa before the arrival of the L.M.S. men from England, they had established a cause of thirteen thousand adherents, and by doing so had broken an agreement. Fields ripen suddenly. If the ingathering is delayed the crop depreciates, as it did in this case. The denominational situation need never have arisen if those who promised had sent laborers into the harvest. The L.M.S. had enough men concentrated on small islands with limited population to have deployed some to Samoa, as Williams had been demanding for a decade. But they were still wedded to the policy of civilizing. It is a lesson so relevant to the missionary world of today.

6

CIVILIZING OR EVANGELIZING
The Voice of History for Our Day

INTRODUCTORY NOTE

THIS CHAPTER purports to draw together in a synthesis the evidence of one of the major problems faced by Pacific missions during the last century. A good deal has been said of this in the chapters on Tahiti and New Zealand. In this chapter I try to relate this to a world perspective, so that one may ask and answer the question, Has history anything to say at this point to the missionary situation today?

I realize that some of my critics will say it is all irrelevant because we live in an entirely new situation which must be judged by its own merits alone and that there are no historical precedents. This type of thinking surely arises from our present alarm at the fantastic potential of this atomic postwar world and the sudden possibility of human extinction.

The scientific features of modern life are certainly new and our direction of the modes and approaches of the church to man must certainly take forms that are relevant in the new environment. Failure at this point may well mean the rejection of Christianity in our day. This would be a tragedy when the same new day offers tremendous potential and open doors and the thrill of exploring new innovations for the presentation of the gospel of God. While it is true that the dangers and possibilities of defeat are more real, the potentials for victory are likewise greater. It is the tempo of life that has changed, and its forms, rather than its content.

We must forget that this age is not *entirely* new. There are some continuous features. There never can be a completely clear-cut break with the past. As long as continuous features remain, history will always have something to say to a new day.

One continuous feature is *mankind*. We glibly say the young nations have cut themselves off from the past and from colonialism. In a practical sense this may be so, but historically this very past has become a current determinant. Present-day policies are determined by lessons learned in the past. Often these changes of orientation can be fixed in a reference point—a Magna Charta, a revolution perhaps. The reference point becomes itself a watchword and a determinant in new-day decisions and behavior.

But the continuity of mankind means more than this. Civilizations have been faced with destruction before. While it is true that the features of destruction have differed scientifically, the psychological reactions of the people have been remarkably similar. The basic relations of man to man, the pressures of his fears, and the satisfactions of his pleasures have been very much the same in every age. The same human problems lie at the root of all his shortcomings and disturbances. His basic needs remain the same, physiologically and psychologically. Only the cultural mechanisms through which they manifest themselves differ. As long as man is man the study of history is a relevant discipline.

Another continuous feature, I believe, is *God* Himself. God manifests Himself in different ways from age to age, but as we are reminded regularly at Holy Communion, "Thou art the same Lord, Whose property is always to have mercy." It is true that many in the West have lost this perception; but millions in the non-Western world have discovered it even in these postwar decades. As long as some people believe in God, He remains a determinative and continuous factor in human behavior.

For the purpose of this church growth study, one may add that as long as God and mankind continue on earth there is a continuous role for the *church*, which brings these two together. For millions of Christians the *Bible* is still the Word of God to man. This too is continuous. It follows also for them that the *Great Commission* is continuous. As long as the gospel is relevant to the human situation, historical studies of the gospel at work among men will have something to say to each new day. This applies particularly at the level of the basic principles that are firmly embedded within the forms, though the latter must change from age to age and culture to culture.

Because I believe in the continuity of God's purpose for man and the continuity of man's commitment to the Great Commission, regardless of changing forms, I insert this chapter on the *continuous problem of priorities* in missionary emphasis.

THE THEORY

The policy of civilizing in order to Christianize was raised in the studies on Tahiti and New Zealand. Some kind of a synthesis is called for, because the theory belongs to a much wider panorama than Southern Polynesia. Furthermore it has emerged in various forms, and as historic experiments these speak to present-day situations.

Though I have criticized the policy I have tried to be fair to the individual missionaries involved. In fairness, one ought to add that this was the view of the church at large and also of academic and political circles. Indeed the theory had three main streams of support.

SUPPORTS OF THE THEORY

The first support of the theory was *the body of missionary policy-makers in Britain.* These men had worked out the theory and were strongly wedded to it, resistant to being convinced of its unsoundness. It was not that the theory was not challenged. Both the L.M.S. and the C.M.S. had to face up to this issue at an early date.

As we have already seen, after considerable pressure from John Williams for a change of policy from sedentary farming to mobile church-planting, his directors had sent commissioners to see the work on the field. This was good sense and the men who went were good observers. Their findings, however, had only the validity of what they had postulated in the first place, *ex hypothesi.* They found evidence of Christianizing and of some civilizing, but they did not prove that the latter was the cause of the former. If they changed their emphasis in any way, it was merely to claim that civilizing was *always* essential, as a preliminary to conversion and as part of the consolidation afterward. John Williams, who had been greatly impressed by the scope for mobility which Leigh the Wesleyan in New Zealand had,[1] must have been a great problem to his directors. He had urged the Raiatéan congregation to become another Antioch. He himself had built a ship in the islands so that no reef could confine him. He had rejected the Society's commercial policy and restated it in terms of local relevance rather than economics. He had forced a policy of church-planting on his mission in contradistinction from the principles laid down by the directors. This clash between field missionary and home authorities has been discussed already in the chapter on the Tahitian web. It was Williams' aggression that led to the spread of the web.

We have seen also that Williams was not the only person to raise this problem. The loss of interest in the Tahiti mission in Britain indicated that church folk at home were questioning this type of mission. The C.M.S. leaders also felt this, and in the chapter on the Maori web we discussed the terms of the appointment of Henry Williams, whom they deliberately sent with "no secular object in view." This, we also noted, while recognizing the shortcomings of the civilizing pattern, did not cancel it.

Although it was John Williams' mobility and priority for evangelism that appears to have brought the responses to the gospel that were to become a great people movement, his directors continued to send out mostly artisans and cultivators. Certainly until the 1830s, the majority of British mission policy-makers remained civilizers at heart. Many of them remained so until the end of the century, though civilizing was conceptualized in different forms later in the century. With the exception of a few brilliant individualists, the mission policy-makers were the first and main support of the theory.

The second stream of support for the theory was that of *the missionaries on the field*. Most of the early men felt that some civilizing had to come first, though they could have found historic precedents to have shown them otherwise. Many felt, like the body of Christian leaders in the days of Ulfilas, that the pure gospel could never be understood in the wild tongue of the Goths. Some refinement was a prerequisite for conversion. Some of them, like Marsden, had written much on the theory. But Marsden's situation was quite different from that of the island missionaries. He had gone to Australia, a land being rapidly peopled by his fellow countrymen. He was dealing with convicts, and especially with freed convicts, who had to be turned into citizens and live with free settlers. Although both Anglicans and Wesleyans made serious efforts to save the aboriginal, these indigenous nomads fared badly under "civilization" and were either exterminated or pushed back into the hinterland. So Australia was hardly typical of the islands, nor was Marsden typical of the island missionary. Strictly speaking Marsden was a chaplain, not a missionary. Nevertheless, because of his establishment of New Zealand missions, his voyages and inspections, his views were determinant in missionary patterns.

It was this second support for the theory that was the first to break. Only sixteen months after the commencement of the Tahiti Mission, Jefferson wrote in his journal:

> The instructing of the Tahitians in any useful art, we suppose, will never be effected by us, at least till the Gospel's powerful and saving influence is felt.[2]

One by one Tahiti missionaries came to the conclusion that civilization did not bring conversion to Christianity, but rather the sequence was the reverse. They were beginning to distinguish between the roots of the tree and its fruit. In New Zealand also, men began to appear who would argue with Marsden. Many of these men, on furlough or retired, were vocal from English platforms on this very matter. The second stream was the first to weaken, and it weakened, not on any rational or theoretical shift, but on a basis of missionary experience.

Buller, after four decades in the New Zealand situation itself, including the years of crisis, admitted that time had proved Marsden wrong. He wrote:

> With his devoted zeal in this good cause, Mr. Marsden fell into the error—not uncommon in that day—that a savage people must be civilized, before they can be Christianized. Experience has proved the contrary.[3]

Even Marsden himself was convinced of this before he died and argued with his bishop against his own former position. The bishop had presented Marsden's own arguments of thirty years earlier and received the following reply:

> Civilization is not necessary before Christianity, sir, do both together if you will, but you will find civilization follow Christianity, easier than Christianity follow civilization.

Marsden went on to argue that the savage needed not "men learned after the fashion of this world, but men taught in the spirit and letter of Scripture."[4] In Africa, Robert Moffat, of "the

Bible and the spade" fame, came to the same conclusion after twenty-six years of missionary service:

> Much has been said about civilizing savages before attempting to evangelize them. This is a theory which has obtained an extensive prevalence among the wise men of this world, but we have never yet seen a practical demonstration of its truth. We ourselves are convinced that evangelization must precede civilization. . . . To make the fruit good the tree must first be made good.[5]

Moffat was a great civilizer, but he had no illusions about where his missionary priorities lay. He knew that "nothing but grace could change the savage" and that the blessings of civilization are best "appropriated after evangelization."

The third stream of support for the theory was that of *a strong and intellectual lay opinion*. This was not a cohesive body, and the motivation was varied, but it included many important people—political, commercial, and social personalities, travelers, men of science, and sea captains. Some had come to their convictions by reasoning at home; others had visited mission stations in far parts of the world and were impressed. Of course, there were some sea captains who were hostile to missions in every form because the trades in which they were engaged or their desire to cater to the physical satisfactions of their crews at the expense of island people brought them into conflict with the missionaries. The documentary records of this type of traveler must be set against those of unbiased scientific men who visited the same places.[6] These men, trained critics and scientific observers, were usually among the strongest supports of the theory of civilizing. They were supported by scholars who had access to missionary and commercial reports from all over the world and time to scrutinize them, and perhaps therefore had a wide perspective that a field missionary isolated on one station did not have.

However, as we look back over the records of a long period of time as well as at the wide perspective, we observe that this third stream was strongly subject to commercial or imperialistic motivation. This accounts for the recurrence of the theory in different forms over the last century and a half. This stream was responsible for the periodic intensifying of the theory at certain points of historic crisis.

Without doubt the Pacific missions that began in the 1830s (Tonga and Fiji) had quite a different policy. In the early twenties England was anxious to civilize Tonga because of its threat to shipping and a bad record of massacres. But the character of the mission was determined by the missionaries themselves. They happened to be a band of holiness preachers, and what civilizing they did (mainly educational and medical) was strongly subjected to spiritual dimensions and was regarded as part of the follow-up of conversion, not part of the thrust itself. These responses might well have crippled the theory but for the fact that the third stream of support stimulated a new approach in the forties based on a number of historic events.

New Zealand became a British colony and was opened for settlement, with many commercial interests involved.[7] Legislation was passed regarding the appointments of colonial bishops, with major consequences for both New Zealand and West Africa.[8] The ecclesiastical economics of this policy required increased settlement in the colonies where such bishops were to be appointed.

At this very time, when colonizing was becoming a matter of English ecclesiastical concern, there came out of St. John's, Oxford, an ecclesiastical writer who wrote a survey of the Pacific scene. He spotlighted New Zealand in particular as a field for *colonizing*, that is, *civilizing*, that is, *Christianizing*. The volume, in which he equated these three concepts, had a wide circulation in that day. It appeared in 1842, and was in its second edition the following year. The title of Dr. Russell's book so speaks for itself that I cite it in full: *Polynesia: or An Historical Account of the Principal Islands in the South Seas; including New Zealand; and the Introduction of Christianity; and the Actual Condition of the Inhabitants in regard to Civilization, Commerce and the Arts of Social Life.*

Such a title at least tells what the book is about. The preface of the volume begins:

> The main object of this volume is to throw light on the introduction of Christianity and Civilization into the islands of the South Sea.[9]

The main points stressed in the preface may be summarized thus:
1. Missions have stimulated a change the consequences of

which are permanent. No converted natives have returned to
paganism.*

2. However faulty some missions have been at some points, the
present state of converts is a vast improvement.

3. Converts readily accept the conveniences and luxuries of
civilized life.

4. Special interest is shown in New Zealand because property
is now available there for settlers on a secure basis.†

5. The book is based on documentary sources from all areas
and stresses the power of civilization to elevate the standards of
morality and taste and direct the convert's thoughts to eternity.
The book was strongly sympathetic to missions, but claimed a
certain objectivity by pointing out occasional biases. It was a
book for the times, and especially for the layman.

Its motivation was to stimulate colonization, but to do so with
the right kind of settler, who would aid in the establishment of
law and order. It was hostile to white adventurers of an immoral
type, who hindered missionary work. The section of the English
public the book sought to win were good colonists to establish
law and order so that the missionary could have support in his
role as "civilizer of the non-Christian world."

> Christianity, which is in every sense of the word the religion of
> civilization, has gone forth among them [the Maoris] attended
> by literature and the arts. . . .
>
> It has been justly observed, that if we stop at the present point
> of our advancement in the attempt to civilize the New Zea-
> landers, there would be room to doubt whether we have not
> rather inflicted an injury upon them than conferred a benefit
> [because they had acquired arms, ammunition, liquor and other
> destructive things by this time]. . . .
>
> The remedy for all these evils is the continuance of the training
> in religion, letters, agriculture and the more simple of the arts.
> Sound and useful knowledge will at once occupy their minds,
> improve their feelings and spread around them the blessings of
> security and competence.[10]

The abiding value of Russell's work is not in the viewpoint he

*In the light of claim 5, how did Russell miss the many references to the
Mamaia movement in Tahiti? His documentary work was either sloppy or
selectively motivated.

†This was written before the Maori wars over the alienation of Maori
lands.

advocated, which was disproved by the Maori wars, the nativistic movements, and the perpetually fragmented state of Maori religious life; but rather in providing us with a historic source for the viewpoint of a powerful segment of English society at the time—a segment which influenced the policy and technique of missions in its day and still has something to say to us.

Russell argued commercial motives under administrative protection, expressing hopes in terms of returns for labor expended. This measure of return is a long way removed from those anticipated by the Great Commission. The end of mission here is clearly in terms of trade and civilization, of establishing "commercial relations with the inhabitants and thereby to aid religious instruction by the resources of civilization." The power to this end is not:

> All power is given unto me in heaven and in earth
> Go ye therefore, and teach all nations . . . (Mt 28:19-20).

but rather:

> The missionary cause will always feel weak and insecure if it be compelled to stand insulated from political aid. . . .[11]

Russell followed this statement with about ten pages devoted to a survey of the trade and trade potential of the Pacific. Significantly enough within a few years the same approach was being presented in the North Pacific, more particularly from Hawaii.[12] Now, wise after the event, we can look back and see how it all worked out. The dream of "commercial relations with the inhabitants" did not work out. For the folk back in England, or the other homelands involved, it became "commercial relations with the settlers," supplies of raw materials from the *new owners* of the land. Russell's claim that "Christianity was in every sense of the word the religion of civilization" had a poignant meaning for the Maori in the sixties.

Meantime on the home front colonization became a Christian duty and appeals were made to all classes of people, who might respond to an empire call for civilizers. The following lines, in the grandiloquent style of the day (necessarily abbreviated), appeared in print at the time, addressed to possible New Zealand colonizers:

> Come bright Improvement! On the car of Time,
> And rule the spacious world from clime to clime.

> Thy handmaid arts shall every wild explore
> Trace every wave, and culture every shore.
> On Zealand's hills . . .
> Where human fiends on midnight errands walk,
> And bathe in brains the murderous tomahawk,
> There shall be flocks . . . and shepherds . . . and
> The village curfew, as it tolls profound.[13]

Not only is this a call to civilize, but it is a call to do so in a thoroughly Western manner.

Perhaps this is the place to pause for a moment and look at the significance of this movement in England. A very large body of public opinion was disposed toward this interinvolvement of colonizing and mission. If the missionaries were wrong, so were the rank and file of thinking people. It is therefore unfair for the secular critic to lay this at the door of the missionary. The charge must be made against the West, which saw its role in "ruling the spacious world" and "culturing every shore," and doing so in terms of its own social patterns. Those missionaries who were caught up in this way of thinking were but the children of their day and its academic institutions.

However, having said this, there is a word here for the Christian church, which cannot be bypassed and which must have a place in our self-examinations. The period of evangelizing by civilizing and/or colonizing shows how the Christian mission can become an instrument of economic and political machinery, being carried along in a stream of public opinion, rather than being a creator of that opinion; being used as a means to imperial, or commercial, or social, or merely secular ends, instead of being about the business of the Great Commission, which is written into the terms of reference of all missionary societies.

Another thing we need to note at this point in our survey is that the character of the New Zealand mission fields changed with this influx of white settlers. The new missionaries who came with the settlers came from the same England with the same perspectives and tempo. The people movements that were in progress at the time were something quite new to them and they were more concerned with building the settlers into a church than with consummating the indigenous people movements. Before the arrival of a bishop the C.M.S. and W.M.S. missionaries had coexisted happily and reaped their harvests side by side, rejoicing in the effectiveness of each other's labors. Thereafter both causes tended to become reflections of their mother-causes at home, with theological distrust at the points of baptism and ordination, and with some rivalry where it had not existed before. We have here an illustration of a principle that is still relevant today—the missionary on the field tends to reflect the characteristics of the home church. The seriousness of this for New Zealand was that the missionaries of the period leading up to the Maori Wars had strong procolonization sympathy and this made it difficult for them to accomplish the consummation of the people movement among the Maoris.

Colonization did not stimulate any church growth. Any growth among the settlers was by migration, not conversion. The Maori people movements were irreparably injured by colonization because of the huge areas of land alienated involuntarily from the Maoris and because the church seemed to take her stand with the settler. The older political and missionary Europeans cried out their warning,[14] but to no avail. The old order had changed. Babbage, in his study of Hauhauism, described the bishop's action in accompanying the imperial troops in battle as "not circumspect" because it encouraged the belief "that the missionaries were leagued with the Government to rob and subjugate the Maoris." He cited missionary sources for his opinion.[15]

The promises of the British civilizers did not work out. This is how Russell stated them in 1842:

> Thousands of our countrymen are hastening thither, carrying with them the arts, the science, the literature and the religion of England; armed too with a moral power which cannot fail to subdue the savage hearts of the aborigines, and furnished with the means of civilization, which, though they were inclined, they cannot long oppose. New Zealand, it is almost certain, will never again witness such sad scenes as passed in it a few years ago, when Christian ministers were attacked and their stations destroyed.[16] (The reference is to Rotorua and Matamata in 1836.)

In our chapter "The Maori Web," we saw that very much more and worse did happen. The documentation was far too gruesome to cite fully. The war dragged on bitterly and generated terrific hatred. By the end of the century the historian of the church, instead of treating the Maori people movements as church history, had relegated the Maori to the category of sociological problems.[17] The bishop himself admitted that the missionaries were seen as government agents "in a deep laid plot for the subjugation of the native people."[18]

Yet back in England through the forties and fifties the cry to civilize was still being heard. A British missionary writing in 1847 on Tonga and Fiji was struck by the different character of these holiness missions. Though he could report tremendous growth and knew the supporters of these missions would be pleased about that, *he felt he had to apologize for it*, because it was entirely within the indigenous patterns and offered no great demonstration of civilizing.

> Very little success has been hitherto made in the civilization of the South Sea tribes in the Friendly Islands and Feejee, nor are the signs encouraging in the matter. Expectations entertained in England are by no means realized on the spot; at least, not with the rapidity which hope had painted, but left experience to correct.[19]

This was Walter Lawry, who had been in the Pacific for thirty years and had truly found his niche as the W.M.S. field secretary. He felt the British missionary-minded public needed reeducating on what a Christian mission really was, for it was a story of holiness conquests he had to tell. Needless to say, his books had their critics, but they are significant evidence of policy and opinion at midcentury. Incidentally two of the strongest of the indigenous churches of the Pacific today have emerged from Tonga and Fiji and they are not without their social outreaches.

In examining the three supports of the theory of evangelizing by civilizing we have shown how *civilizing* became *colonizing* at the beginning of the forties, and especially related to New Zealand. British missionary theory also had other influences which did not emanate from the Pacific, though they were determinants of the general policy. One of these forces was most vigorous contemporaneously with the drive for colonization in New Zealand. Undoubtedly the two reinforced each other, so that I have felt disposed to devote a few pages to this factor that is actually beyond the Pacific theater. It is only when we see Pacific and African issues together that we can really appreciate the British atmosphere in 1840.

The Wider Perspective

One of the expressions of the humanitarianism of the age had been the British Anti-Slavery Movement, which proved its vigor in the victory of 1834 when the Emancipation Act was passed. However, it soon became evident to the missionary communities of Africa that raiding still persisted.

Thomas Fowler Buxton conceived a plan one sleepless night and outlined it in a book called *The Slave Trade and Its Remedy*. He advocated strengthening the African patrol, negotiating with African rulers (both near the coast and in the interior), and making use of the Niger as a highway into the interior to establish posts behind the slaving tribes—Ibo, Yoruba, and Dahomey. To carry out his vision he pressed for the cooperation of the three interested parties: government, commerce, and Christian missions. That such a person as Buxton could seriously propagate such a plan and get enough support for the establishment of a Society for the Extinction of the Slave Trade and for the Civilization of Africa is itself a commentary on the sociopolitical atmosphere of England at the time. It may be worth asking what kind of people stood behind such a scheme.

The public meeting at Exeter Hall in June 1840 was under the chairmanship of the new prince consort, supported by twenty-five peers and bishops and other influential persons, including figures like David Livingstone. The prince defined the task of ending the slave trade as a holy cause to be attended to "under the auspices of our Queen and her Government." Buxton moved the first resolution. He was followed by Samuel Wilberforce (son of William), Sir Robert Peel, the bishops of Winchester and Chichester, the Earl of Chichester (then president of the C.M.S.), the Marquis of Northampton, and several others. Outside the meeting itself Gladstone, Palmerston, and Lord John Russell gave their support. As Buxton pointed out, for once Whig and Tory, Radical and Dissenter, Low and High Church, were united. The outcome of it all was the Niger expedition in 1841. For this the government built three ships, significantly named *Albert, Wilberforce*, and *Sudan*. A four thousand pound fund was raised for establishing an agricultural school on the Niger. The captains and commissioners were Christian men and a chaplain went with the expedition. Buxton insisted that mission stations as well as government posts and trading stations be opened along the great river. The chaplain's prayer is preserved:

> Give success to our endeavours
> to introduce civilization and Christianity
> into this benighted country.

There was some opposition indirectly from slaving interests. Increasing demands for slaves from Cuba and Brazil involved West African supply. A party advocated dispensing with the African patrol altogether on the score of ineffectiveness; but church and missionary leaders supported Palmerston and Russell to carry the day in the House of Commons, and victory on this level permitted the antislavery movement to come through stronger than ever.[20]

Were this an African study I would be bound to discuss how starting missions on this kind of motivation does not necessarily build mission stations at the places where doors are open for the gospel, but Africa is not our theme. The incident shows, however, the strong body of very important persons in political and social life who stood behind these colonial moves with what they took to be a moral dimension. The capacity of Buxton to unite religious and political rivals and to tie government, commerce, and church in such an organization on such a scale was no mean feat. The establishment of colonial bishoprics in West Africa and New Zealand was part of the same complex of forces and manifested the humanitarian temper of England. One can see how civilizing and colonizing and Christianizing were so often equated and so rarely differentiated.

It explains why Lawry felt he had to apologize for Tonga and Fiji for an absence of the civilizing dimension. Ultimately it was the slavery issue that was to tip the balance and receive Fiji into the empire about three decades later. By that time there was a strong evangelical church there with a good indigenous pastorate. It presented an entirely new kind of situation to the British administration, in which they had to establish relations with a Christianized people whose church had no episcopate and put more stress on sanctification than on civilizing.

MISSIONARIES AND IMPERIALISTS

I have already pointed out that the second stream of support for the policy of civilizing was the unstable one of the three. It is significant that over the years the most outspoken opponents of the theory have been field missionaries, frequently men of long-term service. Many of the clashes between missionaries and their directors have been at this very point. Although civilizing and evangelizing are not necessarily exclusive it is seldom that one finds men midway on the axis between these two poles: most missions and most missionaries tend to be nearer one of the poles than the other. When a missionary with a personal conviction for the priority of evangelism finds himself tied down to sedentary institutionalism without outreach he is a miserable person. This is a present-day form of the problem.

In the reports of the London Conference, 1888, one finds the chairman and speaker standing at the opposite poles in this very matter. On the day in which the sessions were devoted to Oceania, Alexander McArthur, M.P., whose advocacy had persuaded the government to accept Fiji's offer of cession, spoke of missionaries as civilizers, of their opening the way for British merchants and manufactures, of fresh markets and the extension of commerce.[21] Then he called on the speakers.

They represented four great missionary forces that had worked the Pacific area. Bishop Stuart of New Zealand considered the early vitality was due to the open Bible, but added that "the spreading tree was cut down" because of colonizing land wars "not to our honour" and a "check to missionary effort."[22] James Calvert, W.M.S. veteran missionary of Fiji, set his values on the translation and circulation of Scripture, the extensive use of indigenous agents, and the numbers brought to the penitent form in Pentecostal outpourings and the motivation of the Great Commission.[23]

Dr. S. Macfarlane (L.M.S. of New Guinea), the third speaker, stated flatly that his society had started with the wrong ideas, but that the lessons had been learned. It was not civilizing but the indigenous agent who had spread the gospel. He said that it took the artisans nearly twenty years to get converts, but the indigenous agents accomplished this in as many weeks.[24] The fourth speaker did not address himself to the problem we are considering but discussed the translation and circulation of Scripture in the northern Pacific as a means of growth.[25] The voice from the platform was uniform: Scripture translation and circulation, the use of indigenous agents, and the patterned movement of the Spirit. These were the factors the field missionaries felt had built the Pacific churches. They all appear to have ignored the chairman's remarks. The imperial thrust in missionary policy may have been strongly felt still in Britain, but the outstanding long-term missionaries of the day were not at all impressed by it.

Yet despite this attitude of experienced men the marriage of missioning and civilizing was kept intact. It was stimulated in those periods marked by a race for European colonies. It stifled numerous moves toward autonomy on the promising mission fields and fostered paternalism which has lasted to our own day. This was a direct hindrance to the growth of young churches. There were also indirect hindrances. International agreements about colonial frontiers split ethnic groups and divided people movements along the cleavages of the different political administrations, thereby injuring the entity and cohesion of the young church that should have emerged. This was not confined to Africa. The imaginary line across New Guinea, the separation of Bougainville from the Western Solomons, and the division of Samoa are three examples in the Pacific. Such imperialistic lines have created untold problems for missions and have hindered growth. Missionaries have been forced to cast policy within political structures that had no ethnic foundation.

Missionaries and administrators have not always agreed, especially in the areas of morals and the discipline of indigenes. Sometimes missionaries have taken their stand with the indigenes even against the administration, especially on the score of indigenous rights. Although the missionary personally loses much by opposing the administration, sometimes his action has worked out for good, because at a deeper level it is apparent that all white men are not similarly motivated. However these are crisis moments. Government-mission antagonism is not a good thing and hinders the work of both. Usually the indigenous church has grown better where there has been no colonial administration, though life may have been more dangerous for the missionary. On the whole, missionaries have lived far closer to the people than administrators; the former aiming at identification, the latter preserving the isolation of status. Where missionaries have allowed themselves to be too attached to political leaders their work has become, more often than not, foreign in character and static. No matter how one examines this marriage of colonizing and missioning, one finds no evidence of church growth because of it. Colonization per se has set more obstacles before the emerging indigenous churches than one cares to tabulate, yet in its day it was argued by ecclesiastical scholars as a means of spreading the gospel.

MISSIONARIES AND COMMERCE

If a church-state identification has its problems, an association of church and commerce has perhaps even more, yet the cry of that day was "Civilizing by organized cooperation of government, commerce, and church."

One of the outworkings of the economics of missions has been the establishment of trading stations and plantations, with the idea that missions should become self-supporting. On the surface this sounds attractive, but let us probe a little.

What is the motive of self-support? All through the missionary records we come across that phrase "free of cost to the Society." If this means to free Society funds for another field where doors are open, this is good—though the records seldom suggest this. The motivation for self-support ought not to be related to the home society, but rather to the importance of planting churches that can stand on their own feet, a principle which should be built in from the beginning. But the self-support of a mission or mission station is a very different thing from the self-support of an indigenous church. A self-supporting station with plantations producing copra and engaged in other commercial revenue-producing activities is more likely to bind the emerging church to an institutionalized mission control. It is in the very places throughout the Pacific where missions have followed this policy that the indigenous self-supporting church has failed to emerge. Even though it is long since the islanders came out of paganism, the organic growth of the church and the development of pastoral dimensions have been very slow indeed.

The second factor brought to light when we probe this matter is the tremendous amount of time and labor required to run these establishments, both missionary labor from overseas and indigenous labor, either for a small wage or a work-to-learn program. One cannot enter the commercial world without being involved in such factors as time, wages, and labor. We may add the burdens, problems, and time-consuming concerns of supervision. The question which many folk ask is, Is this the Christian mission? Was this implied in the Great Commission? And there are a hundred and one aspects of this. For instance, plantations are sedentary and often operate against itinerancy; they imply a movement which is centripetal rather than centrifugal, and this never leads to real church growth; they concentrate mission personnel at a point of agricultural or economic opportunity rather than a point of evangelistic opportunity and many other aspects.

All this, which emerged very strongly as general missionary policy at the end of the century, is but another variant of the civilizing policy. The first Tahiti missionaries had to make themselves personally self-supporting. Some of them did it very effectively, clearing four times as much in a year as was paid to the holiness missionaries farther west by their home authorities. They had to acquire land, fence it, cultivate it, harvest it, and market the produce. The early years were, as every pioneer planter or farmer knows, times of heavy labor and time demands. Industry had the priority, not evangelism, and of course, there was no church growth.

The difference between the early and later years of the century was accounted for by the passage of time, the emergence of strong colonies in New Zealand and the Australian States with nearer markets, and the increased availability of shipping and more regular means of communication. The difference at the level of missionary policy was simply that the earlier artisan missionaries had to take the responsibility of economic management of their own affairs; at the turn of the century the new missions in Melanesia were officially engaged in commercial and plantation ventures. They were establishing mission, not missionary, plantations. The distinction is important because the Societies were supported by public funds solicited for the carrying out of the Great Commission. Much jurisdiction for some of these Pacific missions had been transferred to Australia and New Zealand, where there were independent churches by this time. It is possible that the mission supporters from these churches accepted the policy, as the establishment of plantations had been well publicized in the colonial missionary journals of the day. Furthermore they were themselves the sons and daughters of colonists. Even the Wesleyans, and they are much involved at this point, were stressing less their holiness emphasis and were impressed with what they called industrial missions.

Industrial missions were not only plantations. They included ship-building yards, carpentry and other types of workshop. They aimed at training the indigenous people for industrial work in Western forms considered relevant. Many of the carpenters, seamen, and printers of the Pacific have received their training in this type of institution. In itself this is a good work and deserves praise. However it does not appear to have led to any church-planting, nor to have had any noticeable effect on church growth either numerically or in quality. Here and there young persons were converted while at the institution, and some of these were to become useful Christian advocates in the villages later. On the whole they trained good carpenters rather than built churches. Some of the graduates of mission institutions have actually become the opponents of Christianity, and some of these I know personally. If we feel the cultivation of such social services is the role of a mission, then the matter warrants investigation on its own merits. This will be the outworking or fruit of the gospel in society. That involves the question which is still very much with us: Whether these essential services are the role of the government or church. That is one thing, but it is quite another matter to present industrial missions as the method of winning a pagan community for Christ.

Toward the end of the century the theory of civilizing emerged in this new form of industrial missions and it was a world trend. It was strongly advocated at the Keswick Convention in Britain in 1890. At the same time it had its hostile opponents in its own day. Some of these critics were Christian men who had lived in countries where missions operated and had watched missionary activity as observers from the outside.

One of these critics was a British lawyer who had spent a long term of service in the Indian Law Courts and had been disgusted with missionary trade involvements which had brought them into court. So impressed was he with the tragedy of this type of situation that he wrote a volume on missionary methodology. It received little hearing because the fixed missionary policy was so dead against it, and missions were so involved economically with vested interests. Nevertheless it was an important statement and is of great historical value in the study of the theory of mission. He classified industrial farms, trades, manufacturing and fisheries as *bad methods* (his term), not merely because of the unhappy commercial entanglements they involved, as he observed, but because as a lawyer he found the missionary's terms of reference in the Great Commission.

> When it is proposed to have a pious Industrial Superintendent, or an Evangelical tile-manufacturer, or a Low-church breeder of cattle or raiser of turnips, I draw the line, and fall back on the Great Commission, and sternly reject all adjuncts.

On this basis he objected to turning the "preacher, teacher and friend" into a "farmer, trader and employer." He had no objection to the presence of a Christian farmer—a farmer known as a farmer yet a supporter of the church. He strongly objected to a farmer posing as a missionary.

> Augustine did not teach our Anglo-Saxon forefathers the art of building ships, or starting manufactories, or breeding oxen. . . . He brought a nation that was heathen to the knowledge of a Saviour.

Of the Bishop of Sierra Leone, whose financial appeal for industrial missions stimulated an approving resolution at the 1890 Keswick Convention, this lawyer wrote, "The good bishop cannot be called a missionary, nor his episcopal charge a mission." He went on to deal with a series of missions engaged in similar pursuits in different parts of the world.[26]

But the lawyer, Cust, was fighting against the stream. Christian missions were about to pass into a heyday of institutionalism which lasted until the last war and reflected some unhealthy registrations in church growth statistics, and led to ingrowth as opposed to outreach. Although I did not agree with all that Cust wrote or the way he said it, I personally felt it was an important critical analysis of missionary policy. The lawyer had his criterion in the missionary terms of reference. He objected to any modification of the Great Commission.

THE SUPREME VALUE

I have already suggested that the Pacific islanders watched the missionaries and fixed their impressions as to their supreme values. They may have been wrong in their verdict. But they formed their impressions on a basis of what they observed. If the major concern *seemed to be* cultivating tobacco, spinning cotton, manufacturing oil; or preparing goods for market either locally or for overseas; or administering a compound, caring for drains and legal matters for tenants living on surplus mission lands; or sitting in control of affairs at an office desk—no matter how spiritual the man's personal life might have been—these things were taken as his supreme value. But if, on the other hand, a missionary set out to learn a language, translate Scripture and devotional aids, seeing that these were made available to the inhabitants; training them to use them and witness among their friends and relations; itinerating rather than remaining always at the station or business centers—if in this way it seemed that his one supreme concern was to introduce men to Christ, and to help them use the Book that reveals Him, then he established himself within the terms of reference of his missionary commission.

There was no doubt about the matter to the observers. The latter activities might bring persecution or great growth. The former activities created a wrong impression, might be tolerated for economic or social reasons, but they never planted churches. I am writing of pioneering days, while the mission is still confronted with a pagan environment. Second- and third-generation work is a matter for another book. But there are many confrontations with paganism still today where these principles apply. The study of the history of Christian missions in Southern Polynesia shouts aloud to all pioneer missions of today, Beware of the impression you create as to where your supreme value lies, for this is received as the gospel you preach.

John Turnbull, who had little patience with the Tahitians and some admiration for the missionaries, visited those islands, a decade after they commenced their mission. He has described the personal homes and gardens and their public gardens, well fenced, stocked with fruit trees, taro, indigo, and corn. He felt that such an example should have stimulated the Tahitians to emulate their industry and share its obvious reward. Their indolence, he considered, was beyond the cure of any common remedy.[27] A little later Captain Beechey similarly described the missionaries living "in superfluity."[28]

Thus both before and after the people movement which we have shown to have come from other causes, the islanders saw this same value pattern—prosperity as reward for industry. When Beechey visited Tahiti the missionaries had been there for thirty years, the congregation still had no Bibles of their own, the ten missionaries in all the islands of Eastern Polynesia were close together, six of them in Tahiti itself,[29] and John Williams on the fringe, straining to get beyond the reefs. The officials of the Society, who visited Tahiti just a little earlier, were concerned with acquiring suitable land for a cotton mill. Here is a focal point for a study in values and all documentable. We may well ask the question, How did this appear to the Tahitians?

Against this example of industry as a softener of the way for Christianity, there is the alternative of the Great Commission. It is an alternative and a different approach to mission because it was cast by the Lord Himself in terms of power encounter, not mere example.* The test of our terms of reference then is, Does this or that method bring men into encounter with Christ, and then lead them to go forth into the world as Christ's men for confrontations with the forces of evil? True, industry is a good thing, and should be a fruit of the gospel. It is no substitute for evangelism, however, by our criterion.

The theory of civilizing has a slightly more subtle form today. The ethical life and the way of love, education, medicine, relief organization, and literacy campaigns are all part of the missionary thrust today. I have no objections to this. But the test of our terms of reference must be applied. Are they merely "good works" for their own sake in the hope of influencing or softening a way for some later generation to present the gospel? Or are they bringing folk into encounter with Christ, converting men and women, and planting churches? Are they presenting an example or an encounter? Is the supreme value ethics, education, relief work, or medicine per se, or is it conversion to Christ? It is important to note that all these good works have to be done, and it may well be the job of the church to do them. I am not discussing that issue; this is not a book on applied Christianity, but on Christian missioning in terms of church-planting and church growth. I can cite cases where medical work, for instance, contributes significantly to the Christian mission. On the other hand other cases exist as ends in themselves with no planned purpose of mission at all. Yet sometimes these very institutions have absorbed funds contributed for the church's obedience to

*Matthew 28:18-19. The *therefore* of verse 19 implies the antecedent verse 18, in terms of "all authority."

the Great Commission, when doors for evangelism were open nearby and left unsponsored.

We hoodwink ourselves when we confuse applied Christianity with Christian mission; not because the former is not our duty, but because it often becomes a substitute for mission, so that the real encounter which Christ commanded is avoided. Furthermore, applied Christianity in a so-called mission district should be springing as fruit from a live indigenous church. We have to be careful that the applied Christianity of a sending church does not become foreign aid and lead to a dependent church on the field. There are right and wrong ways of giving help, but be this as it may, it must never be a substitute for direct encounter with Christ. The W.C.C. Consultation at Iberville put it thus: "A Church without a dynamic missionary purpose belies its own true nature."[30]

A Continuous Missionary Problem

In this analysis of the problem of civilizing versus evangelism in missionary policy I have sought to establish that we are dealing with a *continuous* problem. The form may vary with the character and patterns of each period of history, but in some form or other it reemerges, and with each reappearance it is found to have some bearing on the growth (or nongrowth) of the church. The astonishing fact is that each age of missionary strategists has had to relearn the lessons for itself.

Missionary strategists, like some social scientists, are so convinced that the problems of their day are new and the context has not existed before, and therefore requires treatment purely on its own merits, that they overlook the great continuities of history.

In the last few pages we have seen how the perfectly legitimate applications of Christianity in social service can become so preeminent that the encounter of the gospel itself—that is, the Word of God unto salvation—can be left unattended; so that missions can become social services and unfaithful to the Great Commission. Is this a new situation and a new problem peculiar to our day? Certainly not. Its form may have varied but in essence it goes back to the apostles themselves.

The twelve called the multitude of the disciples unto them, and said, It is not reason that we should leave the word of God, and serve tables.

Wherefore, brethren, look ye out among you seven men of honest report, full of the Holy Ghost and wisdom, whom we may appoint over this business.

But we will give ourselves continually to prayer, and to the ministry of the word (Ac 6:2-4).

The social elevation of mankind is an important business. If it had not been so important it could not have been substituted so often for the demands of the Great Commission. But it is not peculiarly Christian. It is something Christianity shares with the best organizations of Hinduism and Islam, for example. A Christianity without its social outworkings is, of course, unthinkable; but the uniqueness of Christianity is Christ Himself and the gospel He commissioned us to present to men.

In every period of the history of mission the church has been tried at this point in some form that appealed to the mind of that day. So we go back step by step from relief programs to industrial missions, to commercial imperialism, to colonization, to civilizing as a softener for evangelism. Always we find the conflict between the missionaries involved—one man building the ship that will take him beyond the reefs and the other setting up his sedentary cotton mill. We are dealing with a recurring phenomenon.

My study of it has been confined to the last century and a half, and the first Pacific missionaries have been defended because they had no antecedents. The truth is that at this very point they did have antecedents, but they still had to learn the lesson for themselves.

Those missionaries must surely have read the story of Egede's mission to Greenland, the pattern of its financing, the attempt to prepare the savage for Christianity by civilizing him, and fifteen years of failure before Egede's retirement. Then, in the end, the gospel was discovered through Scripture translation, so that the word of the cross triumphed where civilizing had failed.[31] Yet missionary promotion also failed to learn the lesson of the Greenland failure. They idealized it as a drama of human endurance, so that the *Duff* missionaries did not expect quick returns. Yet the evidence was there all the time for those with eyes to see it, as the Moravian Mission historian of a later day pointed out:

There is no need of preparing the way for the gospel, it makes a way for itself. . . . The very alpha of the missionary's office in the tropics or at the poles is to deliver the message of Him who has sent him. 'Look unto me and be ye saved.' . . .[32]

It was for one who remained after the return of Egede—John Beck—to speak of a Scripture passage he had translated to an Eskimo from another locality. "Is that true?" he burst out. "Why didn't you tell us that before?"

So the story had to be repeated in Tahiti. The day came, after many years of labor, when Henry Nott read his translation of John 3:16 and immediately there were enquiries: "Let me hear those words again!" This is the heart of Christian theology, the very depths of the gospel—and a long way from cotton culture. These men had feared putting the words of life into the profane Tahiti language. Had they known more church history they would have realized that a missionary to the Goths had disproved that position a millennium and a half earlier.[33]

We have drawn so much in this study from the lessons the L.M.S. men had to learn that I propose terminating this unit by citing three references from the work of their own official historian, as he looked back over their archival records of the century. They view the subject from three different angles.

Referring to the religious questions asked by the converts of Raiatéa and Huahine, and the spiritual depths they reflected, Lovett saw something that mere civilizing could never have stimulated:

It is conceivable that civilization might have, in time, suppressed the infamous Areoi societies and checked infanticide. But civilization, apart from the gospel, could never have started such questions as these, and could certainly have held out no comfort to such troubled souls.[34]

As to the sequence of civilizing and evangelizing he gave his verdict as follows, the italics being his:

Whereever the gospel has come, *civilizing has followed* in its train. In Tahiti not a native would work regularly, or admit that any of the observances of civilized life were preferable to his own customs, until he had embraced 'the new doctrine'. It was only after Christianity had conquered that a civilization, even then very halting and imperfect, so much as *began* to establish itself.[35]

Throughout his researches Lovett has frequently observed an aspect of "civilization" that continually hindered the planting of churches, and did not hesitate to express it in terms of a superlative:

> One of the deadliest foes to true progress in the Pacific has been the presence and influence of unChristian "civilized" men. . . . It is from observers of this class that many of the oft-refuted and oft-repeated slanders upon Christian work in the Pacific have proceeded.[36]

The African scholar Parrinder made a similar appraisal for that region, feeling that "civilization" could be a tragic hindrance to progress.[37]

Civilizing, direct or indirect, in whatever form an age may employ, does not plant churches or promote their growth.

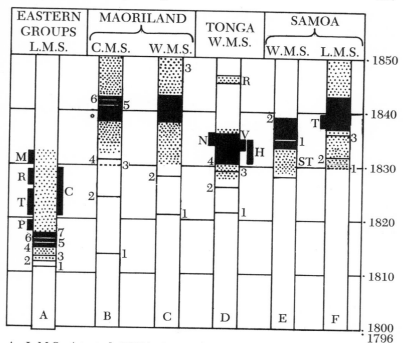

A. L.M.S. (started 1796) 1. Pomare II seeking baptism. 2. Turtle episode. 3. Oito episode. 4. Patii burns idols. 5. Bunaauia. 6. Postwar episode, conversion of Tahiti complete. 7. Society Group complete. Local movements—P: Paumotus; T: Tubuai; R: Rapa; M: Manahiki; C: Cook Is.

B. C.M.S. 1. Start. 2. Rangi converted. 3. Inland itinerating began. 4. 20 members. *People movement intense, 20,000 converts in 2 years, Central area. 5. Spread into eastern area. 6. Bishop Selwyn arrived.

C. W.M.S. 1. Start. 2. Location shifted. 3. Concentration on new colonists.

D. W.M.S. 1. Lawry's unsuccessful start. 2. Official start. 3. Seven baptisms. 4. Vi converted. Local movements—H: Haabai; V: Vavau; N: islands toward Samoa; R: revival movement.

E. W.M.S. ST. Tongan overflow. 1. Turner's arrival. 2. Withdrawal.

F. L.M.S. 1 & 2 Williams' visits. 3. Missionaries arrived. T: Tutuila Wesleyan-type of movement.

Pl. 13. People-movement intensity in Southern Polynesia:
1810–1850.

7

THE STRUCTURE AND VALIDITY
OF PEOPLE MOVEMENTS

WHEN WALTER LAWRY went to live among the Tongans in 1822 he knew well their reputation for treachery and massacre. After having lived among them for a year the reputation was confirmed, and he was able to add further detail on such gruesome accompaniments as human sacrifice. He felt the people regarded him not as a missionary but as a "harbinger of soldiers" so that he was always "treated with suspicion."[1]

In biblical terminology both for the L.M.S. victims of 1797 and the Wesleyans in 1822, the field was not ripe unto harvest. Stated anthropologically, there was nothing latent in the situation that disposed the islanders toward the acceptance of the new innovations being advocated.

In 1847 Lawry returned to Tonga as the area secretary of his Mission and found the whole situation completely transformed. Not only had there been people movements from paganism to Christianity, but there had been consummation movements and revival. Turning from Tonga to Fiji he found the pattern spreading apace. He recorded his feelings about Tonga:

> I am bound to record my testimony, that the great work of God is manifest on every side and that there is much more to cheer than to discourage those who labour among the Tongans. The spirit of the people is generally open and benevolent, cheerful and happy. In their devotional exercises they are solemn and earnest, like men who think as well as feel. . . . I speak of the general state of public morals when I say that I have never seen the wheat so free from chaff in any part of the world. . . . There is conformity of heart and life to the Christianity of the New Testament, surpassing all that I have seen elsewhere, and such as is truly gratifying to witness. . . . What but the gospel of the Lord Jesus Christ could have produced such a change in this once deeply-polluted people? Surely Acts of Parliament could not; counting beads and crosses could not; baptismal regenera-

tion and priestly assumption could not; the teaching of a Christless morality could not. No: the Author of this work is God.[2] This is a valuable record, not only as a statement of the Wesleyan point of view,[3] but also because it shows Lawry's conviction that a tremendous change had come over the people in the interim and that it had qualitative depth.

The same thing was said in vastly different style by numerous scientific travelers[4] and sea captains, some of whom disagreed with some aspects of the new morality and Sabbatarianism[5] but admitted the tremendous reality of the change. Furthermore they saw not merely a few changed individuals, but changed societies. The waves of people movement, which I have charted on a plate (pl. xiii) in this volume for comparative purposes, were real and dramatic and are well-documented.

The purpose of this chapter is to probe deeper into the matter of their structure and validity. To meet the requirements of this book, the analysis will require dimensions of both social structure and religion.

People Movements in Terms of Culture and Structure

There are two important cultural features of people movements that call for comment: the structural workings and the symbolism.

The Structure of the Movement is Multi-Individual

The term *mass movement* is a bad one. It envisages a fearful, hysterical crowd acting as an irrational mass. Any figure of speech implying irrationality fails to meet the requirements of the phenomenon we are investigating. They have been called *people movements*, and *peoples' movements*, the former suggesting the multi-individual character, and the latter the structural entity. The former is valuable for describing the conversion of a village or a family, the latter for differentiating between, say, the Tongan and the Maori movements. In this work I have spoken of people movements and I imply that they have specific structures, that the groups involved comprise individuals who have specific places and rights. The group does not exist as a living organism unless the individuals act and interact, each according to his specific role and rights. Biblically the church is conceived in the same terms as a body. The total group is really the decision-making body, although it may be for one individual to make the pronouncement as the representative of all. In many communal societies there is no decision without unanimity in the village or tribal councils. The decision-making group may be a family, or a village, or a lineage, or a caste. This is a basic determinant in people movements.

In many societies the man who acts alone as an individual is guilty of treason. This does not mean that he cannot think or speak as an individual and claim his rights. The very existence of the men's house in a village implies that there are matters which call for the men getting together for the expression of opinion. The elders, or "complete men" (as the married men are called in some places), often have a communal authority, the franchise being open to all who carry the responsibility of the tribe (marry and contribute to its strength). In some societies there is no chief at all, the group itself being the authority. In others a purely representative chieftaincy rotates among the family units. In still others the chiefs are an administrative class, but such societies usually have other classes—warriors, fishermen, craftsmen, priests perhaps—each with its independent decision-making group. In these cases the chiefs may determine the politics of the whole, but the priests attend to the religion of the whole and the fishermen have monopolies and rights. Such societies have a network of interclass institutions for coordinating decisions that affect the total society.

In all these patterns freedom in decision-making is limited by the pattern of society, as it is in the West;* but in none is the individual deprived of his right of individual opinion and an approved means of expressing it. Those of us who have lived with people like this know how their discussions go on for weeks, till every angle has been probed and unanimity is reached; then, and only then, will there be decision and action. It is multi-individual.

Church growth studies demonstrate that responses to the gospel have been more effective where missionary advocates have directed their appeals to autonomous decision-making groups, who have power to act, rather than to individuals who have to rebel against the group to act alone. Winning converts out of, or against, or in spite of their families may build a few strong

---

*We are free, but within limits—taxes have to paid, traffic rules have to be observed, certain employment demands joining a union, house-building is restricted by building regulations, our marriage must subscribe to legal patterns. Rebellion means penalty.

individual Christians, but it throws up tremendous group barriers against the Christian appeal. It also isolates the Christian from his natural environment and social structure and makes him dependent on foreign resources. The bulk of the church in the Pacific has been won by people movements; that is, not isolated individuals, but by individuals acting within their own social patterns and by means of their own decision-making mechanisms. Thus the total structures have been won. On a smaller scale numerically, the same principle applies even with Asians in the Pacific. For example, among the Indian communities in Fiji, there was no appreciable growth of the church until the missionaries began to see the significance of the family unit.

The prolonged discussion which will precede the majority of people movements will take place within the autonomous local units and also as "table talk" and during communal work projects. Christianity will be examined, both as a gospel and a value system. At first there will be but a few advocates within the group, but they will increase; not only because of the reasoning but because they have been alerted to the possibility of a change of religion. They may invite a missionary to visit the group and state the case for Christianity. Always the effectiveness of the old gods will be critically examined, and frequently at this point the Christian advocates within the group get their breakthrough. Social and economic aspects will be discussed. There may be resistance here, especially from those who have grown rich from the old religion. One whose prestige is threatened, say the leading warrior of the group, may also oppose Christianity. If a missionary can win the principal priest and warrior of the group for Christ, the group response will be rapid because the resistance is so reduced. But a missionary can also antagonize the priest, and this has the opposite effect. What we often ascribe to "primitive" conservatism may well be the complexity of resolving all the problems anticipated by the decision-making group. Although people movements give the impression of suddenness I have been impressed, from my study of missionary correspondence over the period, with the way these movements have cast their shadows before them. Resistance must have been rather obviously exhausted, for example, for Nathaniel Turner to write officially to London of what ought to be done "in event of all Tonga turning. . . ."

A social structure means a great many things to those who live in it: the organization of daily life, the security of group values, the entity of their group in a hostile world in which they are confronted by other entities, and the perpetuity of their society and way of life. Individuals are free to express themselves in their own ways provided the ways of life and group values are not injured thereby. The society is not opposed to change. Change that betters society is welcomed, but radical innovation which might threaten security and group values is suspect. This is specially so in our own Western religious communities. In animistic societies the function of religion is the maintenance of society, the preservation of social values, the assurance of safe passage through the life crises, the avoidance of catastrophes, and the satisfaction of physical and mental needs by means of prayers, rituals, and taboos. The prayers, rituals, and taboos of Christianity were seldom if ever an obstruction to decision for Christ. But acceptance of Christianity—that is, its substitution for the old religion—had to supply all those needs the animist felt were covered by his old faith. Animistic religion has been described as the *integrator* of society. It was not, as alas with the West today, a mere compartment of life, which can be (to change the metaphor) removed like the appendix from the body. For the first generation converts, those actually making the break with paganism, Christianity as a functional substitute had to meet specific needs and satisfactions. Furthermore it had to be thought out in specific thought-forms—of mana, of powers and counter-powers. Here in the area of power encounter Christianity had to prove itself.

Thus the tribal fetish had to be destroyed if Christ was to take its place. Who can destroy a *tribal* fetish but a *tribe*? How can a deified progenitor of a lineage be rejected as a god but by the lineage? Henotheism can be discarded only by henotheistic rebellion. One individual can resist a tribal god, but the belief of the tribe continues. This individual is a rebel, an "atheist," a destroyer of the cohesiveness of the tribe. Such radical individualism threatens security. It calls for discipline—or maybe ostracism. For himself, he can say perhaps that he no longer believes in the tribal god;[6] but the belief in the god continues, stronger than ever, and Christianity is seen as a danger so that the group as a whole orientates itself for resistance. Belief in a tribal deity can only be destroyed by a tribe.

The individual can be as vigorous as he chooses in the tribal mechanisms for discussion and disagreement. Here he can advocate Christianity without fear. His advocacy will at least be heard because he respects the pattern of tribal control. This has some advantages over our own patterns. Mere majority decision does often lead to schism. Our own splinter movements in Western Christianity have been a great hindrance to the acceptance of Christianity among other cultures. Decision by unanimity may be slow, but it has its compensations; and if in communal society a lineage, a village, or a family desires to do its decision-making this way, who are we Western individualists to say them nay?

However, it follows that if none but the tribe can destroy the tribal fetish (the chief as representative, acting in the presence of the group), none but the family (with the family head as representative) can destroy a family god, and a personal fetish can only be destroyed by the individual himself.

In our study of the Samoan *fono* we saw how the group exercised control over any signs of absolutism on the part of the principal chief. We saw that each communal group had its organ for discussion and mechanisms for bringing group pressure to bear on any individual whose operations savored too much of self-aggrandizement. Yet it was always open for any individual to speak his mind. The dominant drive of the *fono* pattern was to achieve an acceptable consensus of opinion, after having allowed all individuals to express themselves freely. It was natural that such procedure would lead to communal action. When a chief visited another village where a teacher was established, listened to the preaching, and observed the worship forms, and then returned to his own village to repeat the performance himself, we need to remember that he was not forcing his opinion on the group. He was their representative acting in accord with the wish of the *fono*—not majority wish, but consensus.[7] This had some great advantages for the young church. It provided a fellowship in which new converts could act and in which their experiences could be developed, because Christianity per se had been approved by their *fono*.

In the case of Pomare II of Tahiti, we have seen that he was for long the sole advocate of Christianity, despite the denial of baptism to him. It was his practice to press the claims of Christianity on certain persons. But—what persons? He had tried to win the leaders of households with kin ties with his own domestic unit, and those who were tied politically. That group movement which we recorded before the Battle of Bunaauia comprised the Pomare II segment of society, represented by the families shown on the ancestry table of Pomare II (illustrated in this book, pl. 2) plus a unit from Huahine.[8] His opinion had not been acceptable to the group for some time but his persistent advocacy won through in the end, especially when he put their old gods to the test in a power demonstration and showed them impotent.

In the case of Malietoa of Samoa, it will be remembered, a test was applied. Although his sons desired to take the risks of eating the sacred fish at the same time as their father, the family *fono* determined otherwise. Malietoa and a segment of the group would make the experiment alone. If they were wrong, they alone would suffer, and the sons would carry on the fortunes of the family. The sons disliked the idea of dividing the group, but agreed because the question of the perpetuity of the group might be involved. Anthropologically this is interesting, showing the strength of family cohesion in a rivalry-orientated society. The *fono* had decided on a six-week test, but the sons could not endure this. Actually they followed the father's course of action after three weeks, but not without first pressing their desire in the *fono*. Malietoa had been quite convinced personally, but he was aware that some of the family doubted. The test was Malietoa's suggestion as a power demonstration on their behalf. That some who partook with him subjected themselves to countermedicine and emetics shows that Malitoa knew well what he was doing. He had faith himself, and insight into the fears of others.[9] Yet with all his power and personality Malietoa dare not push decisions through as an individual, except through the decision of the *fono*.

Across the frontiers of Polynesia in Fiji, we find again the significant function of group discussion. Ratu Cakobau of Bau has been pictured as an absolute authoritarian by some, yet he called three different conferences before his own public acceptance of Christianity. There was a private discussion with his principal wife and the missionary when he personally faced up to the convictions in his heart. Then he assembled the extended family to which he belonged, spoke his mind, and threw the matter open for discussion. Then he called the leaders of the political entity known as the Kingdom of Bau for a similar conference. In each case there were individuals who expressed doubts without fear. There was none who tried to change his attitude, or insisted that he was wrong; but in both the family and political conferences the matter for debate was whether or not the time was opportune. Eventually unanimity was reached and Cakobau made a public confession, together with a social segment represented by the second conference.[10]

The writings of occasional visitors and travelers often suggest the absolutism of Oceanic chiefs of the period. The records of the missionaries show otherwise: there was invariably a group of some kind with free expression of opinion, and an unreadiness on the part of the chiefs to involve their people in major decisions of culture change without reference to those groups. It was because of this that the physical structure of the Christian church was so acceptable to the island people. The absolutism of the paramount chief was within known and approved limits.

MULTI-INDIVIDUAL ACTION IS EXPRESSED IN GROUP SYMBOLISM

The missionary face to face with paganism will seek to know the locus of its religious power, for it is here that any power encounter must take place. Is there a concentration of religious energy in the spirit of the progenitor of the lineage, or in a high god, or in a multiplicity of domestic or local divinities, or for each man in the ghost of his grandfather? Again, is there some material object in which this spirit manifests himself—an image, some natural feature of the landscape, an ancestral skull, a monolith, a fetish, or a human being? Is it an idol, a shrine (form of embodiment), or a repository of *mana*? A missionary in Oceania may meet any of these expressions, and he will need to know in which of them the people of his concern are particularly interested. All these objects are symbols of the power "from beyond man himself" on which he draws to deal with those mysterious problems of life which require something beyond his knowledge and competence to handle. Quite often the symbol counts as the deity itself, although when pressed, the islander will differentiate the spirit and the shrine. In any ocular demonstration of power encounter, the symbol must be involved. The destruction of the

symbol is highly significant with people who conceptualize alle-
gorically. So too is any evidence of disrespect towards it.

When Pomare II ate the sacred turtle without any of the expected accompanying rituals,[11] and Malietoa ate the forbidden
totemic mullet,[12] the significance lay in the symbolism of their
actions. In both cases there was great excitement and fear among
the spectators, for here indeed was a public rejection of a power
which had bound them all for ages. It was a complete and deliberate fracture of a sacred belief. When Pomare II took the Tahitian temple pillar and set it up as his kitchen post,[13] such contempt demonstrated clearly a radical change of faith and values.
As long as these men, these offenders, lived without retribution
from the despised gods, those symbols had become mere material
objects; their power and the fear of them were gone.

When Patii burned his idols, and the Tongan chief murdered
his idols by hanging them, those gods died. And when, time having passed by, no punishment fell on the offenders, the fear of
those gods passed away for ever. They were dead, burned in the
fire and hung by the neck. As the prophet said of old:

> *Shall not the isles shake*
> *At the sound of thy fall?*[14]

The blow of the soft banana-stalk club would only stun the
possessed priestess and spill her half-emptied kava bowl; but it
killed the god and the cry went forth that the god had been
"clubbed while drinking kava."

There are some islands where it is merely said that the god or
goddess went away. There is no final decisive issue to the power
encounter. The god did not die. Such gods can and sometimes
do come back. When a god dies, his cause dies with him. Often
the contests were staged, with date and hour proclaimed before-
hand, with intense excitement among the multi-individual crowd
of spectators. Was Mount Carmel the prototype?

PEOPLE MOVEMENTS IN TERMS OF CHRISTIAN BELIEF

When in doubt on any matter, missionaries usually seek their
prototypes in Scripture. However well I may document this book
and however carefully I may reason the case, there will be some
who will appraise it by other norms. They will ask, What is the
biblical basis for this approach to conversion? It is a fair question,
and my answer is that the apostolic church of New Testament
record grew greatly by such a method.

IN TERMS OF BIBLICAL THEOLOGY

In the New Testament the church itself is conceived as a structured, corporate entity, and although each individual has to make his own personal decision, he is never an isolated individual. He is always an individual within a group. The theological imagery of the church in the New Testament includes such figures as the temple, with its parts fitly framed together; the flock of Christ; the vine with its branches; the "church which is his body"; and the differently functioning but interrelated parts of the body; the household of God; the brethren; and the fellowship.[15]

With such a concept of the nature of the church, we do not wonder that the early Christian evangelists left small groups—flocks, fellowships, households—wherever they carried the gospel. The conviction that comes from the Philippian jailer is transmitted to his whole family, who enter Christianity as a household, as did the family of Narcissus, Aristobulus, and others. The household was the autonomous unit in the towns. When the Lord healed the demoniac, and found him with a desire to join the disciples and Himself, He rather sent him back to his own home unit to testify to them what the greatness of his salvation was. The woman of Samaria came as an individual—and a lonely one at that—but was sent back for her kin.

Where the autonomous unit was the village rather than the family, then we meet a whole village turning to the Lord, after some demonstration of power. Lydda was such a case and Saron was another.

In Samaria, Philip's demonstration of power in healing and exorcism was accompanied by great excitement and people movement. In Ephesus a small group of followers of John the Baptist was converted as a sodality and experienced the charisma apparently as a group, about twelve of them.

The burning of the books on the black arts and the magical paraphernalia also at Ephesus has a strange fetish-burning quality about it, worthy of the New Guinea highlands of today. If the theological validity of Oceanic people movements depends on biblical precedents I think we have plenty.

IN TERMS OF BIBLICAL METHOD

Jesus Himself stimulated a people movement on the village level at Sycar. The incident shows two interesting things.

1. In spite of the cultural barrier, the Jews having no dealings with the Samaritans, Jesus broke through the ethnocentric position of His own race, because he saw these particular Samaritans as a "field ripe unto harvest" and therefore set His approval on the cross-cultural approach.

2. The method was used by Jesus before the Holy Spirit was given to men at Pentecost. Because He used it the approach stands in its own right as legitimate. It is religious, but it is also sociopsychological. It speaks of an opportunity opened and accepted.

Jesus had converts by doing an unprecedented thing—tarrying for two days in a Samaritan village. The people believed, not because of the woman's saying, but because, having heard Him for themselves, they *knew* (an emphatic word of personal experience) that this was "the Christ, the Saviour of the world." In this record we are concerned with a study in personal dynamics. Jesus saw the potential in the situation, for the winning of a group as a group. It had to be this way; where would an isolated Samaritan have stood in Jewish or Samaritan society as a follower of Jesus? There had to be a multi-individual unit, a fellowship. Jesus recognized the possibility in the situation, pointed out to the disciples that the fields were ripe unto harvest, and He moved in across cultural barriers for an ingathering.

Now, let us move on to the experience of Pentecost. Here we are confronted with the winning of three thousand converts in a group, and a continuing process thereafter, in Jerusalem, in various parts of Judea, the villages of Lydda and Saron, over the border into Samaria and in particular the city of Samaria. Through the preaching of the apostles the power of the Spirit flowed through many localities from Azotus in the south to Caesarea in a series of people movements, which jumped across cultural, racial, and class barriers.

The power manifestations at Pentecost shocked many of the Jews, but it was no meaningless babble. Each man heard something meaningful, the Spirit breaking through into his own language and speaking to his individual heart—a multi-individual experience, not mass action. Yet there was great excitement, we can't escape the truth of that, so much so that they were accused of intoxication, which possibility Peter felt had to be denied.

And it did not end with the Bible. We need a history of the

Christian church written from the viewpoint of the dynamics of its growth rather than the development of its thought. Savonarola and Luther and Knox would stand out as prophetic figures who consciously or otherwise tapped huge reservoirs of power. The movements mostly studied for their theological and philosophical content would be seen in terms of multi-individual people movements. The emphasis would pass from disputations to movements, and the half-forgotten Christian communities of history would speak their message to church growth principles for us today. I long to find a history of the perceiving of ripening fields and how they were harvested. It would be interesting to see the "important" subjects which would have to be crowded out of such a volume and the new importances which would emerge. There is a chain of links through the centuries from New Testament times to the period studied in this book, with names like Augustine and Patrick and Boniface, who witnessed the people movement experience when ripening fields were harvested.

Our Lord found Sychar a ripe field in His day, recognized the situation, and gathered in the harvest. But the remainder of Samaria was not then ripe. By the day of Philip's itineration there it had ripened over a vast area. He recognized it and reaped the harvest. If incidents like these, and passages such as Acts 16:6-8 (in which the Holy Spirit guided Paul away from his intended field of labor) mean anything at all for the present-day missionary, they must signify that all fields do not come ripe for harvest at the same time. This involves us in the task of recognizing a ripe field and attending to the ingathering even though it mean deployment of personnel from unripe areas. The concept of the ripe harvest is very closely tied in Scripture with people movements.

The Lord wanted Paul in Europe where the harvests were ripe. He frustrated Paul's purpose of going into Bithynia and gave him a vision at the end of the Asian road to help him recognize the opportunities in Macedonia. This is the biblical way of saying it.

Anthropologically, a situation with something latent in its state that represents a readiness for change or large-scale innovation is open to listen to advocates. The Bible calls for laborers for the harvest *now*. The anthropologist points out that there are many kinds of advocates, any of whom may be able to secure acceptance of his proposed innovation by good advocacy. That means that if

Christianity doesn't move in to harvest, Islam or Communism may well do so. In our day, where we have recognized harvests and put forth laborers, we have experienced people movements. We have seen other fields ripen, only to be swept into the garners of Islam. It does not follow that the scores of thousands of missionaries are all in ripe fields. Perhaps we should be paying more attention to the number of laborers in Bithynia when they ought to be in Macedonia.

PEOPLE MOVEMENTS IN TERMS OF PSYCHOLOGICAL PROCESSES

The psychologist Sherif conducted experiments with the auto-kinetic effect to see how observers would react when asked to define the characteristics of an objectively unstabilized stimulus field. The anthropologist Barnett has related the results of Sherif's experiments to what he calls "subliminal demands for orientation," which is precisely the issue with which we are concerned.[16] It seems to be reducible to five findings.

1. An individual deprived of objective means of stabilizing his perceptions establishes his own point of reference. If effective it becomes standardized.

2. Groups of individuals confronted with similar situations will establish similar reference points. If aware of that established by one person, they may well select the same reference point. It too becomes standardized.

3. Separated from the group, an individual confronted by the same situation will establish his reference point according to the group norm.

4. Individuals with previously established independent reference points, brought together in a group and continually subjected to the same situations, will modify their orientation to approximate to one another. Group effect is undeniable.

5. When a group is suddenly confronted with an unstable situation, in which the members had no previous orientation, what happens? The result is not chaos, but selection and establishment of a common norm.

As this complex of findings is the result of experimental testing we may use it as a basis for examining our own data, at least in two respects.

FIXING THE SYMBOLIC REFERENCE POINT

Malietoa's reference point of eating the *aitu* appears to have been individually fixed, though with the consent of the group. Pomare II's eating of the sacred turtle without the usual preliminary offering to the deity was also individually fixed—partly to convince the missionaries, who had refused him baptism, that he was sincere. (Actually they accepted his sincerity but not his standards.) Patii's decision to burn all the gods he had served was individually fixed. All these patterns of behavior became standardized for other individuals and for groups. After Buna-auia, Pomare II himself accepted Patii's reference point for the disposal of sacred objects and idols of wood and fiber, as distinct from forbidden food. The key post of the temple presented another unstabilized field and called for a new reference point. He degraded it by making the holy thing (hitherto a shrine which the god would enter for purposes of communication) a mean domestic kitchen post. Here again Pomare II himself fixed the reference point, which became a set pattern for other temples as word travelled through the nearby islands.

In the same way ancestral skulls were ceremonially buried in the Eastern Solomons, because this was the procedure first adopted. In West Irian, fetish-burning began in the Ilaga Valley, became the norm, and the pattern swept with the spread of the gospel through the Baleim Valley. The reference point of the first locality became standardized for the area of cultural inter-relationships and across political barriers (war fences). Where the patterns were totemic, the eating of the *aitu*, once standardized in one locality, spread to a wider area for all individuals who wished to become Christian.

It is interesting to note that at the two extremities of Southern Polynesia, in Tahiti and Tonga, where idols of wood and fiber were found, different reference points were fixed. This may be accounted for by the fact that two different webs of people movement were involved. In the Tahitian web the reference point fixed was a public stripping of the ornamentation of the idol, the consignment of these decorative objects to the fire, exposure and display of the wooden residue of the idol itself, and then the unceremonial casting of this also into the fire. In the Tongan web the reference point was the public desecration and murder of the god by hanging the idol, and eventually after this humiliating death of the god, casting the body ignominiously into the fire together with the god-house, or inside the god-house. The Tonga reference points did not become standardized beyond Tonga because the movement spread into stimulus fields that were culturally different. Tahiti and Tonga at this point were sufficiently similar for comparison, but the two movements were independent of each other.

The two webs met in Samoa; but there were no idols there. The reference point fixed by the Samoans approximated Pomare II's eating of the turtle. It is quite possible that the missionary John Williams or Fauea had informed Malietoa of this act.

When the Tongan movement swept beyond the Polynesian frontiers of Lau into the Melanesian area, it confronted a new situation. The locus of power lay in what was known as *ai tikotiko ni vu* (the dwelling place of the founder of the lineage). This was the grove where the deified spirit of the original ancestor lived. Central in these open-air places of worship was a cairn of stones and conch shells, a short stone pillar beside a flat slab of stone. Here the libations of *yaqona* (kava) were poured forth. With the conversion of Ratu Cakobau he determined on the destruction of the sacred place, the scattering of the sacred stones and uprooting of the pillar, and the disfiguring of the trees. Once this pattern was fixed it was adopted in all the wide area under Bauan influence on the mainland of Viti Levu and in the islands of Lomaiviti. Yet there were other parts of Fiji where Bau paramountcy was not recognized, and in these the cairns and pillars still remain for examination by the archeologist. I think we may assume from this that the area over which a reference point is stabilized may be culturally defined. At the same time a comparison of reference points ought to indicate the origin and course of people movements.

The one feature that is common in them all is the fact of symbolic destruction. The old god must die.

REFERENCE POINTS AND SOCIAL LEVELS

A highly important question is, *Who* should perform the act of destruction? Sometimes destruction were ceremonially done. At other times it was deliberately degrading with a complete absence of ceremony. This in itself was symbolic. Where the performance was more respectful we may assume the perpetrator was less sure of himself, more experimental, and leaving the way of return open in case Christianity did not work out. But the aggressive iconoclast was clearly a man of personal conviction. However, whatever the mood of the person involved, the act had to be performed by the correct person. It was the chief or priest or representative head of the group concerned: a tribal authority for a tribal deity, a family head for a family deity, a village official for a village god, and each individual himself would cast his own fetishes on the pyre as a personal act. The occasion always involved a public gathering at which all members of the group were present, so that when these movements involved a great lineage, scattered residentially over a wide area, there were some huge gatherings. The occasions did not bring chaos but were systematically and rationally structured.

In such events observed in the last few years in West Irian, fetishes and charms have been publicly burned, first their common lineage god, and then systematically through the families to the personal level. Although accompanied by intense excitement and agitation, there is no loss of control. It is a sober and rational event, a multi-individual performance, with a total lineage involvement. Every participator in the event (sometimes thousands involved at a time) is personally involved in the death of the god of the lineage as well as his own private fetishes.[17]

Psychologically the passage from the old way to the new is real. Until the skull, fetish, forbidden fish, wooden idol or grove—the locus of past fear or power—is abused, treated as a mere secular thing, the way is not psychologically open for a restructuring of the individual's orientation to the new way of life in Christ. No advocate (missionary or indigenous preacher) can force this experience on people. They themselves have to make the decision, and make the decision meaningful by means of a practical demonstration. It has to be a step in which the new faith is put to the test at the old locus of power. This has to be significant *for the convert*, whether or not it is meaningful to the missionary.

The reference point, having been fixed by performance, passes on into time. Thereafter one hears such comments as "This has not happened in our village since the day we burned our god-houses," or "That was a long time ago. It was before my time. Ask old Joni about it. He remembers the time they destroyed the sacred grove." To those who look back and measure the past on a calendar of events rather than years, the reference point marks the passage from the old way into the new. It is as real to them as B.C. and A.D. are to us: *

PEOPLE MOVEMENTS IN TERMS OF POSITIVE-NEGATIVE POLARITY

In discussing the character of people movements we are dealing with the physical and psychological factors and social mechanisms that determine the forms of social behavior. Men express their feelings through patterns which are both similar and different according to motivation. Thus a people movement may be what McGavran calls "a Christward movement," or on the other hand it may be a movement away from Christ. Men are not saved by a people movement, but it is a social mechanism which brings men to the Saviour. It has been much used of God. The mechanism itself, however, being *amoral*, has also operated in the opposite direction. Like public speaking, it can be for good or bad, for bringing people to repentance or for stimulating revolution.

Sudden rises on a line graph of church growth suggest people movements; so do the dramatic drops that appear from time to time. The church is currently confronted with many of these in Melanesia. We may speak of these as positive and negative people movements in discussing church growth. They are movement-gains and movement-losses. As an individual may fall from grace and become a backslider, in the same way there can be multi-individual backsliding, either in our own or communal society. The group has made a deliberate corporate choice. In Western society groups such as political clubs, cliques, and street gangs, multi-individual movements are away from recognized social norms. In this study we have seen in the Mamaia and Ringatu movements a deliberate choice of rejection of the church and resultant multi-individual loss. This is a major problem in Melanesia in these postwar days, where there has been a wave of prophetism and millenarian or messianic dreams. Even in the day he made it, Russell's claim that there were no such losses was promotional wishful thinking. Neither then nor at the present time can it stand up to testing.[18]

In our studies of the positive movements into Christianity I

---

* My experience has been that these reference points remain fixed for two or three generations in communal societies, but they are lost sight of by those who migrate to the towns in these postwar days.

have always maintained the complicated character of the network of factors responsible—this against certain historians and anthropologists who have often simplified these matters to a single cause.* The same applies at the negative pole. People do not change their life orientation on a whim or a single point, although a single point may precipitate the actual step. Much has been written by anthropologists on the causes of negative people movements—acculturation, economic factors, war, administrative policies, and so on—and, more important to us, the imposition of Western forms of Christianity on converts. However, there seems to be one generalization we can safely make: the basic causes are latent in the situation and have been so for a period of time until they reach a crisis and suddenly become manifest. We could say, They ripen unto harvest.

These neopagan resurgences, set up in opposition to the church, may be either belligerent or coexistent in type. The former will usually assume an antiwhite or antiforeign character that may become politically dangerous, like the John Frum Movement in Tanna, Marching Rule in the Solomons,† and Hauhauism in New Zealand. More often than not they are religious movements, since supernaturalism is a major institution used for fighting the foreigner. The coexistent type is usually highly syncretistic and establishes a rival sect, until such time as it obtains official recognition as a church. Ringatu and Ratana in New Zealand have achieved this. The Peyote in the United States is another example. There is a case for putting Mormonism in the same category.

Whatever form they assume, these movements arise from latent discontent, the character of which is often indicated by the visible symbolism adopted by the cult. This may be military discipline (marching, saluting, using the flagpole), legal administration (use of a chair and rule as symbols for veneration), extreme phallic forms (resistance of moral discipline, or concern over population), Western wealth and goods (transports, cargoes, stores, aircraft as symbols of a golden age about to dawn) and drinking ceremonials (resistance to prohibitions).[19] All these are pointers that help us to recognize some of the problems. People who have lost their tribal lands and see foreigners making wealth

---

*A specific case of this is examined as a type in the appendix to this volume.

†Marching Rule was a purely political movement. Religion was not involved in any way at all.

from them, or who have become a minority people in their own country or perhaps a subject people, who see the power of wealth, property, military authority, and commerce (which do not seem to have been worked for) and, above all, who suffer from voids in their corporate life left by the things that have been taken from them; people in any of these predicaments have latent forces that may well ripen for manifest negative people movements.

A church which establishes itself with indigenous autonomy is unlikely to be seriously worried about negative movements away from its ranks. But a mission that remains a foreign and ruling body, creating an economic complex that can never be handed over to an indigenous church and never opening up its highest offices to indigenes, and establishes legal prohibitions of pre-Christian cultural elements without functional substitutes, may well expect in the second or third generation an emergence of some negative people movement. The best way to safeguard against this, from a religious point of view, is to see that the original Christward people movement out of paganism is properly followed up or consummated. The consummation must bring young converts into significant roles in the life of the church, roles which will give them the responsibility for action and decision-making within the emerging church.

THE WORD OF THE PAST TO THE PRESENT SITUATION

Although this has been a historical study of movements in the last century, it cannot be relegated to the past as mere history. It has something to say to the world Christian mission today. These movements followed in the aftermath of the Napoleonic wars, in the days of the opening up of the Pacific to Western exploitation—sandalwooders, whalers, and bêche-de-mer traders at first, then sedentary planters, labor displacements, struggles between international powers, the opening up of colonies and the introduction of industries. These were the social and foreign factors responsible for a widespread state of disequilibrium in Polynesia. Throw a society into imbalance, with threats to its entity, perpetuity, and security, and it becomes a situation propitious for dramatic innovation. Because religion is the configuration on which animist society depends for securing these things, society is ready for *religious* innovation. This potential was in the situation when missions invaded the Pacific.

The anthropologist Wallace, who is also a competent historian, has worked out a table of religious movements among the Delaware Indians. His research produces a demonstration of war periods followed by periods of religious movements. It is a convincing case.[20]

Today in Oceania, Indonesia, Africa, and elsewhere, where similar factors are responsible for states of change or disequilibrium, and where people are open for major innovation, there are particular openings for large-scale religious movements. The stresses, latent and manifest, in these situations will have to be met. Large structural social units and whole races are either changing their religious allegiance or will do so in the next ten or twenty years. The church grows by leaps and bounds in New Guinea. There are ethnic segments with great growth in Indonesia. In Africa there are hundreds of movements, variously classified by scholars, many of which seem to me to be coexistent movements in the process of becoming churches, somewhere along the axis between our positive and negative poles. There is in the animist world today a terrific latent capacity for Christianity, and to all these situations this book is relevant. If history does not literally "repeat itself" there are at least many types of situation that recur.

But there is one thing about the present situation which is more or less new. A century ago, apart from the appeal of secularism itself, Christianity was the only competitor. Today there are other choices. Communism is one. Islam is, in some fields, a stronger and more growing cause than Christianity. Even Buddhism and Hinduism at some levels are renascent. So the fields which ripen now for change are open for any effective advocate to harvest. Or, if none be effective, some neopagan syncretism may emerge under the guidance of an indigenous prophet, who has received his organizational training as a mission catechist, or as a teacher or as a police officer. In time a Christopagan church will receive recognition. We do well to remember that the animistic world is receptive today, and Christianity is not alone in the field of advocates that claim a hearing.

Although it is clear that no two situations are identical—indeed, every one must be dealt with on its own merits—I feel these documented studies of Southern Polynesia do have something to say to the world today.

To illustrate, I cite a tragic case from a currently active area in

Oceania. Six thousand persons were involved in a multi-individual decision to burn the lineage fetishes in an act of faith, turning from their old sources of power to Christ. Of course they had not yet been instructed in the teachings of Christ. All they knew was that they were turning from the powers which their fore-fathers had believed and feared for centuries, and were ready to turn to the mission for guidance in the Christian way. One day, unexpectedly, the missionaries were confronted by a huge as-sembly of excited people and witnessed the remarkable act of destruction. Then the missionaries concerned thought it over. They felt it was too easy (but fetish-burning is really never easy), that these people really didn't understand the theology of salva-tion, and therefore the movement was not of God. So they re-jected it. Actually it was an overflow of a people movement in a nearby valley, where thousands had turned to Christ, were re-ceiving sound instruction, and where a good church was growing. But at this station, six thousand were turned away. Now, the Bible has something to say to this very situation:

> The evil spirit returns to the house and finds it empty, swept and garnished (cf. fetishes burned and discarded), but finding no good occupant or positive substitute for the removed evil, "taketh with himself seven other spirits more wicked than himself, and they enter in and dwell there: and the last state of that man is worse than the first" (see Mt 12:43-45).

This book has something to say to this kind of current situation.

The Westerner tends to shy from any demonstration of a highly emotional encounter as if it were unreal or irrational. Fetish-burning is, on the contrary, both real and rational. The sym-bolism is not the symbolism of thought and ideas (and let the Westerner remember that these are also symbolic of experience) but of power conflict. The symbol becomes, as it were, the locus of power. It is destroyed because of the reality of a greater power. The two powers struggle to possess "man-soul." The theological dimension here is that of the doctrine of the sovereign Lordship of Christ. The first confession is "Christ is Lord" and religious knowledge follows under instruction. But instead of being rea-soned as set out in a textbook of theology it is experienced in terms of a symbolic and real power encounter. Without such a demonstration of conquest, the animist convert is in danger of never really losing his polytheism. Christ for him may well only coexist with other gods. This is why it isn't enough for a god to go away; he must die.

I think this may account for some of the apostasies which worried Bishop Selwyn in New Zealand at one time. The Maoris in question had not destroyed their *tapu* objects, that is, the shrines of their ancestral and other spirits, which they consulted on all occasions of domestic and military importance. These reverently guarded objects would supposedly answer in half-whisper, half-whistle; that is, the *atua* would answer through the *tapu* shrine. The *atua* was the sovereign of their lives. Now Christ claimed that sovereignty. Where the *tapu* shrine was destroyed, or buried, or secularized, the matter was clear enough. But in some cases the *tapu* shrine was not destroyed: its *atua* was consulted: "Is the message of the white teacher true?" According to H. W. Tucker, who organized Selwyn's material for publication, in every known case, the *atua* gave an affirmative answer.[21] Thus, sometimes with reluctance and with little personal conviction, Christianity could be accepted, on the word of the *atua*. As the Scriptures put it, "The devils knew him too." But the oracle that validated the truth of Christ by the same token also validated itself, and was not destroyed either symbolically or intellectually. Christ was thus accepted not as sovereign but a (perhaps stronger) coexistent with the old *atua*, who was (be it well noted) still consulted from time to time, when the new Christians desired to do so. The ocular demonstration of the destruction of the *tapu* shrine is the symbolic passage from polytheism to a doctrine of the absolute sovereignty of Christ. Expelling the demons, in the Scripture narrative, was not enough. They had to enter the swine and be demonstrably destroyed. This is not irrational.

In the title of this chapter I used the term *validity*. We may now answer the question, What is the validity of these people movements? The validity is one of *means*, not of *ends*. A people movement is a meaningful procedure or form of action by which communal people register symbolically their acceptance of cultural change. In nonliterary societies this is as much a legally binding act as when, in the West, the bride, groom, witnesses, and officiating minister sign a marriage register (a symbolic action). It is the approved social mechanism for the public proclamation of accepted change: the valid means.

Anthropology has demonstrated that peoples do not make changes until they are ready; and that a group ready for a change is bound to make it sooner or later. To put this into biblical and church-growth terminology, "Doors open! Fields white unto harvest!"

The Christian church should be continually on the lookout for opening or ripening fields, and be organized for action, even if it means deployment of personnel and funds. Other faiths and ideologies will act, when we pass by, or when neglected opportunities have led to neopagan revitalization movements. I can document a case in Oceania where doors were open along a primitive trade route for twenty years. During that period frequent requests for teachers were made to a nearby mission station from various locations along that route. The answer was always, "No money; no missionaries!" Then that door closed to Christianity and closed firmly. A neopagan cultic revival swept along that trade route in the very locations that had asked for teachers. This is a recent incident of our own day. I think this book speaks to this kind of situation.

In our own day we have observed how negative people movements tend to become ends in themselves. A positive movement into the church is valid not as an end in itself but as a means to that one great end, the sovereign Christ. The movement is not the end, but it opens the way to that end: the valid means of bringing people in communal society into His church.

Finally, people movements are valid because they recognize what John Collier calls *grouphood*. He described the ruin brought upon the Indians of America as "through the white man's denial of their grouphood."[22] The people movement recognizes society and preserves grouphood. The group entry into Christianity is in line with communal traditions in which important "religious occasions and ceremonies," as Beals and Hoijer point out, "are social functions which help to develop social cohesion and group solidarity."[23] It has been one major function of religion to keep society in a state of balance. When pagans turn to Christianity, is there any reason to expect less from their new faith in view of the numerous New Testament concepts of Christian grouphood: the congregation, the flock of God, the household of God, and the fellowship?

APPENDIX A

THE COMPLEXITY OF THE CONVERSION
OF THE TAHITIANS
A Statement on the Use of Documents

I CITE HERE three different examples of reporting a single event.

THE ANTHROPOLOGIST

The first missionaries had very little success in the conversion of the people, though the material goods they brought were much appreciated. The missionaries were opposed, and many of them left the island in despair. When a fresh set of missionaries arrived some years later, Pomare was in a more chastened frame of mind. He had been defeated in battle and had taken refuge on the neighboring island of Mo'orea. The missionaries accompanied him there and began to make headway with him. Pomare had begun to distrust his gods because of his lack of success against his enemies. He began to flirt with the missionaries, in the hope that their god was more powerful than his own and would bring him the military success he wanted. At the same time he was chary of abandoning his own gods entirely. Thus, though the missionaries had hopes of converting Pomare, they could not get him to abandon his gods publicly. In view of the prospects, however, the missionaries ranged themselves on the side of Pomare and regarded his enemies as "heathen." In 1815, Pomare's enemies on the island of Tahiti invited him to attend a conference with them. Pomare, accompanied by his supporters and some of the missionaries, sailed over to Tahiti and, on a Sunday morning, he and his people attended a service conducted by the missionaries. During the service, the enemy was observed advancing with a large armed force, evidently to attack. The congregation became alarmed and the missionaries were prepared to break off the service. Pomare, however, ordered the service to be continued to its proper ending and stated that the enemy could be attended to afterwards. The missionary writer, Rev. W. Ellis, had praised Pomare's piety and faith in the face of the enemy. The truth is that any religious ritual that was broken off was regarded by the Polynesians as an ill omen for future success. The gods being invoked for assistance turned against their worshippers if the ritual was not properly completed. It was not Christian piety that induced Pomare and his followers to go on with the service but the fear of a broken ritual. At the end of the service both Pomare and his followers had plucked up courage in the hope that the Christian god would assist them in gaining the victory.

From the outset of the battle which ensued, fortune smiled on Pomare. The opposing leader, whose rank was immeasurably superior to that of Pomare, was killed with a musket-ball. On the death of their leader, the enemy retired and victory lay with Pomare and with the Christian god who had supported him. The power of Jehovah having been demonstrated, Christianity was accepted by the whole island of Tahiti, and Pomare became king of the group. Pomare handed over the material symbols of his native gods to the missionaries to be sent to England to show the people of that country what fools the Tahitians had been. A lucky shot had done more than seventeen years of preaching had been able to accomplish.[1]

THE MISSIONARY HISTORIAN

Pomare II walked in his [father's] footsteps ["fickle and brutal, offered thousands of human sacrifices to his gods"] until the missionary outlook became as dark as possible.

Prompted by the grave reports received from the field, a special meeting was called in London in July 1812, to pray for Pomare's conversion, and in that very month he gave up his idols and asked for baptism. This was the turning point of the work in Tahiti. Idolatry was completely overthrown, the king sent for a printing-press to prepare Bibles and hymn-books for his people, and at his own expense he built a huge church, where, in the presence of four thousand of his subjects he was baptized. The light spread not only over all Tahiti, but also from island to island and other groups, through the efforts of the Tahitian Christians as well as from the missionaries and Tahiti will ever be known as the seed-plot from which the gospel was scattered far and wide over Oceania.[2]

THE MISSIONARY THEORETICIAN

After the missionaries had been laboring through a long night of fruitless toil lasting for years, the king made known his wish to be baptized. If after so many years of disappointed expectation the missionaries had been eagerly ready to grant the desire of the royal applicant it would not have been surprising, but for four years he was kept back until more satisfactory proof was given of his knowledge of the Gospel. The earliest missionaries were the children of the revival of the Eighteenth Century, and they took with them to their work standards which united Puritan severity and evangelical spirituality, and they looked for and were not satisfied until they thought they had found evidence of a radical change of heart.[3]

At first it must be difficult for the reader to see that these three passages are each records of the conversion of Tahiti. Each at one point is sound and at other points quite wrong. Not one can be documented as it stands. All are faulty with respect to time depth, dynamic factors, and the total configuration. The historical reconstruction of both anthropologist and missionary historian is appalling. They create quite wrong impressions, and all suffer from oversimplification.

Each writer naturally has a different motive. There is no harm in this, nor in the selectivity this may involve, provided the integrity of the context is not distorted thereby. In this respect the anthropologist's manipulation of his source material is shocking.

The anthropologist is concerned with showing the acceptance of Christianity to have been a simple matter, almost an accident, the matter of a lucky shot. He would presumably argue also that the great war of 1914-18 was entirely *caused* by the shooting of an Austrian archduke. To arrive at his conclusion he has to deliberately omit a great body of facts that hold together firmly within the very sources he uses.

The motive of the historian was to write a world survey. World surveys are by nature unreliable because they have to reduce complexities to simplicities and in doing so lose sight of patterns. By compressing a field of history worthy of a whole volume into a paragraph, both focus and time depth are wrong. They give the impression of something that just never happened. The one contribution is an allowance for the divine element. This is missing from the others.

The theoretician is concerned with an issue of missionary technique and cites the incident out of its context to illustrate his theoretical point. This is a common procedure; but it throws the responsibility on the writer, either to verify or document his source for the historical information on which the theory stands. Many of the myths of history are the supports of all kinds of theory. The third writer is quite correct in pointing out the slowness of L.M.S. baptisms, and the fact he stresses seriously under-

mines the other two impressions; but not only is his own legalistic
picture quite devoid of a dynamism that was certainly in the historic events, but he is careless about his figures. Whether Pomare II was kept waiting four or seven years does not injure his
argument, as it happens, but this figure is the very support of his
theory, and he happens to be wrong.

The anthropologist did contribute an interesting cultural point
that was not in the historical sources. It came from his special
knowledge in his Polynesian background, he being a Maori. But
that same background has given Buck a mental set against the
taking of Polynesian gods to England to show what fools the
people were, and the iconoclasm of destroying ancient Polynesian
sites, which we know from other writings also of this man. We
see him in his own specific class—a salvage anthropologist*—with
a certain cynicism which militates against his capacity for objective analysis when the question of missions is involved. Buck
is denying missionary value-judgments any validity (yet he is
categorical in his own), drawing his own opinions of Pomare II,
distorting the evidence of those who knew him face to face, and
getting away with it because of his own Polynesian connections.
He was, in the majority of his work, a good anthropologist, and
because of this his opinions of Pomare II have been widely cited
by other anthropologists as beyond dispute.[4] Yet his personal
grievance against the Tahiti Christian teachers has been so vocal
in other writings that we ought to be warned at this point. After
all, if an anthropologist appeals to history, he is obligated to respect the canons and criteria of historical method. If, out of his
special knowledge, he can add something interpretive, this is
good; but he cannot select, omit, and distort the facts as set down
in the documents. He may disagree with them, but he must state
them and deal with them.

Glover and Kane give us the impression that the reason for the
whole train of events lies in a certain prayer meeting held in London in 1812. It gives an impression of the complete overthrow of
paganism because of Pomare II's conversion, and that the Bibles
came from the press he sent for and that he was baptized in a
great newly-built church, and so on, one sweeping sequence of
events in a limited space of time. All this was incorrect. The

*A salvage anthropologist is one whose main concern is to salvage cul-
tural items.

picture eliminates all the dynamics of the local events. Pomare II ate the turtle alone. He was kept seven years for baptism. No serious biblical translation work was done for another twenty years. As far as prayers were concerned, the evidence is that those of Tahiti were far more fervent than those in Britain. I have no doubt about the value of prayer, but to pin it to one particular meeting in Britain in 1812 is far too facile.

A brief analysis of the chronology of Pomare II's quest for baptism from sources that were public and not difficult for any of the writers to obtain will expose the weaknesses of each description.

> Pomare first asked for baptism after a conversation with Nott, who did not disclose it to the brethren at the time, lest they build hope on a vain boast.[5]
>
> Either he must have feared disagreement on the matter among the missionaries or he himself was unsatisfied. Some time later Pomare pressed his claim again, but during the interim he had been trying to win the support of some of his relations of status [Tamaloa, his father-in-law, and Tapoa, both high chiefs of nearby islands] but had failed.[6]

Seven missionaries had written to London about this. Pomare's words to the missionaries were, "You do not know the thought of my heart, nor I yours, but God does." This in itself is a simple statement of faith, which was worthy of support. He was told that two things were customary: first, instruction in the Christian way, and then a period during which his walking in the way would be observed and tested. That was all before July 1812. It shows Pomare II's leaning to Christianity and requests for acceptance long before the battle described in the first report, and before the London prayer meeting. At the beginning of 1815, three years after the prayer meeting, the situation was still the same. Some two hundred of Pomare II's people had been received before him by this time, as we have seen in the movement of the *praying people*. Pomare II was still being instructed and observed. At this time the missionaries wrote:

> The case of Pomare grieves and perplexes us. He wishes to be baptized . . . but we are far, very far from being satisfied that he is a proper subject. He has extensive knowledge of the doctrines of the Gospel, but is a slave to drinking.[7]

After the Battle of Bunaauia, when Tahiti had actually become nominally Christian it was another four years before Pomare was

eventually baptized—May 16, 1819.[8] This makes the report of the
1812 prayer meeting look rather foolish. And Buck said Pomare II
was chary about leaving his own gods, and drops the story of his
eating the turtle from the source where he gleaned his other facts.
Yet the documents are quite clear that he strove with the missionaries for baptism for at least seven, possibly eight years.

These passages have been arranged side by side to show the
importance of critical testing and the folly of oversimplification
like trying to reduce conversion to a single factor. We are deal-
with highly complex configurations that build up over a period
of time. While we are never certain of having observed all the
factors, we can and must observe all the factors in the available
sources. The three writers have given us cartoons, exaggerating
one feature at the expense of the others to the distortion of the
general effect. This is not good enough in anthropology, or history, or theory.

On the other hand, if only the published sources are examined
carefully, it will be quite apparent that *structurally* there were
several configurations of conversion movement operating in Tahiti and the neighboring islands. There were "praying people"
building up into a small Christian fellowship. There was a large
segment of Pomare II's family connections, both by blood and
marriage, which he himself set out to win, and he was so engaged
over a long period of time. Others were impressed by the idol-
burnings started by Patii. Only the rebel units came over after
the battle, and only indirectly as a result of it—it was the post-
victory policy of Pomare II ("Spare the rebels but destroy their
religion"), not merely a "lucky" shot. All this is found in the data
in the printed works of the missionaries and the officially published history, although none have worked out the patterns.
Church growth research assembles such data and seeks out the
patterns, because knowledge of those patterns is of tremendous
importance to all engaged in church-planting today.

APPENDIX B

NOTE ON IO, THE MAORI SUPREME GOD

THE AUTHORITY on the nature and work of Io, the supreme god of the Maoris, is the *Whare-wananga* (secret college of Maori priests), of which we have a Maori account. This was written down by Whatahoro, the Scribe, from the teachings of Te Matorohanga and Nepia, priests of the Whare-wananga of the East Cape region. Part 1, *Te Kauwae-runga* ("Things Celestial"), tells what is known about Io. In 1913 the Polynesian Society published the Maori version and an English translation with a commentary. S. Percy Smith was the translator, and the memoirs (2 vols.) are known as *The Lore of the Whare-wananga: or the Teaching of the Maori College on Religion, Cosmogony and History.*

Io, the supreme god, creator of all things, dwells in the Twelfth Heaven (*Te Toi-o-nga-rangi*), or the Uppermost Heaven, where no minor god might enter except by the command of Io. All things were subservient to Io-the-great-One, hence his many names.[1] "The name, Io, was so sacred that it was rarely mentioned. . . . The priests alone had a complete knowledge of him and ordinary people knew nothing. . . ."[2] He was conceptualized however in an anthropomorphic manner, for example, his conversation with Tane.[3] The view of his work in creation has some similarities with the Hebrew concept,[4] a series of acts by which the world and its living occupants are created one by one. The process builds up to the creation of the bodily form of man, to which Io then gives a human spirit.[5] Gatherings of the Maori College commenced, when the door was shut to outsiders, with a liturgical recitation to Te Toi-o-nga-rangi, the abode of Io.[6]

The performance was completely secret and not for many years did the missionaries understand that the Maoris did have a concept of a Supreme God, who was like Jehovah in so many ways. Had they been aware, they most certainly would have been more cautious in their selection of a Maori name for God. This is not to say that they would have chosen to use *Io*, but they would not have elected to use the subordinate term they did.

NOTES

CHAPTER 1: The Tahitian Web

1. The major British missionary societies were formed within a period of three or four decades. Those marked with an asterisk (*) are involved in this book.
   1786, Dr. Coke's Wesleyan mission
   1792, Baptist Missionary Society formed
   1795, London Missionary Society formed*
   1796, Edinburgh Missionary Society formed
   1799, Church Missionary Society formed*
   1799, Religious Tract Society established
   1804, British and Foreign Bible Society formed*
   1813, Wesleyan Missionary Society formed*
2. Instructions are set out in W. Wilson, *A Missionary Voyage to the South Pacific Ocean, performed in the years 1796-8 in the ship, Duff, &c.,* p. xcvi.
3. The official account is in Wilson. See especially chap. 2 and pp. 11, 13-14, 49, 53-54. For further detail on the Marquesas see Edmund Fanning, *Voyage of Discovery in the South Seas, 1792–1832,* and John Davies, *The History of the Tahitian Mission:1799–1830,* ed. C. W. Newbury. For Tonga see W. Ellis, *Polynesian Researches . . . ,* 1:102.
4. This is clearly set out in Wilson. The party was comprised of thirty men, of whom six were married. Four were ministers. Others included carpenters, joiners, cabinetmakers, bricklayers, shoemakers, hatters, weavers, tailors, a butcher, a cooper, a surgeon, a gentleman's servant, a shopkeeper, a gardener, and a smith (Wilson, pp. 5 ff). They were to represent a cross section of Christian civilized society. The role of some was to improve the mind and assume leadership, and of others to work at crafts with their hands. When dividing into smaller units the balance of this structure was to be retained—an "indispensable requisite"—and it was thought better to have only one establishment than to endanger the whole project. The missionaries were directed to a particular site because navigators had reported it as being productive of cotton and sugar cane (ibid., pp. xciii-iv, xcvii, cxiv-v).
5. Tenerife was named for grapes and wheat and also livestock; Rio de Janeiro for sugar, chocolate, cochineal, and tobacco (ibid., p. xci). Tobacco indicates that more than subsistence was involved in the policy—the men had to make their own living. The second party (1800) was instructed, "Let cultivation of the ground be diligently attended to, for the supply of your own wants and the advancement of your useful influence over others" (Davies, p. 19).
6. Ulfilas resisted this misconception. The leaders of the church insisted that the pure gospel could be translated only into Greek and Latin. Ulfilas created an alphabet for the Goths and transmitted the gospel through it. Max Müller said of this, "Prophetic sight and a faith in the destinies of those half-savage tribes."
7. From the official instructions; see Wilson, p. xcix.

8. The translation program was ineffective until Nott, knowing his time was running out, concentrated on it in the 1820s and 30s. He went to Tahiti on the *Duff* in 1796 as a bricklayer, age twenty-two. Now, at sixty-two, he was returning to England with his Scripture translation. When one considers the size of the party, and the linguistic material they had for use on the voyage (ibid., pp. 13-14), the slowness is surprising. Elsewhere it was done in half the time. (See W. Butler, "New Zealand," in *Cyclopedia of Missions*, ed. Harvey Newcomb, pp. 569-76.) Richard Lovett (*The History of the London Missionary Society: 1795–1895*, pp. 793-95) lists the missionaries to these islands over the period. After two decades of inaction the directors urged the translation of Scripture for the islanders (letter, Dec. 19, 1815). The missionaries replied that they were afraid of corrupting the sacred Word by mistranslation (letter, cited by Lovett, p. 204). The gospel of Luke was translated into Tahitian in 1818 (Lovett, p. 216) and John by 1821. A script of Acts was available by 1823 when the official deputation was in Tahiti. By 1825 the Pauline letters from Galatians to Philemon had been translated and also Mark, but the whole New Testament was not translated until 1829. Nott finished translating the Old Testament on Dec. 18, 1835, but five more years passed before it was available in printed form in Tahitian (see ibid., pp. 300-304).

9. Ellis, having seen the work of his colleague, John Williams, and also that of Henry Williams in New Zealand, took a stand on this matter. After a long description of arts and crafts, he wrote, "During the early periods of their residence in the islands, our predecessors often endeavoured to rouse them . . . to build more comfortable dwellings, to wear more decent clothing, to adopt . . . the conveniences and comforts of Europeans. . . . While the inhabitants continued heathens, their endeavours were altogether unavailing. . . . The people said, 'We would like to see some of these things but we cannot have them without working. . . . Bananas ripen on trees . . . pigs fatten on the fruit beneath them, even while we sleep.' . . . They furnish a striking illustration of the sentiment that to civilize a people they must first be christianized" (Ellis, 1:451-52). A similar shift of emphasis was observed among the leaders of the Church Missionary Society in 1822, when they appointed Henry Williams as a corrective to the priority of civilizing (Eugene Stock, ed., *History of the Church Missionary Society . . .* , 1:213).

10. "Civilize in order to evangelize" became "Evangelize in order to civilize." But for "civilize" we may, in point of fact, substitute the word *Westernize*. This is not a safe generalization for all the Pacific, but it was so for Tahiti. Christian instruction aimed at better houses, more cultivation, Western clothing, and domestic habits. Ellis states the motives as "to increase their wants" and to make the "comforts and decencies of society" desirable, and to "incite permanent industry" by increasing production of raw materials for exchange for "manufactured goods" from "civilized countries" (Ellis, 1:452-53). The follow-up of conversion was thus economic advancement toward Western ways and comforts. This was to be achieved by the following methods:
    1. the cultivation of cotton for export (prototype specifically stated as sandalwood and kauri trades)—clearing, fencing, and cultivating land, and ingathering were more attended to by women than men, they being more desirous of foreign possessions;
    2. working for missionaries in clearing, cultivating, and harvesting coffee, sugarcane, and cotton (note the missionary role of employer);
    3. developing industry sponsored by the missionary society (described as "developing the genius and spirit of Christianity and exercising its practical virtues," showing the term *Christian* as equated with being civilized and industrious);

4. manufacturing sugar for export to Port Jackson and the cultivation of tobacco and its preparation for market under missionary guidance (considered to be a "lucrative branch of industry" until New Holland [Australia] put heavy duty on it)

To assist this business the directors of the L.M.S. engaged a plantation manager with Jamaican experience, and procured machinery and apparatus for processing sugar. The manager reached Tahiti in 1818. Each of these industries had a varied history, but enough is provided here to establish the character of the policy in civilizing the converts. By this date, the mission had operated for over twenty years. It was another decade before it turned to serious Scripture translation. The missionaries contented themselves with producing statements of Bible facts, until the directors suggested Scripture portions (Ellis, 1:453-65; Davies, pp. 162-63).

11. Davies' contemporary account of the Tahiti mission, though not published until 1961, provides many references to the futility of the work through the barren years.

1801, people listened to preaching when addressed, "but when they had satisfied their curiosity, they had in general no further desire for these things" (Davies, p. 41);

1803, some evangelistic effort was made: itinerating, preaching, and teaching children; after two years "no fruit appeared" and all was still "unproductive of good" (ibid., pp. 67, 82);

1804, "some knowledge of these doctrines did spread among the people, notwithstanding their indifference and inattention" (ibid., p. 70);

1806, "The poor natives remain as before: no success has attended our labours, so as to terminate in the conversion of any, and there is no apparent desire after being instructed" (ibid., p. 86)

12. One is astonished at the number of foreign vessels that visited Tahiti during this period. Acculturation must have been considerable. The fact that missionaries, as British subjects, could and did seek the aid of sea captains saved them from many a situation. It is true that this factor has been much overrated by some historians (e.g., Henderson, of Fiji), but even so it was important. In this case the missionary letter to the captain began: "We, the missionaries on Tahiti, subjects of His Britanick Majesty . . . in imminent danger . . . request the detention of your vessel for 48 hours. . . ." They charged this to the Society (ibid., p. 119).

13. Several letters from the directors expressed disappointment at the lack of results in Tahiti. Then letters stopped coming at all. Occasionally the missionaries received rebuke for views that were "erroneous and inconsistent" (see ibid., pp. 43, 91). Ellis, writing of the same period (Ellis, 1:127-32), has numerous references like these: The missionaries "were cheerless and apparently useless"; "——— relinquished his missionary pursuits and sailed for Port Jackson"; "discouragements every day increasing"; "the gloom and discouragements that depressed their spirits, on account of the total want of success attending their labours"; and "the painful and protracted discouragements, by which, at this period, they were depressed, were of no ordinary character"—all these within half a dozen pages. The loss of interest in England was communicated by a medical missionary named Warner who arrived in 1808 (Davies, p. 113 and fn.). Ellis insisted that the directors had failed to answer letters or to correspond. Writing in 1806, he said there had been no mail since 1801—"neither supplies nor letters from England" (Ellis, p. 130). Davies spoke of "six years without a line or an article being received from England" which he considered "sufficient to exercise dissatisfaction and 'even suspicions' that in respect to them and their affairs *neglect* had certainly occured somewhere" (Davies, pp. 92-93). In 1808 the brig *Perseverance* brought goods

and mails, but nothing from the directors. The missionaries were very much offended (ibid., p. 116), because there had been no scarcity of shipping.

14. Ibid., p. 85; also W. Butler, "South Sea Islands," in *Cyclopedia of Missions*, ed. Harvey Newcomb, p. 686.

15. Davies, pp. 78, 102; Ellis, 1:128.

16. Davies tried the general language-teaching experiment for three months, but discontinued it, selecting a few of the brighter persons for a special class (Davies, p. 109). The method of their approach was specific: learn the language, start to preach, do some work with the children; but nowhere was there any response. Davies wrote in 1807, after a decade of missionary activity, "If by success be meant the renunciation of heathenism, a change of heart and conduct, in other words the conversion of sinners to God, we must answer with grief, that we have not hitherto seen anything . . . permanent and satisfactory" (ibid., p. 101).

17. The missionaries occupied their lands by permission of Pomare I and Pomare II, whom they accepted as legitimate sovereigns. This was also the official view of the directors and of the British sea captains. The latter would lend sailors to Pomare II to restore order if need be (e.g., Captain Bishop in 1802 [Davies, p. 54; Ellis, 1:114]). When one of the missionaries—Bicknell—was sent as a plenipotentiary to the rebels in 1802, he was asked whether or not the English would join Pomare II in his wars. He told them "the English only acted in self-defence, and were men of peace, and wished to be in peace," and then he urged the rebels to return home (Davies, p. 49).

18. The anthropologist Peter Buck, a better anthropologist than historian, did not allow for this in his appraisal of the situation. (See App. A in this vol.) When the missionaries were in danger, they expected Pomare II to protect them, and they would send him help if the rebels threatened his authority. They treated Pomare II as a feudal monarch, appraising the situation in the light of their knowledge of medieval Europe. In this they were wrong; but of course administrators in many colonies have been similarly wrong down to recent times. As Newbury pointed out, "Overtones from European feudalism have obscured the picture of Tahitian society and its rulers" (C. W. Newbury, ed., *The History of the Tahitian Mission: 1799–1830*, p. xxxiii). Buck's statement that "in view of the prospects [of Pomare II's conversion] the missionaries arranged themselves on the side of Pomare" (Peter H. Buck, *Anthropology and Religion*, p. 65) is an unworthy appraisal. The missionaries acted throughout as if they were confronted by a feudal society under a king; it was an honest mistake.

19. Davies, pp. 90-91.

20. I have mentioned a specific case (n. 17, above), in 1802. During a devastating attack by Pomare II in 1807 the missionaries received and protected rebels and tried to negotiate peace (Davies, pp. 97-98). This involved a risk of disloyalty. In 1808 again they tried to bring the parties together to negotiate peace (ibid., p. 121).

21. Most of the missionaries shifted to Huahine on Nov. 10, 1808, with their women and children; only three men remained to watch their valuable property (ibid., pp. 121-22).

22. The prophetic role of Meetia in the behavior of Pomare II has not been sufficiently stressed. Davies' term for Pomare II's attitude toward the prophet is *infatuated* (Davies, p. 130). See also Ellis, 1:137.

23. The captured cattle were offered to the god Oro at the *marae*. The portrait sent to Pomare II of the British king was also devoted in the same way. The flocks of sheep and goats were lost and the houses stripped and burned. The hogs also were lost. Thus ended twelve years of civilizing (Davies, p. 130). This was not the first time they

had suffered large-scale loss. In 1805 in one hour they had lost their fences, coconuts, limes, citrons, oranges, and six hundred plants (Ellis, 1:128).

24. Davies, p. 136; Ellis, 1:137-38.
25. Davies, p. 138.
26. Details of the deaths of Lewis, Jefferson, and others, loss of faith and retirements, with comments on motives, are preserved in the primary sources that have been published: Butler's long survey compiled from annual reports in 1854 (Butler, "South Sea Islands," pp. 678–724); Ellis in his vol. 1 (he having been one of the missionaries); and Davies' contemporary account, only recently published.

The journal of the *Hibernia* missionaries shows that they felt there was little probability of Pomare II regaining his authority, even with the aid of chiefs of nearby islands. They imagined a general state of anarchy. At the same time they wrote: "We may add that these two vessels lately from Port Jackson gave us no reason to think that the directors of the Missionary Society trouble themselves much about us." The departure was not a sudden decision made because of the presence of a means of escape in a time of crisis. They had met to discuss the possibility six months earlier (April 14) and they were almost unanimous. They recorded the following reasons: many years of hard work without success; the state of the islands (war), particularly Tahiti and Eimeo (now Moorea) because of the instability of the government; "above all the persuasion that the Directors of the Missionary Society had given up the mission, or at least left it to take its chance"; and there were other reasons considered but not recorded (Davies, pp. 126, 131-32).

A few weeks later the missionaries addressed a letter to Pomare II with heavy theological overtones, depicting Tahiti "under the displeasure and anger of God" and claiming that had Pomare II harkened to their message things may have been very different. This last clause was quite true; the rebellion was largely because of the arrogance and misrule of Pomare II, which Ellis described in the following terms in 1808: "The dissatisfaction of the farmers, inferior chiefs, and lower orders of the people, with Pomare's conduct, was daily increasing, and his recent massacre of the Atehurans had greatly strengthened their determination to destroy his authority . . ." (Ellis, p. 135). Prior to departure the missionaries observed a day of fasting, humiliation, and prayer because of the unprofitableness of the mission (Davies, p. 133). There is no doubt they took the matter very much to heart. On Oct. 17, 1809, after three fruitless months at Huahine, they left for Port Jackson, via Fiji. Thus ended the project as an attempt to evangelize by means of civilizing. Missionaries Nott and Hayward remained in the islands. For the text of the *Hibernia* journal, see Everard Im Thurn and Leonard C. Wharton, *Journal of William Lockerby.* . . .

27. This point marks the end of a particular pattern of rule in Tahiti and also the end of a particular pattern of missionary approach. The political situation was friendly neither to Pomare II nor to the missionaries. After the missionaries left, the tempo and tone changed dramatically.

28. Hayward was at Huahine, Nott at Eimeo, and Crook quite forgotten at the Marquesas, shortly to be rescued and to join the men at the Society Islands. (I use the name of the group because the original station on Tahiti was unoccupied.)

29. Davies, p. 138; Butler, "South Sea Islands," p. 686; Ellis, 1:138.

30. When the missionaries built themselves a little chapel in the early days, Pomare I sent them a fish to be devoted to Jesus Christ and placed in His "temple" (Butler, "South Sea Islands," p. 686). Po-

mare II was the same kind of man. Jefferson recorded, in his journal of Pomare I, that "nothing was sin to him but neglecting prayer and sacrificing to his gods. In these things he was exemplary" (written on the death of Pomare I, Sept. 3, 1803, and cited by Lovett, pp. 181-82).

31. This loss of faith in these gods is evidenced in behavior as well as in words in 1810, when, soon after his defeat, he met one calamity after another, despite his offerings to his old gods. He found them deaf and impotent. This decline of faith in his old gods can be traced from early in 1810.

32. This was probably late in 1811. Davies gives no date (Davies, p. 138), nor does Ellis; but from the latter the date of Pomare II's demonstration of faith can be calculated as "ten days before the death of Mrs. Henry" (Ellis, 1:191), which is elsewhere (ibid., p. 188) recorded as July 28, 1812. This gives us July 18, and shows that Pomare II was in this state of suspense for about two years. He became a keen advocate of Christianity, pressing its claims with the chiefs of Raiatéa and Huahine. Ellis was quite satisfied of his sincerity as an advocate. All this is within the Oceanic pattern (ibid., p. 193).

33. Ibid., pp. 192-93; Butler, "South Sea Islands," p. 686.

34. He began observing Sunday about a year before his conversion (Butler, "South Sea Islands," p. 686). There must have been a deep and long struggle in the mind of this man which brought him to sincere conviction as to the impotency of his gods in the presence of the power of Christ. The experience was experiential and dynamic rather than rational.

35. Ellis, 1:191-92. Butler's survey, composed from the contemporary annual reports, uses almost identical words. See also Lovett, p. 197.

36. Davies, p. 153, fn. 2.

37. Davies does not narrate this incident but says that Pomare II was fully determined in July 1812 "to cast away his false gods," and again asked for baptism (Davies, p. 153).

38. The experiences of the *Hibernia* missionaries upon arrival in Australia is narrated by Davies, who was one of the party (ibid., pp. 140-51). That was in Feb. 1810. This highly important statement leaves us with more sympathy for the missionaries than for the directors. In Sydney they received a quantity of correspondence which answered a number of their problems (ibid., pp. 140-42). The attitude of the Committee was merely that they should "trust exclusively on God, and to expect assistance and success alone from Him" (ibid., p. 143). Marsden, the agent of the Society in Australia, wrote to them: "The mission to the South Seas does not now rest with the directors, but with you; they have been anxious to meet your wishes by sending out persons to co-operate with you. . . . If you now relinquish the missionary work, from any other motive than necessity, your own conscience will condemn you, the religious public will condemn you and the Searcher of hearts hath told us, 'he who putteth his hand to the plough and looketh back is not fit for the kingdom of heaven.'" He went on to speak of their call, about "fighting against God" and about "leaving the heathen to sink" and left the matter with them "for the happiness of each individual concerned in time and eternity" (ibid., pp. 144-47). In the imagery of the world of convicts to which Marsden partly belonged, he knew how "to use the screws" on missionaries. However, the occasion and the speech cleared the air. Several of the single missionaries were married, and Marsden did press the claims of all the missionaries for better communications. Most of the party returned to Tahiti, and though this is spoken of as "the resumption

of the mission," we should not overlook the fact that Nott and Hayward remained at their post in the islands throughout (ibid., pp. 149-50). The directors were hard men with fixed ideas and more inclined to make excuses than to see their own faults. After any applauding of missionary perseverance they would add, "We feel disappointed at the small degree of improvement made amongst the natives in respect of industry and civilization" (ibid., p. 151).

39. Ellis, 1:198–201; also letter to London, Sept. 8, 1813, cited by Lovett, p. 201. It is strange that the anthropologist Buck eliminated both these incidents of the mental changes and turtle-eating of Pomare II, and the growth of this prayer group, seeing they were both narrated in the source he used.

40. Ellis, 1:202; also W. Butler, "South Sea Islands," p. 687.

41. The meeting was held at Eimeo, where there was also some sign of movement (Ellis, 1:200, 205). Davies says that three men had actually gone to Eimeo from Tahiti in May to inquire about salvation (Davies, p. 156). The prophet of the god Oro found it necessary shortly afterward to start terrifying the people. We have three independent lines of evidence: one through Davies, another from official reports and Ellis, and also a letter, dated Sept. 8, 1813, cited by Lovett (Lovett, p. 201).

42. Davies' spelling is *Ariois*. The publication of Davies' manuscript in 1961 has been important. Quite apart from its confirmation of a great many things, in which we have hitherto had only Ellis' word, the places where the two sources differ are significant. We can now establish that Puru (Davies) was the same as Tehei'ura of Mahine (Ellis) and Taaroarii (Butler). This means that the responding chief was the man on whom Pomare II had been working for some time. Butler says the priest was Matupuupuu, chief priest of Huahine (Butler, "South Sea Islands," p. 687).

43. I note that Pahi, judge of Raiatéa, had burned his god and baked breadfruit with it. He then ate the breadfruit. This was before Pomare II ate the turtle and the incident greatly angered Pomare II. It may however have influenced his thinking (Jas. Montgomery, ed., *Journal of Voyages and Travels by Revs. Daniel Tyerman & George Bennet . . . ,* 2:32).

44. Very little was done for the first five years. They had only been around the small island of Tahiti itself twice by the beginning of 1803 (Davies, p. 59).

45. Newbury, App. 1; Ellis, 1:193, 198, 202, 206-207.

46. Ellis, 1:220.

47. Davies, p. 183.

48. Ellis, 1:210.

49. Davies' style is formal and factual. He was concerned with problems and reasons, and left much of the dynamic situation unrecorded. Ellis and Davies are good correctives to each other. Davies dated this service and discussion as Feb. 14, 1815; but merely recorded that Patii publicly committed his god to the flames. Ellis gave a full and dramatic description, which was largely confirmed by Butler, The service had been at Teataebua, five miles from the mission, where Nott had been speaking to an encampment of people from Huahine. Lovett also provides an account of these events (Lovett, p. 206).

50. Ellis, 1:210.

51. Ibid., pp. 210-12; Butler, "South Sea Islands," p. 687.

52. *Epistle to Diognetus,* chap. 2.

53. Buck's oversimplified interpretation of Tahitian conversion bypasses all these data, which he had at his disposal. What happened at Eimeo was relevant in Tahiti. The Tahiti prophets were deeply concerned

about it. As we have seen, one went to Eimeo to terrify the people out of becoming Christian (Davies, p. 156).

54. Davies, p. 184, fn.
55. Ellis, 1:211-14 (passage cited, p. 214); Butler, "South Sea Islands," p. 687.
56. About the same time, when food was being presented to the "queen" (Mar. 28. 1815), in the presence of many heathen, Farefau, a chief, forestalled any heathen rites by blessing the food in the Christian manner, thus rendering it unsuitable for a heathen offering, and leaving the dominantly heathen assembly thunderstruck (Lovett, p. 207). This was still 102 days before Bunaauia.
57. Davies, p. 184, fn. See also George Pritchard, *The Missionary's Reward . . .* , p. 50.
58. Ellis, 1:234-35; Lovett, p. 208.
59. It was indeed an unholy union, but indicates the growth of the *Bure Atua* (Ellis, 1:239).
60. Ibid., pp. 239-42; Davies, pp. 188-89.
61. This took place at Narii, near the village of Bunaauia, in the district of Atehuru. The "king" had taken a regular force of selected men. Clearly if there was to be a showdown it was to be with a Christian following (Ellis, 1:246-47).
62. This is not the impression Buck gives, yet it is a summary of Ellis's eleven-page account (Ellis, 1:247-57), which Buck used. The musket firing was at the start of the service, not during it. The contest went on after the death of Upufara, the enemy leader. Fortune had not smiled on Pomare II from the outset. Sure, the death of a leader affected the result; but only as one of a great complex of factors. There is also another source: a missionary letter sent to London, Aug. 13, 1816, and cited by Lovett (pp. 209 ff).
63. Davies, pp. 194-95; Ellis, 1:257-60; Butler, "South Sea Islands," p. 688; Montgomery, pp. 160-61.
64. Numerous biographies of John Williams have been written but none reflects better his motives and methods than his own *Narrative of Missionary Enterprises in the South Seas*. The Preface shows his wide interests in nature, man, culture, customs, and language. Even more, it reveals that first and foremost he was a Christian missionary responding to what he himself called the *imperative* of the "command of the ascending Saviour" (Williams, p. x). In eighteen years he sailed over 100,000 miles (ibid., p. vii) and eventually lost his life trying to take the gospel to a Melanesian island, doing what he had been advocating, against considerable opposition, for a decade and a half. If he was a civilizer more than most of them, he was certainly no sedentary farmer.
65. This was the *Messenger of Peace*, 60 feet long, 18 feet broad. She took fifteen weeks to build and then went on a trial run of 170 miles to Aitutaki. The narrative is told in Williams' *Missionary Enterprises*, pp. 141-55.
66. John Williams to the directors of L.M.S., July 7, 1820 (cited by Ebenezer Prout, *Memoirs of the Life of the Rev. John Williams*, pp. 81-82).
67. Appraisal of Tyerman and Bennet, L.M.S. deputationists, by Joseph King, *Christianity in Polynesia*, pp. 78-83.
68. Montgomery, p. 550.
69. Ibid., p. 205. Civilization had increased their wants and the means available for supplying them. Industry was thus essential (p. 95).
70. John Williams to the directors of L.M.S., cited by Prout, p. 157. The date appears to be 1822, but it could have been earlier.
71. Murdered by pagans at Eromanga, New Hebrides, Nov. 30, 1839.

72. Peter H. Buck, *Vikings of the Sunrise*, pp. 67, 84, etc.
73. Instructions written July 6, 1823, preserved by Prout, pp. 172-78.
74. Williams to the directors of L.M.S., cited by Prout, pp. 263-64, but no date given.
75. Dr. McFarlane (L.M.S.) speaking at the London conference, 1888, said, "Not only the directors, but Christian men generally thought that civilization must precede the introduction of Christianity" (S. McFarlane, cited in *Report of the Centenary Conference on Protestant Missions of the World: London 1888*, ed. James Johnston, p. 336).
76. John Williams to the directors of L.M.S., Sept. 30, 1823. Text cited by Newbury, pp. 341 ff. Another missionary, Darling, felt the same way and wrote to London Dec. 25, 1827, stating that there were too many missionaries in Tahiti. His mind had been to go to the Marquesas, but the brethren disapproved. Text cited by Lovett, p. 298.
77. Although the Eastern Polynesians succeeded in gathering groups for worship in Tongatabu and Oneata (Lau, Fiji), in neither case were they effective, because of communication difficulties.
78. Williams, pp. 428 ff.
79. These figures have been calculated from those given by William Wyatt Gill, *Gems from Coral Islands*, 1:161, 182, and from annual reports of the societies concerned.
80. Dr. McFarlane said in 1888, "The gospel has gone from island to island, and mainly by native agents; whereas the first white men, who went to Tahiti were some twenty long years before they heard of any converts, the native teachers have not been, perhaps, so many weeks without hearing of some good result" (cited in Johnston, p. 337). The observation is sound but exaggerated. Nearly all Pacific missionaries recognized the superiority of their indigenous brethren in this.
81. Heath estimated the figures at: Upolu, 20,000; Manono, 2,000; Savaii, 12,000 to 13,000; Tutuila, 6,000; smaller islands, several hundreds—total, 41,000. He lived in Samoa at the time, but the fact that better statistics are not available indicates something of the character of the intake from paganism. Communicant figures were better kept. The official figure for 1853 was 2,141 and only one of the fourteen stations recorded the same figure as the previous year. That suggests that the communicant records were being kept up to date.
82. The 1853 figures were collected by Butler in that year.
83. The 1856 figures were collected by Gill (2:298–301, 305-7).
84. The date of Pomare II's baptism is supplied by Joseph King ("Oceania," in *Christianity Anno Domini 1901*, p. 378). He pointed out that it was four years after Pomare II's demonstration of faith. I have indicated already that he sought baptism long before that date. King went on to speak of this "Puritan severity."
85. Figures from the *Missionary Register*, 1840, p. 238.
86. King, "Oceania," p. 378. This is supported by many references in the correspondence of missionaries from other parts of Oceania, from those in which King was particularly interested. Thus, for instance, Watkin wrote from New Zealand to his Committee in London, "I make no haste to baptize, or I might have scores to report. I wish them to know what Christianity really is before they embrace it" (cited in T. A. Pybus, *Maori & Missionary . . .* , p. 21).
87. Nott's report of the 1835 revival, Tahiti, in *Missionary Register*, 1836, pp. 534-37.
88. I take Nott's reports at face value, as they have every evidence of accuracy. The reports of Osmond, another missionary, did not; after careful examination I reject his evidence as bitter invective because of his dismissal from the mission. Too much just does not fit the known facts. See Newbury, p. 361.

89. As, for example, in *Missionary Register*, 1831, p. 90; ibid., 1832, pp. 98-99; and ibid., 1833, p. 100.
90. It was stated as being in the fringe of the congregation "who found moral restraints irksome." This is putting it mildly. The congregation at Maupiti went over entirely to the Mamaia sect. In April 1821 old customs had been renewed in opposition to the law code, church subscriptions, and missionaries. Visions began in 1826. The chiefs and indigenous judges were effective only at the seat of authority in Tahiti. The leaders of the movement were Teao and Hue, who established drinking parties, sensual dancing, and fornication. This is clear in the writings of Davies and in Newbury's footnotes based on missionary correspondence with the directors (Newbury, pp. 252-56), in his Epilogue, and also in Darling's letter of Dec. 25, 1827, cited by Lovett (Lovett, pp. 297-98).
91. Newbury, pp. 328-31.
92. Nott and Shelly in 1812 (ibid., p. 159, fn).
93. Montgomery, p. 93.
94. G. E. C. Catlin, Introduction, pp. 31 ff., in Emile Durkheim, *The Rules of Sociological Method*, trans. Sarah A. Soloray and John M. Mueller, ed. G. E. C. Catlin.
95. Montgomery, p. 150.
96. Ibid., p. 120.
97. Ibid., pp. 95, 205.
98. Lovett, p. 270 (using Ellis).
99. Ibid., pp. 221-22. A letter from Pomare to Haweis, 3 Oct. 1817, discussed the procedure by which the laws were to be set up and the nature of the consultation by means of which the "faulty parts would be corrected." This I found in the Turnbull Library, Wellington, N.Z., misc. ms. 1396.
100. Under the entry of Nov. 20, 1835, Darwin, at Tahiti, wrote his opinion of affairs in these islands. He had read Ellis, Beechey, Kotzebue, and others. He found Kotzebue "strongly adverse to the whole missionary system." Darwin was aware of all biases. He strongly disagreed with the critics who declared the Tahitians had become a gloomy race, living in fear of the missionaries. Though he thought the prohibitions and sabbatarianism overdone, he thought the morality and religion highly creditable. He described Kotzebue's attack as "acrimonious" and says he expected of the missionaries what the apostles themselves were unable to accomplish. He said they overlooked the transformation that had been effected (or refused to see it). "I believe that, disappointed in not finding the field of licentiousness quite as open as formerly, they will not give credit to a morality which they do not wish to practise, or to a religion which they undervalue, if not despise." We are fortunate to have this evaluation by a scientific man like Charles Darwin, especially as Kotzebue has been taken as a major primary source by some recent writers and his comments accepted at face value (e.g., Aarne A. Koskinen, *Missionary Influence as a Political Factor in the Pacific Islands*, p. 95). One does not miss the implication of Darwin's alternatives—they forget, *or they will not remember*.
   Darwin carried his own flask but acknowledged "no common debt of gratitude to the missionaries" for their fight against liquor, the effect of which he had seen in many lands. Darwin also recognized that missionaries alone had no power to impose laws and prohibitions unless they were acceptable to the people. He was also impressed by the devotion of Tahitian Christians, grace before meals, prayers before sleep, and such things as he witnessed where no missionary was present. These findings are recorded in the paperback edition of his *Voyage of the Beagle*, republished after more than a century.

These references to Tahiti are found on pp. 355, 356, 357-58, and 376. This serves to show that the people movements were a real move from paganism into Christianity and the missionaries had an open door for planning the kind of church they desired.

101. Davies, pp. 252-56.

CHAPTER 2: THE MAORI WEB

1. According to Hobbs (June 30, 1851), Hongi and Shunghee were the same person. At times he was the terror of the district. Both C.M.S. and W.M.S. missionaries have left many accounts of his bloodthirsty wars. The key to Hongi's apparently inconsistent behavior lies in his Maori morals. As the leader responsible for *utu* (satisfaction), his behavior is meaningful. At first missionaries were tolerated for economic reasons. His attitude was often conditioned by the fact that the missionaries were serving his people or his enemies. Thus, for example, when the Wesleyans were seeking a new site he nominated Hododo, but they rejected his offer and chose Whangaroa in the enemy territory, for which they paid a dear penalty, which well nigh wrecked their mission.

2. Hall (the joiner) was sent to Hull to learn the ship-building trade and the rudiments of navigation. King (the shoemaker) went to a rope walk to learn spinning. Kendall (the schoolmaster) proved a useful man, serving as farmer, teacher, doctor, and linguist. None had theological or biblical preparation. As with the L.M.S. artisans, they had to maintain themselves after having been given the initial seed, tools, and stock. Their remuneration was only twenty pounds per year. They were really not designated "missionaries" but "lay settlers," although subsequently the schoolmaster was ordained. They were instructed to introduce "the arts of civilized life" as a means of ultimately introducing "knowledge of Christ." In personal life they were to follow specific rules: (1) observe the Lord's Day; (2) maintain family worship (singing and reading loudly enough for it to be observed by passing Maoris); (3) while planting potatoes and sowing corn they were to converse about religion; (4) when possible they could gather children for instruction. In teaching such children they were to stress the following points: be industrious, make yourself self-sufficient, neither give nor receive presents, and handwork can always be sold at Port Jackson (Sydney). Everything was clearly geared to the civilizing process (Eugene Stock, ed., *History of the Church Missionary Society* . . . , 1:206-7).

3. Ibid., pp. 205-6. Even so, Marsden still has many supporters among the secular writers. See A. W. Reed, *The Impact of Christianity on the Maori People*, p. 18, and also Eric Ramsden, *Marsden & Missions: Prelude to Waitangi.* The passages cited, however, are from the official C.M.S. history.

4. Stock, p. 213. The official historian writes that the committee realized "that if Civilization preceded Christianity it was very likely to prove an obstacle"—a conclusion drawn by both committee and historian.

5. The recognition of the importance of direct evangelism came with the appointment of Henry Williams in 1822 (arrived 1823), but the change was not so clear-cut that the C.M.S. ceased to supply civilizers. Marsden sent another farmer and a carpenter before the next minister arrived; and still another carpenter and a flax-dresser accompanied Williams. However, Henry Williams himself was so convinced of the priority of evangelism that he continually argued the case with the others, including Marsden. Eight years later he wrote, "So impressed were we at Pahia of the importance of seeking first the spiritual good

of this people, laying aside every personal consideration, that I have not possessed a house one year out of eight" (Williams to Marsh, Sept. 4, 1831).

Williams could write this because he had seen the only adult baptisms up to that time. He might argue that this vindicated his policy, though it was no real proof, because the sedentary policy and the itinerant policies were used together and the factors in the pattern were complex. Yate insisted that civilizing had great value (W. Yate, *An Account of New Zealand . . .*, p. 241). Taylor, writing in 1868, after many years of missionary experience, described in this way the process of civilizing as it was tried in New Zealand: ". . . Little good from their labours was perceptible; no impression seemed to be made on the native mind by their teaching, they had no moral influence over it. But when men were sent forth to them solely as bearers of the gospel message; when they simply preached salvation through Christ, and regular ministrations were established, then its genuine effects were soon perceived" (Richard Taylor, *The Past & Present of New Zealand . . .*, p. 9).

Fancourt, writing a century after the events, in a period when missions had adopted a strong policy of sedentary institutionalism, and the church was influenced by the doctrines of the social gospel (and New Zealand especially so), was not so sure Taylor was right (H. C. Fancourt, *The Advance of the Missionaries . . .*, chap. 2). One thing we can be certain of from the historical documentation is that both among the field missionaries and the authorities in London, the time did come when leaders became convinced that the notion of "Civilize in order to evangelize" was false.

Williams was right in pressing the positive importance of presenting the gospel in itineration. The sedentary stations did not permit visiting more than a few villages in the vicinity. This tended to identify stations with tribes and tribal rivalries. It militated against wide diffusion of the gospel. The extent to which a missionary cause could become sedentary can be judged by the fact that when William Williams, the second itinerator, arrived at Pahia in 1826 the remainder of the staff included a shoemaker, a gardener, two smiths, four carpenters, a farmer, a herdman, and a flax-dresser and weaver, a number of whom were married with families (F. W. Williams, *Through Ninety Years: 1826–1916 . . .*, pp. 10–11). If the London committee had recognized the importance of itinerant evangelism, they had still not recognized its priority. It was by field missionaries like Williams and Taylor that this was pressed.

6. The official history records the first conversion as 1825, but I am satisfied that it took place in 1824. An error of one year is frequent, owing to the long time it took for reports to reach England. Yate says definitely 1824 (Yate, p. 179). I think it was the baptism, not the conversion, that took place in 1825. The major movement of the family units dates to 1830 (Stock, 1:356), a deeply spiritual movement, "an outpouring of the Spirit." For further details see Yate, p. 180.

7. See W. Butler, "New Zealand," in *Cyclopedia of Missions*, ed. Harvey Newcomb, p. 570, a source based on annual reports.

8. Stock, 1:357 ff.

9. Harvey Newcomb, ed., *Cyclopedia of Missions*, a very good statistical and factual source, and up to date in most areas to 1854, its publication date.

10. Yate reported in 1835 the difference between regulated "Christianized villages in the interior" and those "in connection with shipping." It

did not work out this way in every land under commercial and colonial influence, but it was so in New Zealand.

11. The statistics of these early years have been published by Harrison M. Wright, *New Zealand: 1769–1840* . . . , but there is an error of one year—a statistical lag. Henry Williams' figures (8,760 and 233) agree with Wright's table, though the latter records them for 1840. The date on Williams' letter proves them as for 1839. When he wrote, the 1840 figures were incomplete, hence he speaks only in round numbers: 27,000 and nearly 2000. When completed they actually stood at 29,320 and 584; which suggests he estimated communicants from those being prepared for reception. Actually many of these were not received until the following year, when the figure in one district alone rose by 878 in this category.

12. Williams' references were dated May and September. This shows how Bishop G. A. Selwyn has already passed into New Zealand mythology. Probing the causes of this growth, I was assured by academic persons in New Zealand that it followed the arrival of Selwyn. He was appointed in 1841 and arrived May 30, 1842, so we must look elsewhere for the causes.

13. Bishop Stuart, cited in James Johnston, ed., *Report of the Centenary Conference on Protestant Missions of the World:* London 1888, pp. 330-31. Moral change brought about by these people movements may be judged by the comments of Charles Darwin who visited New Zealand in 1835. Although Darwin did not hesitate to criticize anything he thought out of place, he was impressed by the transformed lives of Christian Maoris, who stood out in contrast with the pagan in appearance, habits, honesty, and humor. (See Charles Darwin, *The Voyage of the Beagle,* entries for Dec. 21, 23, 24, and 25, pp. 361-71.)

14. See, for example, "The Tahitian Web," n. 86, citing Watkin's letter, mentioned in T. A. Pybus, *Maori & Missionary* . . . , p. 21. See also William Williams, *Christanity Among the New Zealanders,* pp. 149, 210, 288-90.

15. The missionary Bishop J. R. Selwyn had something to say of this type of experience: "The Hawaiian queen who stood on the edge of the crater of Kilaulea, and as the waves of molten lava dashed at her feet, braved with contemptuous scorn the deity who ruled them, and who all her ancestors had worshipped, gave proof of a moral and physical courage, which has never been surpassed. And every heathen convert does the same. He braves the wrath of him whom, up to that moment, he has dreaded unutterably (J. R. Selwyn, *Pastoral Work in the Colonies and on the Mission Field,* p. 120).

16. Bishop G. A. Selwyn's report to the committee, 1844, in which he enlarged on these moral reforms and their "deep and earnest feelings of religion." The training facilities were made possible by renting a farm at Waimate. See Butler, p. 573.

17. The church was an imposing structure, 80' x 36' and 40' high, and was described in detail in the *Australian & New Zealand Gazette* at the time. (See also Butler, p. 574.) Sixty acres had been cleared and drained, twenty of which were under crops. They had seventy head of cattle and four teams of oxen. Six thousand pounds had been spent on buildings. Two hundred head of cattle and seventy horses were owned by Maori share-farmers and this a decade after their conversion.

18. Marsden's journal, cited in *Wesleyan,* 1822, p. 90. See also William Williams, pp. 245-47, 260, 286, etc., and Lawrence M. Rogers, *The Early Journals of Henry Williams* . . . , p. 256.

19. Samuel Leigh to the London committee, *Wesleyan,* 1822, p. 291.

20. Thomas Buddle, "The Aborigines of New Zealand," *Wesleyan,* 1852, p. 55.

21. For example, John Bumby described such a case in his journal. He was at Mana Island. See *Wesleyan*, 1840.
22. Peter H. Buck, *The Coming of the Maori*, p. 486. For the various uses of slaves mentioned in this valuable source, written by a Maori, see pp. 338 and 429. Buck also insisted that the slave category was not conceptualized as a social grade (ibid., p. 486). Bernard Mishkin says slaves were recruited in war and not regarded as a static class, because they could marry commoners and their offspring were free. However they held no line of descent, and because of this they lost their *mana*. This loss of *mana* made them useful workers and not subject to *tapu* regulations of many kinds. Thus in pre-Christian society economic efficiency was increased relatively with slave population (Bernard Mishkin, "The Maori of New Zealand," in *Co-operation and Competition Among Primitive Peoples*, ed. Margaret Mead, p. 435). However I note the last point has been questioned by A. P. Vayda (*Ethnohistory*, vol. 8).
23. Yate, pp. 242-43. W. Williams has numerous references to slaves being used in a variety of ways, sometimes bartered like goods, or killed to accompany the dead (W. Williams, pp. 162-63, 255-57, 269). Other references are found in the journals of Henry Williams (Rogers, pp. 103, 291, etc.). The uncertainty with which their fortunes were determined is illustrated in the Rangihona incident (W. Williams, pp. 162-63, 173-80; Rogers, p. 308).
24. Buck, p. 357.
25. The Io cult theology was certainly not understood by the nonchiefly segments of society. The missionaries quickly gained access to the popular animistic beliefs, but not to those of the closed Io segment. Their choice of theological terminology came from the popular religion. Though they learned much about this, they had difficulty in structuralizing it. Yate, who was able to write from twenty to thirty pages about Maori religion, was unable to find a pattern in it, or any idea of God. The same account reveals a strong dynamistic animism at the popular level (Yate, p. 141). This segmentation is also revealed in attitudes. W. Williams discussed the increased interest in Christianity but showed the group conversions as not of the total communities. Some chiefs often obstructed the Christian movement and they were supported by a following, or a Christian group might break away and form a village of its own (W. Williams, pp. 210-14, 245-47). Henry Williams has an entry in his journal (Oct. 4, 1832) which shows strong class feeling. A chief was reluctant to go to the Christian worship service because it was of dominantly slave composition (Rogers, p. 261).
26. "The Maori people who were in occupation of New Zealand at the time of European contact were the decendants of the intermixture of three successive groups of immigrants: the moa hunters and the early *tangata whenua* who came with Maruiwi, the two crews under Toi and Whatonga, and the settlers from the fleet of 1350. The second and third groups came from Hawaiiki, which has been identified as the Society Islands and hence they were recognized as people of Polynesian stock" (Buck, p. 65).

From his researches in skull measurement Buck claims "considerable tribal variation in the percentage of long-heads and broad-heads" (ibid., p. 67). Although these are everywhere mixed in Polynesia, there is reason to believe that the present population of the Society Islands is more broadheaded. Yet these islands were the greatest center from which the early migrations took place and evidence is that at an earlier period they were dominantly longheaded, as they still are in the marginal area (ibid., p. 68). The Manahune were longheaded, the Raiateans broadheaded and so also settlers in the Cook

Islands (Aitutaki, Atiu, and Mauke) still to this day. Buck thought
the Tane worshipers were probably broadheaded (ibid., pp. 69-70).

27. Tauranga, for example, was a strategic center both for economic and
    military connections. It was from this location that the gospel was
    diffused in the interior (W. Williams, p. 286).

28. For example, see references to translations and Scripture distribution
    in W. Williams, pp. 67, 85, 117, 151, 164, 248-49, 260-61, 270, 280,
    286; and Rogers, pp. 38 n, 60 n, 64, 71 n, 72, 98 n, 155, 326 n, etc.

29. In an interview with Rev. G. I. Laurenson (Dec. 9, 1961) I noted
    down his opinion as follows: "There is evidence of the monotheistic
    cult of Io, taught only to the sons of chiefs, a mystical cult of a high
    order, not known by the common people, who were animistic. The
    early missionaries did not learn much of this secret cult, but did learn
    much at the popular level. Thus they chose *Atua* for God, instead of
    Io. For long, the *Tohunga*, the *Kaumatua* and the *Rangatira* (craft
    priests, honoured elders and high chiefs) preferred to observe and
    withhold their decision—till about 1839. Io worship was groping for
    the truth about the god who hid his face. The missionary message
    seemed to offer an answer to this. The Christian Bible and especially
    the New Testament helped to convince them."

30. I believe the main reason for this opinion however was that it mili-
    tated against the civilizing process. Butler, C.M.S. missionary, de-
    scribed his farming, fencing, gardening, livestock, timber cutting, and
    the land he had ready for planting wheat, barley, oats, and peas, and
    his fruit trees and vegetables, and his employment of ten Maori
    farmers and eight sawyers. He then went on to describe the war
    expeditions of Shunghee which "threatens all this kind of thing"
    (*Wesleyan*, 1823). It is a typical passage.

31. In his journal of the voyage of the *Beagle* Darwin recorded between
    two and three hundred Europeans at the Bay of Islands. In another
    paragraph on the same page he added, "the greater part of the English
    are the very refuse of society" (Chas. Darwin, *The Voyage of the
    Beagle*, p. 372). White men who had gone native, known as "the
    devil's missionaries," increased until 1840, then declined in number
    as the Maoris learned to trade for themselves. The statistics are:
    before 1814, 6; 1827, 15; 1830, 50; 1835, 100; 1840, 150; 1845, 50;
    1850, 15; 1853, 10 (Thos. W. Gudgeon, *The History & Doings of the
    Maoris 1820–1840*, p. 46). The Right Hon. Sir George Rose spoke in
    public in England of the solid work of the Wesleyan missionaries in
    New Zealand. He threw this in contrast with the harmful work of
    runaway seamen and convicts and discussed their hindrance of the
    gospel. See report of his speech at the anniversary of W.M.S. in
    Wesleyan, 1840, pp. 513-15.

32. Samuel Leigh to the London committee, Feb. 25 & 27, 1822.

33. Leigh's health trip was in 1819. With C.M.S. approval he returned
    to England and obtained the sanction for a Maori mission (1821).
    His plan to set up at Mercury Bay was stopped by Maori wars, hence
    his commencement at the C.M.S. station (Butler, p. 576). Mission-
    aries frequently shared hospitality. See Woon's correspondence in
    Wesleyan, 1832, p. 53, for his praise of the C.M.S. on this account.
    A report of how Hongi desolated the locality of the tribe which had
    invited the Wesleyans, scattering some and enslaving others, is given
    by Wm. Moister (*A History of Wesleyan Missions, &c.*). Hongi's
    destructive work reached to the East Cape, to Kawia on the West Coast
    and to Cook Strait in the south. Whangaroa had been chosen by
    Leigh against Hongi's nomination of Hododo. Hongi invaded Whan-
    garoa. Missionaries of the Hokianga tribes were his enemies (ibid.,
    pp. 319 ff). (Whangaroa was frequently spelled *Wangaroa* in the
    records.)

34. Mangungu, still in the same tribal jurisdiction, was forty miles from Whangaroa, and had some four thousand people in the river locality who could be reached with little trouble by boat.

35. Butler (p. 579), reporting this movement among the chiefs, gives the names of two of them: Tawai and Miti, the former a famous warrior. Deputations were officially sent from the southern chiefs seeking the gospel. As a good C.M.S. documentary reference, follow Henry Williams' journal entries of his October 1831 itinerancy. He traveled with the chiefs, Taiwanga, Kiharoa, and others (Oct. 24), who presented the message to other chiefs in places where their kin authority held good (Oct. 25, 27). They were received, welcomed, and addressed in the chiefly manner, ceremonially (Oct. 27, 28), and in the same pattern they responded. See this log, cited in Hugh Carleton, *The Life of Henry Williams*, 1:134 ff. Richard Taylor made the point that many of these chiefs were young, the older men being more tied to their traditional beliefs (Taylor, p. 35).

36. Alexander Strachan, *The Life of Samuel Leigh*, pp. 448 ff. The liturgy had a singular effect in worship, especially responses like: "Holy, holy, holy, Lord God of Sabaoth: Heaven and earth are full of the majesty of Thy glory!" Interestingly enough, the *Te Deum* figured conspicuously in Fiji also in Methodist work a decade or so later.

37. Ibid., p. 451.

38. Ibid., p. 452.

39. Ibid., pp. 454-55.

40. The year 1837 was an important one for Scripture publication at the C.M.S. press at Pahia. It included the complete New Testament and a number of Old Testament portions. For a list of early publications in Maori by these presses, see Taylor, pp. 38, 305. The statistics cited here are from Strachan, pp. 476-77. They appear to be for about 1840 though not specifically stated as such.

41. John Whiteley to the London committee, Aug. 20, 1839.

42. Ultimately the New Zealand Land Co. usurped this whole region regardless of custom and endeavored to defeat the aims of the mission by poisoning the minds of the Maoris against the missionaries (Directors' statement, *Wesleyan*, 1840, p. 698).

43. After eighteen months he had been removed for three years. When he returned he found his house and chapel still standing and his little flock remained intact. Bumby and Hobbs saw Whiteley receive sixty-eight adults for baptism. He had prepared them over a period of time. Then they brought their children, so that the baptisms were of households.

44. At the time of the visit Whiteley was undertaking a journey to Mokou to attempt a reconciliation and avoid a large-scale retaliation. One of Whiteley's converts had long awaited the opportunity of retaliation for killing by sorcery. The sorcerer had fled to Padianiwaniwa, a heathen village, and fortified the place, *tapuing* the road. There was much excitement when it was known that the wronged man had broken the *tapu* and was approaching the fortified village. When he announced that, having become a Christian, he sought reconciliation, there was a general astonishment and the visit ended in a feast. John Bumby described the pattern of peace negotiation ("Itineration Journal," *Wesleyan*, 1840, p. 705). Whiteley served the church for thirty-six years in New Zealand and effected many reconciliations at great personal risk. He was eventually murdered on a peacemaking journey, April 13, 1869, at a time when much of the fine missionary pioneering work was undone by the Maori wars.

45. Dated Aug. 20, 1839, at Mangungu (*Wesleyan*, 1840, pp. 699–706).

46. Woon, who had just witnessed the baptism of a hundred and eighty adults at Mangungu and fifty more farther north at Oruru, and had

met fifteen hundred in class, wrote of open doors in the south, and pointed out that fragments of Christian literature were found all along the east coast. He mentioned one area where some two thousand heathen were enquiring about missionaries and books (letter to London, Nov. 28, 1839).

47. Published in the *Wesleyan* magazine in 1845.
48. John Warren to the London committee, July 5, 1849. The work at Newark was static, so Warren watched it from Waima, visiting one week in six.
49. Wm. Woon to the London committee, Nov. 11, 1846.
50. Gideon Smales to the London committee, Jan. 29, 1847.
51. Henry Lawry's report for the W.M.S. Annual Meeting, 1851, in *Wesleyan*, 1851, p. 614.
52. Wright's claim that "by 1845 two-thirds of the Maoris were attending church" seems to me an exaggeration (Wright, pp. 163-65).
53. In an interview Laurenson compared the movement with that of its Tongan counterpart. The religious factors were similar, but not the colonization background. Whiteley's figure comes from Reed, p. 34. Bliss's estimate of two million in 1835 is fantastic.
54. Report in *Wesleyan*, 1851, p. 614.
55. Wm. Woon to the London committee, Nov. 28, 1839.
56. Moister, p. 344.
57. Ibid., p. 345.
58. The early missionaries of the two societies were remarkably alike in faith and practice, and I have been able to locate no denominational disagreements before the arrival of Bishop G. A. Selwyn. The comity agreement was fairly effective, but there were places where the spontaneous expansion of the indigenous church brought a flow from the area of one toward the other, and as a result there were a few personality clashes. This difficulty was slight. The real problem came with Selwyn's policy and attitude toward the Wesleyans as a whole. He discredited their ordination and baptism, and must be held responsible for introducing the theological issues. To the Wesleyans this change of attitude from cooperation to discreditation cut deeply. Apostolic succession and baptismal regeneration were the two doctrines involved. Unfortunately the doctrinal issues were transmitted to the Maori converts. Reed (p. 19) lists this as one of the factors which opposed the gospel.
59. H. H. Turton to the London committee, Mar. 20, 1845.
60. Henry Lawry to the London committee, July 6, 1847.
61. Walter Lawry to the London committee, April 30, 1847—"Things are brisk in New Zealand, and every secular interest thrives, especially that of shipping."
62. Moister, p. 345.
63. Lawry's journal, May 14, 1844 (*Wesleyan*, 1845, p. 301) gives a good example. A public meeting had been held to discuss the possibility of establishing an institution to instruct Maoris in English, in religion and civilization. A committee was established for fund-raising. It was comprised of white colonists and missionaries.
64. This was true up till 1865 when the foundations of the cathedral were laid. This was at Christchurch, "the capital of the exclusively church colony" (Taylor, p. 104).
65. For years Watkin tried to secure the appointment of a missionary for Maori work at Lyttleton in the Canterbury district, but without success. By 1851 he changed his argument and began pointing out the number of Wesleyan migrants who had settled there. He spoke of twenty Wesleyan families in Christchurch nearby. With this appeal he was effective. A minister was appointed to care for one Maori and two

European congregations. (See Watkin to the London committee, Sept. 6, 1851.) The Maori people of that area had been requesting the general secretary for a missionary for over six years (Lawry to the London commitee, July 29, 1844).

66. At the end of 1845 Auckland had a small weatherboard church to seat 200. There were 28 full members. Six years later there stood on the site a brick church to seat 500. There were 185 full status members, mostly (but not all) migrants. This is typical of the towns. (Buddle to the London committee, Oct. 9, 1851.)

67. The same letter refers to three educational institutions: a seminary for the children of missionaries, a day school for children of the poorer people, and a native institution for which a government grant of six hundred pounds had been received. The annual report of the W.M.S. for 1854 reported the church beginning to supply teachers for primary schools under government regulations; agricultural and industrial institutions at Three Kings and at New Plymouth; new projects on foot in Wellington; and the acquisition of property in Christchurch and Lyttleton. The report suggests a strong concentration of interest on towns and institutions.

68. Chas. Creed to the London committee, Sept. 4, 1851.

69. Apparently migrations from the countryside, which constructed villages on the fringe of the towns, as in many parts of the Pacific today. In 1851 Buddle said at Auckland, "Villages arise around us." In 1849 Warren complained that his work at Waima was static because of the drift of people to the town at Taranaki. (John Warren to the London committee, July 5, 1849.)

70. Buller reported to the London committee (April 18, 1851) a pleasing display of Maori initiative in missionary responsibility. They initiated collections for sending the gospel to other lands. Wiremu Tipene advocated each pig owner setting aside one pig, and each squarer of timber one spar. He was supported by Arama Karaka. Two years later the same missionary, commenting on the annoying manner in which land disputes kept coming up at their missionary meetings, described how some thought to discontinue missionary meetings on this account. The popular vote for continuation of missionary activity was expressed by one Maori: "When we give up missionary collections, we have renounced Christianity." (Jas. Buller to the London committee, April 19, 1853.)

71. Fancourt, pp. 95 ff. The termination of *tapu*, polygamy, and slavery are claimed by some to have caused the population decline. Firth thought the effects of *tapu* were beneficial. Bishop Henry Williams thought otherwise. It involved a conflict between religion and magic. (See Carleton, 1:104-5; also Reed, p. 18.)

72. Selwyn's associate, C. J. Abraham, stated this as being so. See letter dated Sept. 16, 1850 (cited in H. W. Tucker, *Memoir of . . . Selwyn . . .*, 1:337). Selwyn himself confirmed the opinion in a letter dated Aug. 11, 1851, cited in ibid., p. 391.

73. These three items were featured by Selwyn himself in his résumé of his first ten years in office. It is given eight pages in his biography and has not one single basic statement on the Maoris (ibid., pp. 379-86). There are two references in the nine pages of the Index. The biographer's appraisal was aimed at stressing Selwyn's own emphasis: "An emotional system of religion without a spiritual system of teaching and discipline had left them without backbone, moral or intellectual, and a time of reaction had to set in. . . . The missionaries, burdened with the charge of enormous districts, had been unable to give to the young the moral and social training which was necessary if Christianity was to be a power" (ibid., 2:1).

74. Statement by Bishop Stuart at the London Conference, 1888 (Jos. Johnston, ed., *Report of the Centenary Conference on Protestant Missions of the World: London 1888*, p. 331).
75. Moister, p. 351.
76. Ibid. The actual figures were 225,000 Europeans and 40,000 Maoris, a ratio of 85% to 15%.
77. Fancourt, p. 100.
78. Johnston, p. 331.
79. Harlan P. Beach, *A Geography and Atlas of Protestant Missions*, 1:176.
80. Maori census figures, 1951.
81. Thomas S. Grace to the Secretary of C.M.S., Dec. 16, 1867 (S. J. Brittan et al., . . . *Letters and Journals of Thomas Samuel Grace*, p. 163); also, Grace to the Secretary of C.M.S., Nov. 28, 1868 (ibid., p. 202).
82. Grace's journal, Jan. 4, 1868 (ibid., p. 177).
83. Grace's journal, Nov. 20, 1870 (ibid., p. 218).
84. Ibid., Nov. 10, 1870 (p. 215). See also Grace to the Secretary of C.M.S., Dec. 18, 1873 (ibid., p. 253); also journal, Aug. 9, 1877 (ibid., p. 265), where the following is found: "With full force their standing objections were brought forward. 1st. Our land buying. 2nd. That we ran away and left them. 3rd. That we went with the troops and burned the people. 4th. That we worked only for money." See also Grace's annual letter, Nov. 1877, in which he argues (ibid., p. 286) that they never intended to dispose of Christianity itself but had "lost confidence in us as a body and look upon us with distrust and suspicion, and have determined to manage their own religious affairs."
    In one of Grace's last letters to the Secretary (Jan. 1879) he expressed the opinion that New Zealand needed missionaries of the old type, who were willing to live among the Maoris and share their lives rather than confine themselves to stations. He claimed the older pattern won them influence and confidence. People came with their sick, sought advice, and listened to instruction. Now: "They tell us plainly that we have forsaken them—not they us!" (ibid., pp. 308-9). The complaint that missionaries were not resident in their districts was a long-standing one. Grace had stated this as an obstacle to growth a decade earlier (annual letter 1868, ibid., p. 202).
85. Grace to the Secretary of C.M.S., July 19, 1877 (ibid., pp. 256-57).
86. Grace's journal, Aug. 9, 1877 (ibid., p. 263).
87. Grace to the Secretary of C.M.S., July 19, 1877 (ibid., p. 256).
88. Grace's annual letter, Nov. 18, 1877 (ibid., pp. 287-88).
89. Leonard P. Tolhurst, *The Religious Concepts of the Maoris in Pre-European Days & a Detailed Study of the Ringatu Church of Today*.
90. At some points allowance has to be made for the fact that Tolhurst's thesis is in the discipline of theology and for a Seventh-Day Adventist seminary. The ax that the author has to grind is apparent. Neither does the thesis always pass as history or anthropology, and the documentation is limited. Even so, it has some valuable material.
91. William Greenwood, "The Upraised Hand," in *Journal of the Polynesian Society*, pp. 1-81.
92. Alexander Sutherland and George Sutherland, *The History of Australia and New Zealand from 1606–1890*, p. 239.
93. Jos. Cowan, *The New Zealand Wars:A History of the Maori Campaigns & the Pioneering Period*, 2:1-20. The government was rewarding troops with land grants from confiscated Maori lands in the Taranaki and Waikato territory. Some colonists and politicians felt the extermination of the troublesome Maoris would be in the interests of colonial development. Thus the land question was important for both sides. To the Maori the movement became fanatically religious and an attempt to reestablish the Maori *tohunga* priesthood by appealing to embittered tribes at the psychological moment. The appeal of

love of country and kin linked tribe with tribe (ibid., pp. 2-4). The prophetic appeal was made on the book of Revelation. The *niu* were usually short sticks used by *tohunga* for purposes of divination before battle (S. Barton Babbage, *Hauhauism: An Episode in the Maori Wars, 1863-66*, p. 29), but the pole was taken from a wrecked ship (Cowan, p. 6), and the flag, marching, and military terms were borrowed from Western military authority. The equation of the *niu* stick with the pole is seen in their common use for divination before action (Herbert R. Meade, . . . *Selections from the Journals & Letters of Lieut. Hon. Herbert R. Meade, R. N.*, pp. 123-29).

94. The word *Hau* literally meant "wind," but its esoteric significance was "the vital spirit of man." It might well be added that one feature of the movement was a rejection of the Christian idea of sex relations. The rationalization and justification for promiscuity was that "their children might be as the sands of the sea for multitude" in the face of population decline (Babbage, pp. 31, 37).

95. The authority for this comparison is William Williams, cited in Babbage, p. 32. Beach (p. 167) says it was "a singular compound of Christianity and heathenism . . . neither heathen nor Christian."

96. The drive of the movement was prophetic but the mechanisms were priestly in carrying the prophetic visions into effect. This was typical.

97. This compares remarkably with observations made of the Papuan Taro cult.

98. Tolhurst, p. 79. He devotes twenty pages to the matter. Cowan also deals with this charge (pp. 223-24).

99. Sutherland & Sutherland, p. 241. Escape and return described in detail by Cowan (pp. 228-34). Ship illustrated.

100. It is sometimes wrongly claimed that Te Kooti did not use the pole. He certainly did until the end of the Maori wars, and the flag he flew on it I have illustrated (pl. 7). It was a war flag and a symbol of their religion.

101. G. I. Laurenson to A. R. Tippett (June 7, 1962).

102. This summary is based on Tolhurst, Greenwood, and Vine.

103. Correspondence on this matter is filed at the Institute of Church Growth now at Fuller Theological Seminary, Pasadena, with details of an actual case.

104. These three points were made by the missionary Taylor, who lived in New Zealand at the time (Taylor, p. 63).

105. Ibid., p. 83.

106. The whole complex was, as Selwyn himself said, "an utter loss of faith in everything English" (Jos. King, *Christianity in Polynesia*, p. 54). In a private letter (G. A. Selwyn to Coleridge, Dec. 26, 1865, cited by both Tucker and Babbage) he showed his mind: "O, how things have changed! . . . The Queen, law, religion, have been thrust aside in the one thought of the acquisition of land." This valuable reference shows his bitter awareness of the change in Maori church life. Indirectly it suggests that the queen, law, and religion were taken by the Maoris as foreign control, and Christianity lost rapport. The good bishop strove valliantly to serve both the Maori and the empire; but his stand beside the official troops was interpreted by many Maoris as an indication that his religion was, after all, a white man's faith (Babbage, p. 71). Secular historians are not alone in making this appraisal. Very soon after the wars missionary records themselves reveal it. The Rev. T. S. Grace, who had been in New Zealand since 1850, was pressing for an evangelistic drive in 1877 in a letter to the Society. He was asking for an outside evangelist, if I interpret him correctly, because " we stand so badly with the Maoris." It is interesting to note the strong terms he used in stating the repeated accusations of the Maoris against the church: "1st. They say with reference to the old Missionary land purchases—'You came to us and taught us

to turn our eyes to Heaven, while you turned yours to the land!'
2nd. "You are all hirelings, and therefore you ran away and left us
in the midst of our troubles' [giving instances]. 3rd. 'You went with
our enemies, the troops, and your prayers made them strong to fight.
Our women and children were burned alive and this made us Hau-
haus'" (Grace to the Secretary of C.M.S., July 19, 1877). Against
such bitter taunts as these you can see the extreme difficulty of spiritual teaching. Grace considered the period of 1863 to the time of
writing "fourteen years of neglect" and wrote in his private journal
on July 10, 1877, "They have lost confidence in us as a body, and
look upon us with distrust and suspicion, and have determined to
manage their own religious affairs. . . . Who can blame them after 14
years of neglect? (cited by Babbage, p. 39). Both Selwyn and Grace
were depressed by Maori defection. They had seen the original victory and knew something was arrested and lost.

CHAPTER 3: THE TONGAN WEB

1. Cook anchored at Maria Bay in 1773 and named the group the Friendly Islands. "In the choice of this name the intrepid navigator showed
misguided judgement, for behind their simulated friendship they were
preparing to club him" (J. Egan Moulton, Jr., "Tonga," in *A Century
in the Pacific*, ed. Jas. Colwell, p. 413).
2. Wm. Wilson, *A Missionary Voyage* . . . , pp. 53-54.
3. Wm. Smith, *Journal of a Voyage* . . . , pp. 137-48.
4. Ibid., pp. 149-50 for the accounts themselves, p. 151 for reference
to the reprisals.
5. A. H. Wood, *History and Geography of Tonga*, pp. 34-35.
6. J. Martin, Introduction to *Account of the Natives*, by Wm. Mariner,
p. xviii. Mariner was a junior clerk on the *Port au Prince* and one of
the few to escape the massacre. He lived for over a decade in these
islands.
7. Wood, Part IV, "The Period of Civil Wars and Disorder: 1797—
1826."
8. Jas. Morris, *A Voyage Through the Islands of the Pacific Ocean, &c.*,
pp. 83-92. Morris was clerk of the *Arrow*, met Mariner in Tonga, and
gives an account of the *Port au Prince* massacre.
9. *Quarterly Review*, April 1817, pp. 1-39.
10. Morris, p. 103.
11. *Quarterly Review*, April 1817, p. 20.
12. Ibid., p. 39.
13. Wood, p. 44. I cannot trace the primary source. There are other
important facts in Wood's undocumented history which show he used
some source unknown to me.
14. See "The Tahitian Web," this book, fnn. 67-71.
15. Leigh made an appeal for contributions in the form of trade goods
in the industrial centers of England—Manchester, Bristol, Sheffield,
Liverpool, and Birmingham—in 1820. He was in New Zealand Feb.
22, 1822.
16. Thos. West, *Ten Years in South-central Polynesia* . . . , p. 275. Apparently the matter of the Tongan mission was discussed in London
in 1820, 1822, and 1823. Leigh had formed an *Australian* missionary
auxiliary (Kenneth S. Latourette, *History of the Expansion of Christianity*, vol. 5, *The Great Century*, p. 160). However, West says that
it was the district meeting which approved Lawry's action (West,
p. 275).
17. W. Butler, "South Sea Islands," in *Cyclopedia of Missions*, ed. Harvey
Newcomb, p. 714. West gives the date as Aug. 16 (West, p. 275).
The craftsmen included Lily (carpenter), Tindall (blacksmith) and a
Marquesan interpreter. (Walter Lawry to the London committee, Oct.
16, 1822.)

18. Burton's statement that Lawry was the first ministerial missionary to Tonga is incorrect (J. W. Burton, *The First Century: The Missionary Adventure of Australian Methodism, 1855-1955*, p. 18). The *Duff* missionaries had ordained one of their artisans to keep the Tonga project within their terms of reference. The event is narrated by Wilson. When Thomas and Hutchinson arrived at Maria Bay in 1826, they were met by one of the men left behind by Lawry, and it was on his advice that they established themselves at Hihifo and not at Mua (Wood, p. 45). Moister records that both craftsmen remained in Tonga (Wm. Moister, *A History of Wesleyan Missions, &c*, p. 360).

19. Moulton, p. 418.

20. Butler, p. 714. Real conversions came at Nukualofa in 1829 after the first lot of baptisms, and by the end of that year thirty-one had actually been received into membership (West, pp. 278-79).

21. This conference is critically examined in the notes of chap. 4 ("Two Webs Meet—Samoa"), where it is more relevant than at this juncture.

22. Turner and Cross arrived Nov. 27 (Moulton, p. 419) and had a school established by the following March (Wood, p. 45). By 1829 there were over thirty full members in the Society and this was doubled in the following connexional year (West, p. 279). However, this does not indicate the numbers under instruction. Turner reported to the London committee that 1,034 were receiving instruction by Dec. 1830. This shows how the door had opened at Nukualofa (Nathaniel Turner to the London committee, May 3, 1831).

23. Butler, p. 715, from which I cite: "Immediately on his arrival, Mr. Thomas began to preach to the natives. He also opened schools for both males and females, which were well attended, chiefly by adults."

24. Ibid.; also, West, pp. 277, 358, 369.

25. Peter Vi's own narrative is preserved by West, and translated fairly literally, West, pp. 360-68.

26. The date is disputed. Moulton (p. 419) gives 1830, and since the chief was catechized from January of that year (Butler, p. 715), this date could have been correct. Wood (p. 46) and Burton (p. 20) give Aug. 7, 1831. Burton ascribed the delay to his fear of inability to maintain the standards required. Butler says Thomas baptized him "after a few months," which would probably mean in 1830. I think it possible these historians have confused two specific incidents: baptism and reception into full membership.

27. "The Missions of Polynesia." This is cited from a valuable volume of collected articles on the Pacific, bound under the title *South Sea Sketches*, at the library of the University of Oregon. The article from which this comes—"The Missions of Polynesia"—is a reprint from *Quarterly Review*, I think from its contents, of about 1853.

28. Some still in the vernacular, others fairly literally translated—e.g., those of Vi, Havea, Bulu, Bulivucu.

29. In the studies of Tahiti and New Zealand we were dependent on the reports of missionaries. Fortunately several missionaries of Tonga, Fiji, and the Solomons saw the importance of having competent indigenes write down their own records. Some of these missionaries, like Lorimer Fison and R. H. Codrington, became important names in early anthropology.

30. The narrative of Peter Vi, cited in West, pp. 366-68.

31. Peter H. Buck, *Vikings of the Sunrise*, p. 164.

32. Wood, p. 46.

33. Vi's narrative, cited in West, pp. 366-68.

34. "The Missions of Polynesia" (see n. 27, above). Two of the books reviewed in this article concerned Wesleyan missions in Tonga and Fiji as seen at a point twenty years later, when the pattern had become firmly established.

35. Basil Thomson, *The Diversions of a Prime Minister,* p. 193. The actual quotation is: "If the first missionaries were ignorant and narrow-minded, so also, according to modern lights, have the apostles seemed, but no less in their case than in that of their great prototypes was their very narrowness of vision a means of success."

36. Ibid. Not without some justification, missionaries have been blamed for forcing prohibitions on the converted peoples of the Pacific. However, the ready critics have seldom evaluated the factor they have observed, making a sweeping generalization and attributing it to foreign puritanism. But this was not always so. Prohibition, or taboo (*tapu*), was an indigenous mechanism. Today, anthropologically speaking, we would say the missionaries often used *functional substitutes.* Their tabus were often highly effective. They were usually quite meaningful. Where they failed it was not because they were tabus but because of their foreign character. It should not be overlooked that a taboo (*tambu* or *tapu*) was often imposed by the islander himself—it was an automatic response within the thought-forms of their indigenous conversion orientation.

37. Thomson's style is *typical* of many Colonial Servants of the period and accounts for their many clashes with missionaries, especially with Australian missionaries, Australia not having reached dominion status at that time. A colonial Wesleyan had more often than not some difficulty in establishing his credentials with men who wore the "old school tie," though the latter frequently built their administrative work on the linguistic research of the former, and not infrequently "prigged" (Fison's word) from the researches of missionaries for the "reminiscences" he published on retirement. This note is not just a "chip" of the writer. This was a real factor in administration-mission relations, and has invalidated much of the writing on the Pacific done by otherwise competent administrators. Basil Thomson himself is typical. His work on *The Fijians* has become a textbook. A large part of it was taken from missionaries and not acknowledged. I have been through the Fison papers and know how he felt about the matter. So much of what Thomson wrote is important, but the person who uses him as a source must remember the peculiar shade of his spectacles.

38. Basil Thomson, *Diversions,* p. 346.

39. Ibid., pp. 347-48.

40. Ibid., p. 349.

41. It is interesting that the secular writer should choose this term *enthusiasm* for this type of experience, half a century before the appearance of Father Knox's remarkable volume on the subject.

42. Butler, p. 715, Missionary Notices VII; West, pp. 159 ff.

43. The standard text and prescribed reading for Wesleyan ministerial trainees in Australia on the doctrine of sanctification was written by one of the missionaries of this Society, who died in Fiji in 1848. It remained the set text until Methodist Union at the turn of the century, having run to many editions but then going out of print. Hunt's *Letters on Entire Sanctification* still remains one of the best biblical studies of the doctrine.

44. I have developed this aspect of evangelism in the South Pacific in a monograph, *The Christian (Fiji: 1835-67),* (p. 24).

45. This conviction was first brought home to me by William Morley's article on "New Zealand" in Jas. Colwell, ed., *A Century in the Pacific* (pp. 376–407). This is in the *historical* section of the survey of a century. The Maori, who is scarcely mentioned, is a problem to the spread of the church (i.e., among the settlers). To go through this looking at the spread of Wesleyanism down to the end of the Maori wars is rather staggering in a *historical* article. The Maori was dealt with as a problem in the *sociological* section of Colwell's symposium.

46. West, p. 279.
47. Wm. Woon to the London committee, Feb. 1832.
48. N. Turner to the London committee, May 3, 1831.
49. Woon to the London committee, April, 1831. See also Woon *Journal*, Aug., 1830-Oct., 1833, Turnbull Library, Wellington, N.Z. A valuable source.
50. Woon to the London committee, Sept. 13, 1831.
51. Woon to the London committee, Feb. 1832.
52. The L.M.S. was Calvinistic and the W.M.S. Arminian. The *Duff* missionaries found one of their number an Arminian, and there was quite a tempest in a teapot until the other missionaries reduced him to submission. The incident is narrated in Wilson's journal of the voyage (1799).
53. John Thomas to the London committee, April 1831.
54. Speech of Rev. John Bowers, regarding the oratorical question in Is 66:8 and 42:4, in *Wesleyan*, 1832, p. 457. Bishop Selwyn cited the same verse when he saw the results of the Maori people movement in New Zealand.
55. Station sheet for 1832 in *Wesleyan* of that year, p. 658. Charles Tucker and Cargill were named. Actually when the time came to transfer from Tonga, Cross and Cargill went.
56. J. Egan Moulton, Jr., as cited in Colwell, p. 420.
57. If a powerful chief determined to become Christian and overrode his household in doing so, the resisters would usually do this. Several of Finau's servants were guilty of it (Butler, p. 713). It seems to me that this, rather than preventing group movement, was a natural and accepted escape mechanism in animist action patterns.
58. Missionary Notices VII, cited in Butler, p. 715.
59. H. D. Tucker to the London committee, from Missionary Notices VIII, cited in ibid., p. 716.
60. Thomson, *Diversions*, p. 349.
61. Moulton, cited in Colwell, p. 420.
62. Tucker to the London committee, cited in Butler, p. 716.
63. West, pp. 163-64.
64. Turner to the London committee, cited in Butler, p. 716.
65. Ibid.
66. This picture has been compounded from seven or eight of the sources cited in the last dozen or so pages.
67. These quotations come from Joeli Bulu's autobiography, written in the Fijian language (he spent thirty-nine years as a missionary in Fiji). *Na Noqui Tukutuku* is still preserved, but because of its length, the translated passages cited here have been much abbreviated. I have worked from the Fijian and also from Fison's English translation (1871).
68. Butler, pp. 715, 717.
69. Ibid., p. 717.
70. From Missionary Notices VIII, cited in Butler, p. 716.
71. Moulton, cited in Colwell, pp. 421-22.
72. Ibid., p. 425.
73. Thomson, *Diversions*, p. 358.
74. Both in Robert Young's official report, *The Southern World . . .* , and in his speeches upon return to England, mentioned in *Wesleyan* magazine.
75. In computing the figures for Tonga membership growth one has to eliminate Samoan and Fijian figures and the migration effects between Tonga and Fiji. Having done this, one is struck by the fact that the membership decline continued until 1858—i.e., for half a decade after the war was over. With the country at peace, and no record of

epidemic or roll-purging, one must ask why. Two factors may be held responsible for the continuity of fall. The lesser was the dispatch of Maafu to Fiji after the war with a considerable force, which became permanently lost to Tonga numerically. Even if there was a continual going and coming, the number of absentees was constant at about three thousand (Wood, p. 55). But I have no way of checking how many of these men were members and how many were new adherents just out of paganism. My knowledge of Maafu's political record and roving in Fiji, and the behavior of those "Christian" troops, would lead me to doubt if there were any members at all among them. Maafu's own record was very up and down. He was converted with each revival meeting and disciplined shortly afterward for backsliding. The Fiji missionaries rejoiced with and wept for Maafu with regular rhythm. The more likely reason was the loss of a generation through the war in Tonga.

76. Not until 1857 did the number on trial reach 150—but not for all Tonga; most of these would come from Haabai and Vavau. There must have been virtually none in Tongatabu.

77. Young, *The Southern World* . . . , p. 268.

78. West, pp. 165-66. Utui was the village.

79. Sarah H. Farmer, *Tonga and the Friendly Islands*, pp. 240-49. Here is found a long account of the 1834 revival and this incident is included.

80. Both references are cited from Young, *The Southern World* . . . , pp. 258-62. Coming from the critical Wesleyan commissioner, this shows how they viewed their mission, its purposes, and its policies. It shows a completely different approach from those who pressed for civilizing first in order to evangelize. It is interesting to note that when Young's report was reviewed by the editors of the *Wesleyan* magazine (1854), they commented that Young's observations "confirm, what everyone seems now disposed to admit,—that in these days, the civilization of a barbarous people, anterior to their acceptance of Christianity, or apart from the influence of the Gospel, is simply impossible." This review of the original edition of Young (*The Southern World* . . .) in the *Wesleyan* magazine was written for the home church, so we may take it that British Wesleyanism in general accepted this position by midcentury. This cannot be said for all the British Christian public. The Wesleyans believed in conquest by Pentecostal action, by "manifestations of Divine grace." It is a pity the term *pentecostal* has been so charged with other meanings in our times. Wesleyans prayed for and expected what Thomson called "hysterical enthusiasm."

81. Richard Amos to the London committee, Nov. 3, 1853. He says that Nukualofa was "an obscure village, with a small population of less than one hundred persons (except when fortified in time of war as a place or refuge for other villages), until the *Lotu* collected from all parts of the island a population peculiarly its own, which now amounts to upwards of one thousand two hundred."

82. A detailed account of the ceremonial and the significance of this occasion was published in the *Wesleyan* magazine for 1846 under the title "Appointment of King George Taufa'ahau as *Tuikanokubolu*."

83. Largely the work of Rev. James E. Moulton, Sr., whose biography has been written and is an essential source for any study on this later period.

84. I note that Moister reported another at Haabai at the end of the 1860s, as a result of which eight hundred members were received (Moister, p. 399). This "generational" pattern is indicated by the movements of 1834, 1846, 1859, and 1869.

85. H. Stonehewer Cooper, *Coral Lands*, 2:161-69.

CHAPTER 4: Two Webs Meet—Samoa

1. Williams changed his plans at Tonga. The trader Samuel Henry was one cause; the W.M.S. request that Fiji be left to them was another. Williams had a personal wish for comity policy. He was also aware of cultural affinities—Tahiti had more affinities with Samoa than with Fiji, though there was a bridge from Tonga to Fiji. (John Williams, *A Narrative of Missionary Adventure in the South Seas, &c.*, pp. 301-2.)

2. The documentation needs critical examination. The Wesleyan accounts, written later to justify reentry into Samoa in 1857, by principles of literary criticism appear to come from a common source. Likewise, much of the L.M.S. material in histories comes from one source. The principal statement is that of Williams, who gives an account of the conference and what they decided. This was published and in circulation at the time of tension, but no Wesleyan disputed Williams' account at the time; indeed, the Wesleyans had already acted on it in Fiji. The action of the men involved toward Takai and Fauea (see below) seems to confirm the account Williams gave. The Wesleyan committee in London was adamant about honoring this agreement—their correspondence was as considerable as it was definite. There are also numerous isolated references in correspondence before the 1857 issue arose. Furthermore, the policy outlined by Williams was the natural and common-sense one in the light of the situation as it existed at that time; however, it changed later on. I think that we must start by accepting Williams' statement. It is hard to think he would distort the fact. It is also hard to think that if he did, the Wesleyans would have let it pass at the time. The onus falls on the critic who disputes this to prove the validity of his position.

   Nathaniel Turner is said to have disputed Williams' interpretation. Turner had pointed out that Samoa was a better field for Tahiti agents than Fiji was. He admitted this in a letter seven years later. I have not seen the letter, but it does not appear to have been cited in Wesleyan interests until twenty-seven years later, when the controversy was running hot; was Turner only referring to island agents? This view creates more problems than it solves. It does not allow for the fact that Cross, the other Wesleyan at the conference, never at any time denied the agreement, and in due time he himself *acted on it* in Fiji. The Wesleyans on several occasions pointed out that they had understood the Tahiti work in Fiji was undertaken with the idea of the W.M.S. taking it over. The journals of the men involved record this. It is also difficult to see why Nathaniel Turner was silent for seven years. Actually, Turner's letter was cited by Dyson, who was writing forty-five years after the event. Dyson's case was that the reentry was justified but unwise. His case has far too many important facts omitted and does not allow for all the personal and district correspondence or for the involvements of the two Societies at home and on other mission fields. His case is based on a *developed* local situation, but the facts have to be seen in the *historic sense.*

3. James Calvert, who wrote the mission history volume of *Fiji and the Fijians,* was in the islands before the withdrawal of Peter Turner from Samoa and was a recipient of the London committee correspondence on the subject. He accepted Williams' account of the conference and says Williams was "*induced* to reconsider and rearrange" his plans, and that the L.M.S. men "abandoned their original intention." Calvert also knew Takai, the Fijian who was in Tonga at the time of that conference and who influenced the decision, and the Tahitians whom he had taken to Lakeba and then to Oneata.

4. In the L.M.S. record, cited in Williams (p. 302), it was "agreed that we should occupy the Navigator's Islands [Samoa], and that they bend their attention to the Fijis. But as we had now an opportunity of

sending them, that whenever Wesleyan missionaries should arrive from England for the Fiji Islands, they should proceed, if they pleased, to the very spot where our native missionaries were labouring."

In the W.M.S. record, an official letter from Tonga District to the London committee speaks of an *"interview"* regarding Tahiti teachers and says, *"We informed them* it was our intention" and "for the above reasons *they assured us."* Such terminology suggests the initiative had come from the Wesleyans. Two things seem clear: (1) plans for Wesleyan entry into Fiji were well advanced; and (2) they had no intention of entering Samoa. It is hard to see how Cross and Turner could bargain for the former and induce Williams and Barff to change their plans without committing themselves in some way with respect to the latter.

5. Jas. Calvert, *Fiji and the Fijians,* 2:9, fn.
6. Williams, p. 141.
7. The London committees of both societies ratified this agreement. Twenty-five years later, when the situation was different, some Wesleyan missionaries raised a question as to whether Cross and Turner had authority to determine what was an inter-Society matter. However, the official bodies did agree about it in 1834, before the Wesleyans had moved into Samoa, and this was immediately communicated to the men on the field. The chairman and the man who went to Samoa delayed until they received the "stinging" communications in Dec. 1838. It ill became them to argue a technical point on authority. From the viewpoint of dynamics, however, we ask, What is the authority of missionaries suddenly confronted with open doors for people-movement intake, doors which open across the comity agreement of the parent Society? This is a problem in our own day.
8. He had written to the directors about Samoa. The incident involving his wife is told in Williams, pp. 141 ff.
9. Ibid., pp. 324 ff.
10. W. Butler, "South Sea Islands," in *Cyclopedia of Missions,* ed. Harvey Newcomb, p. 702; Williams, p. 324; Richard Lovett, *The History of the London Missionary Society,* p. 288.
11. Williams, pp. 325-26; Butler, p. 702.
12. Williams, pp. 326 ff; the passage cited is on pp. 327-28; see also p. 355 for further information on the character of Fauea and his wife, and also Williams' letter, cited in Lovett, pp. 286-89.
13. Williams, pp. 306-7, 330; Butler, p. 702.
14. According to Butler, p. 702.
15. Williams, p. 330.
16. Ibid., p. 354.
17. Ibid., pp. 351, 421 ff.
18. Ibid., p. 327.
19. Ibid., p. 329.
20. This was a considerable concession. The building was public property and used for amusements, dancing, and all public discussions. Malietoa said that they were to use it for teaching and worship, and upon his return from the war, he would erect for them what buildings they needed. (Williams, p. 343 and fn.)
21. Ibid., p. 353.
22. Ibid., p. 356.
23. Ibid., p. 341. See also the section on the bearing of social structure on church-planting in the anthropological unit of this vol. (chap. 5, "Cultural Determinants and the Acceptance of Christianity").
24. I mean permanent church-planting in which a white missionary had established his teachers under a Samoan chief. There had been Wesleyan outreaches from Tonga before this. See section on Wesleyan origins, pp. 54-59.

25. Williams, chap. xxiv; Butler, p. 703.
26. Williams, pp. 400-401.
27. Ibid., p. 413; Butler, p. 703.
28. The port is not given. There were some Christians on Tutuila (see n. 17, above) at Leone.
29. Williams, pp. 414-15.
30. Lovett, p. 375; Butler, p. 703.
31. Lovett says 23,000 by 1838 (p. 375).
32. Ibid., p. 380. I suspect these were people taken over from the abandoned Wesleyan cause, which means transfer and not conversion growth.
33. Wm. Wyatt Gill, cited in Lovett, p. 374.
34. Lovett, pp. 384-87.
35. Ibid., p. 389.
36. John E. Erskine, *Journal of a Cruise Among the Islands of the Western Pacific, &c.*, p. 83.
37. Many Tonga reports were published in the *Missionary Register* and the *Wesleyan* magazine. Statistics of the 1850s are in the minutes of the Australasian Conference.
38. Benjamin Danks, "Samoa," in *A Century in the Pacific*, ed. Jas. Colwell, p. 483.
39. A letter from Tonga to the London committee, June 25, 1829, reveals the thinking on the field. There had been conversions at Nukualofa (Thos. West, *Ten Years in South-central Polynesia . . .*, pp. 278-79), what the Fijian missionaries of the same Society called "a movement among the dry bones." The reference in the Tonga letter is: "If Tonga [i.e., Tongatabu] becomes Christianized we have good reason to believe that not only the Hapaiis and Vavau will receive the truth, but we shall obtain access to the Fiji and Navigators' Islands. There are men at Tonga from each of these places and from what we can learn respecting the inhabitants they are numerous and very mild, excepting the Fijian people." The hope of expansion was there, the atmosphere of expectation, and the awareness of differences between Fiji and Samoa. This was prior to the Tonga discussions of 1830.
40. Danks, p. 484.
41. *Tonga Report* for 1832-33 for the London committee. The committee passed the matter back to the men on the field. At this stage they had not yet made the official agreement with the other London committee. Very shortly afterward, with more facts, they decided against expansion into Samoa.
42. I have these facts from Dyson (p. 14), but he is citing a letter of Peter Turner, three decades after the events.
43. These are the figures which Turner recorded as having found on his arrival in Samoa in June 1835.
44. Williams, pp. 471 ff.
45. In October and June respectively, 1835. The L.M.S. men arrived in June 1836. The fact that the Wesleyans occupied Samoa before Fiji is surprising in view of the long time they had been preparing for the Fiji mission and the fact that the designated men were in Tonga for some time. The transport to Fiji was much more difficult to obtain and very expensive because of the greater risks involved. Even so, they did lay themselves open to misinterpretation by occupying Samoa first under the circumstances.
46. Dyson, p. 19, and Danks, p. 484.
47. Dyson, p. 19, (citing a letter from the *Wesleyan Chronicle*, Feb. 11, 1864).
48. Danks, p. 485.
49. Dyson, p. 27.
50. Ibid., p. 27.

51. A set of typescript copies of these documents is in the Methodist Mission Archives in Fiji. They are severe in that the committee had actually approved the men on the field making the decision in the light of the 1832 decision (see n. 41, above), and the men acted on the assumption that the Holy Spirit had opened the door and the L.M.S. had not acted. To the W.M.S. in London, it seemed better to hand over this opening than to fall out with the L.M.S., which pressed the "gentlemen's agreement." The W.M.S. and L.M.S. were neighbors in many parts of the world. The severity, however, was the only way of dislodging Turner, and it was a rebuke for refusal to obey official instruction from London. If this happened in other places, it could have meant chaos in the central administration.

52. At least they should have been preserved in Tonga or in London. It was a serious matter to destroy official records, especially when he subsequently produced his own personal copies, and cited the figures that were no longer officially preserved. It was indeed a strange way of *terminating* an issue. This destruction of the records is mentioned in Sarah H. Farmer, *Tonga and the Friendly Islands*, pp. 280-81; Martin Dyson, *My Story of Samoan Wesleyanism* . . . , p. 29; and Danks, p. 487.

53. In 1830 Williams had left eight teachers, dispersed as Malietoa decreed: six on Savaii and two on Upolu, in the political segments in which he was particularly interested. To him these appointments were partly status symbols. "My foreigners must not be scattered among other tribes." It was because of this that Tuinaulu of Satupaitea went to Tonga to make his appeal to the Wesleyans. I do not think that either party of missionaries realized at first that their enthusiastic receptions were based on the personal rivalries of the Samoan chiefs. Though their records preserve the evidence, I doubt if they realized its significance. (See Dyson, p. 13.)

54. Danks, p. 487. This is typical island oratory. In one sense the Samoans, Tongans, and Tahitians were all one people. In another sense they were different. Nor does the orator allow for the fact that for many years before this, Tonga and Samoa had been at war.

55. Alaiasa of Falefa, Sosuia of Falealili, Samuela of Vailele. The proposition was put up by the *tulafale*, Masua. Leaders' meetings were continuing at Manono, Atua, Tuamasaga, and Tutuila. (Dyson, p. 33.)

56. Dyson, p. 34; Danks, p. 488.

57. Dyson, p. 35.

58. Ibid., pp. 35-36; Danks, p. 489.

59. Ibid., p. 490.

60. At one point of time his statistics had been better but they fell through his political activities and then remained static. Many Tongan teachers both in Samoa and in Fiji spoiled their work by meddling in local politics. Dyson (rather unconvincingly) argues that Samoa would all have become Wesleyan but for this. Political segments were always on the move. Some returned to the L.M.S. Others poined the Roman Catholic cause, which had now entered the scene. In Manono and Tutuila Wesleyanism virtually disappeared (Dyson, pp. 36-37). In 1847-48 political disturbances led to war and Wesleyan growth ceased. Some returned to their old pagan ways.

61. He addressed a breakfast meeting in Sydney on the matter in 1855 and secured a petition for a plan of reopening the cause abandoned by the British Wesleyans. The upshot was that he (Thomas himself) was appointed to visit Samoa, with Latusele as his fellow investigator, and to make a report. Thomas did not speak Samoan and used island interpreters who were themselves interested parties. His observations were made in the short time the *John Wesley* was in port in 1855. He refrained from obtaining any information from the L.M.S. missionaries

in the group. All the witnesses for either side were partisan. What kind of an inquiry was this? Dyson, who was later sent to reestablish the work, was quite candidly critical at all these points. (Ibid., pp. 46-47.)

62. This also was Dyson's conviction. He had mentioned New Guinea. The entry of the A.W.M.S. into Samoa was one of the first actions of the new Australasian Conference within its new autonomy. The conference was established in 1854, and this decision made in 1856 on a basis of Thomas's partisan report. The Society subsequently extended its work in Melanesia: New Britain, Papua, and the Solomon Islands. Dyson thought these areas should have been explored in 1857, instead of Samoa (ibid., p. 49).

63. The attempt to justify reentry by discrediting the original 1830 discussion was pressed at the time of reentry. It does not stand up to critical examination. The comity agreement was made in London. Latusele's appointment and ordination were both in defiance of that agreement. This action kept the wound open and made reentry inevitable. The only legal justification for "reentry" is that a completely new body (A.W.M.S.) was entering the field and therefore it was not a *re*entry at all.

64. Dyson's own terminology is retained in italics (ibid., p. 48). The use of Dyson by Danks must be treated with caution. Faced with the promotional interests of the Samoa mission in 1914, he cited the "justification" but not the inexpediency.

65. A. W. Murray, *Forty Years Mission Work in Polynesia & New Guinea*, is the primary source. See pp. 121, 122, 130, 131, 132-33, 135-36, 139, 140, 141, 142, 155 ff, and 166. The dates cited are of occasions described by Murray as an eyewitness. No doubt there are others that he did not actually observe himself. A secondary source that gives much of this information from the same primary source is N. A. Rowe, *Samoa Under the Sailing Gods*.

66. The Scottish awakenings were taking place in Kelso and other places (including Jedburgh, Murray's hometown). Revivals in the Perth and Dundee areas continued for roughly the same period of time as those in Samoa, where Murray recorded them as beginning in 1839, at its peak in 1840, and continuing at a slower tempo during 1841 and 1842. Murray, however, is specific in describing the Scottish revivals as "what we afterwards learned" (Murray, p. 125). There were many other fields ripe unto harvest in this way at that time, but the local stimulus in the case of Samoa seems to have been an overflow of the Tongan movement.

67. Ibid., p. 130.

68. Ibid., p. 156. This reference (one of many of its kind) was to events at Leone, Tutuila, June 3, 1840, where the movement had already been in progress for seven months (ibid., p. 155). The congregation was comprised of about a thousand people, and the flood burst loose during the sermon. Many critics of missions say that preaching did not get responses. In Tonga, Samoa, and Fiji it certainly did. Seven months earlier, Murray had met this for the first time, while he was expounding Scripture texts (Nov. 4, 1839), ". . . when to my astonishment and almost alarm (I had never before witnessed anything of that kind) a number of our company were seized with overpowering convictions . . . became more and more ungovernable. . . . It was vain to attempt to restrain or calm them by words, their distress was evidently too deep. . . . Eight were thus affected—three men and five women" (ibid., p. 123). On March 1, also at Leone, there were waves of repentance during the prayer, the sermon, and the Lord's Supper. "Many were completely overcome. Ten or twelve sank down exhausted, and had to be carried out of the chapel in a state of complete prostration. The afternoon service was of a similar character" (ibid., p. 141).

69. Ibid., pp. 132, 135-36. Murray admits the caution.
70. Ibid., pp. 130, 142, 143, 156, 166, and 173-74 for specific cases of transformed lives, which stood up to the test of time fairly well.
71. Ibid., p. 158. Mrs. G. A. Lundie, ed., *Missionary Life in Samoa . . .*, an independent primary source, confirms this account with much detail (pp. 86-87, 113-21, 160-63).
72. Murray, p. 160; see also Lundie, p. 121.
73. Murray has numerous references, as, for example, the following: "One noticeable thing connected with it was the large number of *men* who were overcome by their feelings. *They* were sooner overcome, and in larger numbers than the women" (Murray, p. 162; italics his).
74. In Murray's earlier days Maunga was "the villain of the piece." He was converted June 15. "The proud, haughty Maunga, who has so recently acted such an outrageous part, was among the number . . . who fell under the arrows of conviction. 'Saul was among the prophets.' He was carried out of the chapel in a state of complete prostration" (ibid., p. 163).
75. Ibid., p. 163.
76. Ibid., pp. 165-68.
77. In Tutuila, for instance, where there should have been a large membership intake, there had been only 45 to set off against the losses of 30. Although the largest category in the breakdown of losses was "by death,," the second was "by suspension" and these were more than half as many as the number who had died. For every five new members admitted, one old one was suspended. (See Murray, p. 225.)
78. Ibid., pp. 223, 237. It is clear that the L.M.S. men suspected the movement. Murray was greatly relieved that a senior man, Heath, could witness it with him and pronounce an opinion that "it was of God" (ibid., pp. 135-36). He also gave reasons for the caution: (1) the danger of bringing folk rapidly into church status was the risk of inducing an unfavorable state of mind (pride, I presume); and (2) others might act in a hypocritical way to obtain notice (ibid., p. 121). If these were serious reasons (and I believe they were), they were far too cautious—even distrustful—of their converts. Yet in the same paragraph Murray, after examining twenty-eight candidates, found them "truly awakened" for the most part.
79. "Tonga Reports," *Australian Wesleyan Conference Minutes*, 1856.
80. Dyson, pp. 53-54.
81. The L.M.S. in Samoa had a good missionary staff, educational system, and program of printing, all at work before midcentury (John E. Erskine, *Journal of a Cruise . . .*, pp. 87-88). Theological training was attended to at Malua by two missionaries, with courses on religion, leadership, Bible, philosophy, logic, and general subjects. Yet when we examine their statistics just before the Wesleyan reentry (so as to eliminate any effect that event might have had), we find 41,000 persons at worship, according to Heath. Of these, only 2,141 had been fully received as members (see Butler, pp. 704-5, compiled from official reports) and this twenty years after the people movement. This member/adherent ratio of 5.2 percent is the poorest I know in the Pacific in the last century. In view of the fact that this mission did correct many of the faults of their earlier experiments in Tahiti (e.g., more direct use of Scripture, stress on the use of the vernacular, etc.) and had the advantages of an early people movement, which called for pastors and teachers rather than evangelists, the figure calls for some explanation. It seems to me that their Puritanism and caution were excessive in the extreme.
82. Erskine, pp. 99-100.
83. Ibid., p. 83.
84. Walter Lawry collected a great number of these testimonies and recorded them in his itineration volumes (*Friendly & Feejee Islands*;

Second Missionary Visit to Friendly & Feejee Islands, &c.) and also in his New Zealand journal in *Wesleyan* magazine. The function of the Wesleyan love feast was to develop the member's ability to testify of his own experience.

85. The actual figure for 1862 was 4,962 (Tonga report and statistics, in *Australasian Conference Minutes* for 1862).

86. Ibid., for 1858.

87. Ibid., for 1859.

88. Ibid., for 1860 and 1861.

89. Ibid., for 1862.

90. Donald A. McGavran, *The Bridges of God: A Study in the Strategy of Missions*; see section "Stages in Christianization," pp. 13-16.

91. Written to Dyson from Salelologa, Savaii, after a meeting of the chiefs and leaders, Mar. 1, 1858. Turner had translated thirteen chapters of Matthew into very imperfect Samoan. His followers considered the L.M.S. scriptures apocryphal. The differences were so great that Dyson brought the Wesleyans to accept the L.M.S. version. The same applied to some of Turner's hymns. There were also features about holy days. When Dyson tried to bring Christian forms and devotional aids into line, some of the other camp began to "gloat" and the Wesleyan Samoans felt they were being served very "humble pie" (Dyson, p. 58).

The tragedy of this spirit of rivalry is also seen in their attitudes toward missionary appointments, which provided a rhythm of elation and depression. When the Wesleyan, Rigg, had to leave soon after his arrival, the members of that denomination were thoroughly depressed, especially since the new L.M.S. men arrived about the same time.

"Their ensign floated in the breeze . . . ours drooped at the mast-head." When Brown arrived to establish Wesleyan theological training, the rivals having predicted there would be no more Wesleyans, the elation-depression emotions were reversed. Wesleyans "were jubiliant"; the others "put on sackcloth." These are actual terms from the primary sources, and I cite them to show what can happen when rival denominations enter a rivalry-oriented society.

92. There is in the Archives of the Methodist Overseas Missions in Sydney a letter-book of correspondence to Tonga, 1856-58 (lot 30). Letters written by the secretary Eggleston show quite clearly that the church was hard put to find a man for Samoa and the appointment was made under extreme pressure from the District. The mind of the missionary leaders in Australia was generally against opening work in Samoa, both for staffing reasons and on principle. Eggleston described the position as "delicate and painful" and thought the Tonga chairman should learn to speak Samoan and go there himself and persuade the Wesleyans to join in with the L.M.S. (Eggleston to Dyson, Dec. 18, 1857).

In 1858, after Dyson's arrival, Eggleston had a long session with Murray (L.M.S.) and held to his views. Whatever he thought of the original decision, he believed the unhappy situation had been brought about by Turner's unwillingness to cooperate. Perhaps when Turner's statistics reached London the committee ought to have reversed its decision, but they had not done this and that should have been the end of the matter. Thus Dyson was not encouraged to expand his work. If the Wesleyans had to remain in Samoa, it should be a policy of peaceful coexistence.

It is significant that the Australian Conference refused to probe the matter further, but left things to the Tonga District. Eggleston did not agree "that it would be irresponsible to leave the Samoa Methodists without instruction [Dyson's claim] because *I believe their prejudices* to have been created by one of our agents while smarting under a sense of what he deemed to be a deep injustice done to him by his

own and the other committee" (Eggleston's letter, Mar. 25, 1858).
On April 13, Eggleston confirmed this in another letter, sent to the
District, in a form which suggests to me that the Conference had not
been at all confident about the whole business.

Eggleston's opinion is supported by a secular reference in Chas.
Wilkes (*Narrative of United States Exploring Expedition during the
Years 1838-1842*, 1:188), where, in 1838 (the year of withdrawal), the
naval officer said that the disagreement between the two bodies was
settled amicably and added, "Only one individual was uncharitable
about it."

93. Dyson, p. 59.
94. Ibid., p. 62.
95. Ibid., p. 67.
96. Ibid., p. 68. By such gifts as a fine whaleboat, for example.
97. Ibid., p. 73.

CHAPTER 5: CULTURAL DETERMINANTS AND THE ACCEPTANCE OF CHRISTIANITY

1. Robert H. Lowie, *Primitive Religion*, p. 75.
2. Ruth Benedict, "Religion," in *General Anthropology*, ed. Franz Boas.
   Her reference reads: "In some cultures, like Samoa, supernaturalism
   is at a minimum, while in others, as for instance in New Zealand,
   which belongs to the same culture area, the concern with the supernatural is almost omnipresent and is deeply felt." Annexation, colonization, and the great alienation of lands in New Zealand, leading ultimately to war, stimulated supernaturalism as a defense mechanism.
   The whole complex of Maori religion and magic was revived to fight
   the invader, as we have seen in the chapter on New Zealand (chap. 2,
   "The Maori Web"), in which I have described some of the neopagan
   nativism. It was the sum of these historic events that weighted Maori
   culture toward supernaturalism.

   In the case of Samoa, there was no annexation at this time, land
   alienation was voluntary, the cultural structure was preserved, and
   church organization and education fitted into the culture pattern.
   There was no competition between Polynesian and foreigner. Events
   fortified the social patterns, which were weighted toward prestige and
   status. There was no need to call on supernaturalism as a defensive
   mechanism—though it was there all the time. Even in the more sober
   L.M.S. meetings, emotionalism ran high at times, causing the Calvinist
   missionaries some concern, as the records of Murray and Lundie show
   clearly. Rowe cited half a dozen pages of this (N. A. Rowe, *Samoa
   Under the Sailing Gods*, pp. 52-57), describing it as *flummery*.

   Benedict failed to allow for differences caused by historical events—
   accidents (S. F. Nadel, *The Foundations of Social Anthropology*, pp.
   16-17).
3. Benedict theorized on data supplied by Margaret Mead ("A Lapse of
   Animism Among a Primitive People," in *Psyche*, pp. 72-77); yet it
   seems to me that Mead was more aware of the real situation. She
   was presenting her concept of "accidental cultural pre-occupation" and
   reported how Christianity had *not* destroyed animistic attitudes, but
   had validated the supernaturalist viewpoint for the Samoans. "Native
   pastors share the superstitions of their flocks" (ibid., p. 73). She
   demonstrated their preoccupation with social arrangements, status,
   and relationships, and added that it was not the work itself that was
   important, but *who* was participating. Old taboos became trappings
   of etiquette. Sacrifices disappear but feasts remain. At the power
   level the old religion has gone, but taboos are still set up to operate
   against present-day Samoans who steal. Her theme is that animism is

dying (and supernaturalism), not because of education and science, but because of cultural preoccupation. Then she tells of some interesting survivals. At the level of mat-making, carving, etc., which all bear on prestige and status, the emphasis is on the number of mats one gets at the mourning feast presentation; but at the level of dye-preparation, full pre-Christian supernaturalist rites are used. Mead is right in her claim of preoccupation as a factor in change, and right about the supernaturalist survivals, but wrong if she thinks that Christianity did little to destroy animist attitudes.

4. Felix M. Keesing, *Modern Samoa: Its Government and Changing Life,* p. 400.

5. Ibid., p. 48.

6. This is Keesing's definition, and undoubtedly does represent a structural entity of some kind and an indigenous conceptualization. Grattan apparently sees a village as a planned unit, comprising two lines of houses and a village green, and today at least one church (F. J. H. Grattan, *An Introduction to Samoan Custom,* p. 57). Is a village a number of people with a specific relationship to each other, or a planned locality of habitations?

7. Kraemer (cited in Keesing, p. 48) provides the following statistics of Samoan villages: Savaii, 36; Upolu, 44; Tutuila, c. 36; Manua, 6—total, c. 122. Official figures cited by Keesing were: Western Samoa, 170; American Samoa, 66—total, 236. If we accept Grattan's definition we must allow for some traditional clustering of villages. If we accept Keesing's we must allow for some segmentation.

8. Grattan, p. 10 and fn., pp. 16, 17.

9. Keesing, pp. 48 ff, where the names and locations of the old divisions are given, and where further information is supplied about the mutual relationships of the villages within these larger political units. He also shows that villages and subdistricts had specific privileges, roles, and duties: Where would the capital be? On whose square would assemblies be held? Who would provide the orators? Who would lead in war? Who would provide the fighting canoes?

10. Lowie, p. 76.

11. Ibid., pp. 77-80.

12. Julius Lips, "Government," in *General Anthropology,* ed. Franz Boas, p. 524.

13. Grattan, pp. 135, 139.

14. Ibid., p. 19.

15. Ibid., p. 16; Lowie, pp. 79-80.

16. Grattan, p. 19.

17. Ibid., pp. 20, 134-35. Other priest groups included diviners (ibid., p. 135), custodians of sacred objects (ibid., p. 134), workers of craft rituals, etc.

18. Margaret Mead, "The Role of the Individual in Samoan Culture," in *Source Book in Anthropology,* ed. A. L. Kroeber and T. T. Watterman, pp. 555-56. Unfortunately, in this worthwhile article, Mead generalizes from "a point of time." She may be right but some of her points are not verified as generalizations.

19. Ibid., pp. 557-58.

20. Ibid., pp. 560-61. If Mead is right we should have in Samoa a church which is capable of evolving a new organizational pattern in two decades, rather than a conservative body that ripens slowly for a dramatic change at a point of time. I am not sure that she is right. The matter needs further study.

21. Grattan, pp. 13-14, 20.

22. This custom (*mavaega*) helped to prevent disputes and segmentation of a group when candidates for succession were of equal merit. Neither would feel disposed to lead a party against the will of the deceased, whose spirit could be angered thereby (Grattan, p. 14).

23. A good model of a preserved tradition of an ancient dispute of this kind, which shows several mechanisms for maintaining equilibrium at work, is in George Pratt, "The Genealogy of the Kings and Princes of Samoa," in *Proceedings . . .* , p. 658. Cases of clans selecting a chief, severing connection with the parent tribe, and joining another, were apparently not rare. Ella says it happened "occasionally" (Samuel Ella, "Samoa," in *Proceedings . . .* , p. 631).

24. Keesing devotes a good deal of space to Samoan individualism within the communalism, in economic life, in land-holding, in the *matai* system, and in education (Keesing, pp. 144, 247-51, 255, 269, 273-90, 326, 333-37, 340, 345-51, 434, 437-39). This supports my claim that communal societies do not engage in mass movements and activities, but are multi-individual. This charge has often been made by critics of people movements from paganism to Christianity. I have devoted a chapter to this matter elsewhere in this book (chap. 7, "The Structure and Validity of People Movements").

25. Robert Mackenzie Watson, *History of Samoa*, p. 35.

26. In *A Brief Account of Methodist Missions . . .* , officially published after Methodist Union in Australia, to acquaint the other groups in the union of Wesleyan missionary activity (p. 5). See also John G. Wheen, "The Mission of Australian Methodism," in *Australian Methodist Missionary Review* (Oct. 4, 1913), p. 9.

27. Martin Dyson, *My Story of Samoan Wesleyanism . . .* , p. 27.

28. British missionaries all over the South Pacific were jittery after the Tahiti affair. Even a rumor of the proximity of a French warship caused the deepest concern. A good, brief, unbiased and officially documented account is found in John M. Ward, *British Policy of the South Pacific (1786–1893)* (chap. xii, pp.127-37). For the real missionary reactions to the affair, one has to go to the mission sources. Thomas Heath (L.M.S., Samoa) sent a memorandum to the Foreign Office on French activities and intentions in the Pacific. Britain appointed a consul in the Pacific in 1843. In 1844 Heath's predictions about Gambia and Wallis and Futuna came to pass. But the policy of minimum intervention was reaffirmed in 1848. George Pritchard's *The Missionary's Reward . . .* (pp. ix–xxxvi) has a vigorous statement. Pritchard figured prominently in consular affairs. After the French occupation of Huahine, Borabora, and Raiatéa (1845), the L..M.S. officially protested to the Foreign Office. Treaties were made and not honored. Pritchard's warnings were justified when "France seized New Caledonia in 1853 and took the British government by surprise" (Ward, p. 146). Many private letters of British missionaries show their widespread fear lest all their labor be lost through the "bishop in the gunboat." A set of letters, written by Joseph Waterhouse from different stations on his voyage through New Zealand, Tonga, and Fiji, reflects this tension (Jos. Waterhouse, typescript copies of correspondence, Meth. Overseas Mission Archives, Fiji). In some localities (Tonga, Samoa, Fiji, etc.) the Roman Catholic priests attached themselves to rival segments. This usually meant a rebel unit, because Protestant missions tried to approach people through their accepted chiefs. Sometimes they worked on disgruntled units like the Wesleyan groups in Samoa. In Samoa they also won the support of the chief, Mataafa. He was a rival of Malietoa, who supported the L.M.S. and tried to keep Christianity for his own area of power. (Watson, p. 35; Benjamin Danks, "Samoa," in *A Century in the Pacific*, ed. Jas. Colwell, p. 485.) The Wesleyan Turner had also linked up with anti-Malietoa factions (Dyson, p. 27), but none were as adept at this as the priests. Rivalry continued "with honour" and the prestige of having a missionary (Richard Lovett, *The History of the London Missionary Society: 1795–1895*, p. 383). A very important collection of

Pritchard documents on the French affair in Tahiti: is housed at the Turnbull Library, Wellington, N.Z. (G. Pritchard, "Aggression of the French at Tahiti," Ref. 9MS/184/P). Another set of the Waterhouse correspondence is also at the same repository (Ref. Ms. Papers 203). The originals are in the Mitchell Library, Sydney.

29. Witness Heath's statistics of member-adherent ratio, cited in chap. 4, "Two Webs Meet."
30. Dyson, pp. 55-58.
31. Grattan, pp. 10-11.
32. Margaret Mead, *Coming of Age in Samoa*, p. 45.
33. Erich Schultz, "Samoan Family Law and Law of Inheritance," in *Journal of the Polynesian Society*, pp. 43-44.
34. Grattan, p. 11.
35. Ibid., p. 16.
36. Ibid., p. 17.
37. Ibid., p. 21.
38. Schultz, p. 45. He also says that the more outspoken *matai* are regarded as the representatives of the others, and are called on by the others. Even so, they know they have the backing of the others before they speak. Thus they are really advocates.
39. Grattan, p. 12.
40. Ibid., p. 154.
41. During the decade of the second world war, four hundred new *matai* were created (Grattan, p. 156).
42. Ibid., p. 139.
43. Dyson, p. 32.
44. George Turner, *Samoa: A Hundred Years Ago and Long Before, &c.*, p. 18.
45. Laulii, *The Story of Laulii, a Daughter of Samoa*, ed. Wm. H. Barnes, p. 39.
46. William Wyatt Gill was a prolific writer and a good researcher. For much early Polynesian material he is the only source. He has a score or more entries in Taylor's *Pacific Bibliography*, and his personal archival material has been appraised in the *Journal of the Polynesian Society*. Dr. Turner's work on Samoa is the best collection of ethnological data on Samoa as it was in the early days. It is pure description without speculation or interpretation. He did other writing also. These men, with others like Fison, Fox, and Codrington, were all missionaries who laid the foundations for the study of Pacific anthropology.
47. This viewpoint was developed by Rowe in *Samoa Under the Sailing Gods*, where a chapter is devoted to each of Williams' voyages. It is true that Williams did repeatedly describe himself in these terms (which led some other Pacific missionaries to question his humility). In his *A Narrative of Missionary Enterprises* . . . (p. 339), he and Barff were "two great English chiefs." On p. 414 (ibid.) he reported being told that "a great chief from the white man's country, named Williams . . ." had done certain things. Williams accepted the prestige system and his place in it. This suited the Samoans and gained acceptance for Christianity.
48. The Samoan aristocracy was comprised of three families—Malietoa, Mataafa, and Muangututi—but the kingship existed only when one individual held all five titles (*Ao*), each gift of a different province. The kingship (*O-le-Tupu*) had been with the Muangututi, but after the death of this king the position had been vacant until usurped by Tamafainga, then war priest of Manono. This explains the prominence of Manono at the time (Rowe, p. 61).
49. Lips, p. 524.
50. Mead, *Coming of Age*, p. 67. She says, "His title may be taken away

from him when he is old, or if he is inefficient, but a lower title will be given him, that he may sit and drink his kava with his former associates." See also Grattan, p. 16.

51. Grattan described the possibilities of expulsion and ostracism for a *matai*, for not accepting the unanimous decision of the *fono*. His family with him can only be restored by an apology and an offering. He is not bound to leave the village, however, nor is the village bound to restore him (Grattan, pp. 17-18).

52. Ibid., p. 18.

53. Ibid., pp. 18-19.

54. Dyson, pp. 27-28.

55. Ibid., p. 76. However, this was not confined to the Wesleyans. There were so many converts in the revivals that only a few were selected and admitted at each church meeting, for reason of caution (Mrs. Lundie, *Missionary Life in Samoa . . .* , pp. 84-85). Many were kept back "lest their ministers should be entirely overwhelmed" (ibid., p. 83).

56. This value still survives on the social level. Keesing (p. 30) points out, however, that this distribution of wealth is reciprocal. It is, in fact, a mechanism of distribution—the family of the bride gives mats and women's goods, that of the bridegroom supplies the pigs and food (and nowadays money): "My chief gives me goods and entertainments today, knowing that when the appropriate occasion arises I will return him my wealth and service." Even so the organization, conduct of the festivities, and psychological experiences earn him prestige and contentment.

57. Generosity is simple because there is little need to store very much for the future, and because people have the capacity to produce more than their needs. "People with no worries about the future see no need to accumulate to the exclusion of others," says Ruth Bunzel ("The Economic Organization of Primitive Peoples," in *General Anthropology*, ed. Franz Boas) of the Samoans. But with the coming of Western money economy, generosity (even in church collections) can mean giving away tomorrow's breakfast.

58. E. S. Craighill Handy, *Polynesian Religion*, p. 321.

59. Ibid., pp. 323-28.

60. Turner, p. 77.

61. Ibid., pp. 23-77.

62. Ibid.; these examples come from pp. 26-31.

63. Grattan, pp. 130-33.

64. Turner, pp. 52-54.

65. J. B. Stair, "Jottings on the Methodology and Spirit-lore of Old Samoa," in *Journal of the Polynesian Society*, pp. 33-57.

66. Grattan, p. 131.

67. In the Fijian language the verbal root *liā* means to change the bodily form. By using this as a prefix with a noun like stone, wood, or man, we have *liāvatu, liākau,* or *liātamata,* indicating the kind of body involved in an incarnation.

68. For a detailed summary of references to Tangaloa in Samoan contexts, see Robert W. Williamson, *A Missionary Voyage to the South Pacific Ocean . . .* ,pp. 78-84.

69. Turner, pp. 36-44; cf. Williamson, pp. 75-76.

70. Williams, p. 410, also fn.

71. Ibid., p. 327.

72. Ibid., pp. 410-11.

73. Ibid., pp. 412-13 (Tutuila episodes).

74. Ibid., p. 415 (episodes in Leone district).

75. Examples are easy to find. The writer was recently engaged in research in the Solomon Islands and observed that in the village of Kidu a group which had broken with the local church had assumed a title

and wore a flower in the hair as a symbol of their new allegiance. In the island of Malaita, the islanders felt they had to categorize anthropologists, who did not seem to fit any known behavior patterns. Now they are spoken of as "custom men," and are no longer a problem because they have entity. That entity is accepted. The formation of entity is important in the emergence of an indigenous church.

76. Williams, p. 417.
77. Ibid., p. 418.
78. Ibid., p. 425.
79. Ibid., p. 418.
80. Ibid., p. 431.
81. Ibid., p. 448.
82. The families of Mataafa of Amaile and Letufuga of Safotualafai. Both Stair and Turner made note of the practice. See also Grattan, p. 130, fn.
83. Grattan, p. 133.
84. Stuebel is the writer, cited by Grattan in fn. on p. 131.
85. The question arises as to whether an *aitu* was ever a fetish. I think not, but Williams gave an account of a convict who took part in Samoan wars, using his firearms with deadly effect. After his death, the chief whom he served had his fractured head pieced together and sewn with coconut fiber, making it into an *aitu*, which he worshiped. I wonder if it was Williams himself who categorized this as an *aitu*. What word did the chief use—was it *aitu*, or *tupua*, or something else? Did he deify the spirit of the convict, with this as his shrine, or was it a sacred object? (See Williams, pp. 462-64.)
86. W. Butler, "South Sea Islands," in *Cyclopedia of Missions*, ed. Harvey Newcomb, p. 704; also Williams, pp. 432-36.
87. Williams, p. 435.
88. Ibid., p. 434.
89. Ibid., pp. 436-37. In this case the *aitu* was rescued by some teachers, who followed in another canoe. After they had disposed of it, it ultimately found its way into the British Museum. The disposal of this kind of material to missionaries and sea captains did permit the preservation of much cultural material, but it was never as effective as a power demonstration of a change of faith.
90. Laulii, pp. 251-52.
91. Williams, p. 351.
92. Turner, p. 18.
93. E. B. Tylor, Foreword, p. ix, in Turner.
94. E. N. Hawker, L.M.S. missionary in Tutuila, cited in Jas. M. Alexander, *The Islands of the Pacific: From the Old to the New*, p. 218.

CHAPTER 6: CIVILIZING OR EVANGELIZING?

1. John Williams to his father, April 23, 1822, cited in *Wesleyan*, 1823.
2. Journal entry Dec. 31, 1798, cited in Richard Lovett, *The History of the London Missionary Society: 1795-1895*, p. 161.
3. Jas. Buller, *Forty Years in New Zealand*, p. 262. Miss Tucker says it was an "increasing conviction among them all" (*The Southern Cross and Southern Crown*, p. 89).
4. J. B. Marsden, *Life and Work of Samuel Marsden*, pp. 208-9.
5. *The Leisure Hour*, Nov. 1883, cited in John S. Moffat, *The Lives of Robert & Mary Moffat*, pp. 372-73.
6. To cite one of many examples, Dr. Coulter, surgeon of H. M. S. *Stratford*, visited the islands and wrote in a manner calculated to appeal to conservative Englishmen. After allowing for possible criticism, he spoke of "transition from heathenism in all its barbarism to mild Christianity." He said, "One could at once know and feel where the missionary had been," and that "the power of Christianity had completely

altered the character of the native." He discussed how conditions were
bad "where the shipping lies," and that Papeete was worse than the
rest of Tahiti. His work was cited and reviewed with approval in an
article, "The Missions of Polynesia," in the *Quarterly Review,* which
also supported the policy in question. Much the same thing was written
by Charles Darwin in *The Voyage of the Beagle.*

7. The House of Commons published a factual report about New Zea-
    land in 1838. The New Zealand Company was established in 1839
    (after several failures) and a shipload of settlers sailed in May. The
    queen's sovereignty was proclaimed in 1840.

8. The Bishop of Australia visited New Zealand in 1838 and reported the
    need for planting the Church of England in "the full integrity of its
    system" (*Missionary Register,* 1839, p. 552).

    Upon the declaration of sovereignty, the C.M.S. pressed for the ap-
    pointment of a bishop, and offered a subsidy of six hundred pounds
    per year to his support for the time being (Eugene Stock, ed., *History
    of the Church Missionary Society . . . ,* 1:413).

9. M. Russell, *Polynesia . . . ,* p. 5.

10. Ibid., pp. 372-73.

11. Ibid., pp. 419-20.

12. A good example is the writing of Henry T. Cheever. His *The Island
    World of the Pacific* contains an appendix covering statistical, trade,
    commercial, and population data (pp. 377-407). His *Life in the
    Sandwich Islands* surveys conditions in 1850 (pp. 259-79).

13. The poem was called "Pleasures of Hope" and cited in a document
    called *Ships, Colonies and Commerce,* and addressed to New Zealand
    colonists. I have not seen this publication, but the poem was cited by
    Russell, with approval in a fn., pp. 429-30. It was to him "a beautiful
    anticipation." I have reduced it to its essential thought, eliminating
    such things as tigers (if you please) from the New Zealand hills.

14. Sir Wm. Martin, later chief justice in New Zealand, wrote a pamphlet
    on land tenure in 1846. Several letters cited in the *Wesleyan* magazine
    have already been mentioned in this book in chapt. 2, "The Maori
    Web" (nn. 53, 57, etc. in that chap.).

15. S. Barton Babbage, *Hauhauism: An Episode in the Maori Wars,* p. 70,
    citing both Grace and Selwyn.

16. Russell, p. 414.

17. Wm. Morley, "New Zealand," and Wm. Slade, "The Maori of New
    Zealand," both in Jas. Colwell, ed., *A Century in the Pacific.*

18. Addressing the Third Synod at Christchurch.

19. Walter Lawry, *Friendly & Feejee Islands, Missionary Visit, 1847, &s,*
    p. 136.

20. For further detail see S. Dearville Walker, *The Romance of the Black
    River . . . ,* pp. 1-20, of which these two paragraphs are a summary.

21. Chairman's address June 13, in Jas. Johnston, ed., *Report of the Cen-
    tenary Conference on Protestant Missions of the World: London 1888,*
    pp. 328-30.

22. Bishop Stuart's address, in ibid., pp. 330-32.

23. Jas. Calvert's address, in ibid., pp. 332-35.

24. S. McFarlane's address, in ibid., pp. 335-38.

25. It was Dr. E. W. Gillman, Secretary of the American Bible Society,
    whose address is in ibid., pp. 338-40.

26. Roger Cust, *Essay on the Prevailing Methods of Evangelization of the
    Non-Christian World,* pp. 16-17, 19.

27. John Turnbull, *A Voyage Round the World . . . ,* p. 261.

28. Capt. Beechey, *A Narrative of the Voyage . . . ,* p. 234.

29. Ibid., p. 235.

30. Cited from par. 2 of the statement drawn up by a special consultation
    convened by the W. C. C. Dept. of Missionary Studies at Iberville,
    Quebec, Canada, July 31—Aug. 2, 1963.

31. Hans Egede's mission to Greenland comprised a colony of some forty persons under his secular leadership. He was also their pastor and missionary to the Greenlanders. He had to make explorations and seek remunerative openings. His company had been established by stock subscribed by Bergen merchants; had to be helped by means of a lottery, which failed; and a tax levied on the people of Denmark and Norway. After the company disbanded, the king withdrew his support, though the missionaries stayed on. The Eskimo had mocked, mimicked, and taunted the missionaries. After fifteen years Egede returned to Europe after preaching his farewell sermon to the missionary community on the text, "I have laboured in vain, I have spent my strength for nought" (Is 49:4). In Europe he was appointed superintendent of a seminary to train missionaries.

   Shortly after Egede's departure, John Beck was copying out a gospel translation when a group of Southerners passed by the station. One asked what was in the book. He read and explained the word of the cross. One listener, Kaiarnak, began asking questions and was led to believe. He returned to his group and witnessed to them. Before long three Southlander families pitched their tents near the mission. Kaiarnak later went south again and returned with his brother's family. (Summarized from accounts in Augustus C. Thompson, *Protestant Missions: Their Early Rise and Progress* (pp. 243-53) and idem., *Moravian Missions* (pp. 195–201).

32. Thompson, *Moravian Missions,* p. 252.

33. No one will question the sincerity or devotion of either Egede or Nott, but of the former, Thompson said, "His heart was right but his theory defective" (ibid., p. 253). Of the theory he says that the organization of a colony with stockholders and colonists was a commercial venture. "Its originator had to be a leader . . . morally bound to look after the secular interests . . . looking out for places and sources of more profitable trade . . . experience constant chagrin at the inadequate financial returns. What in the way of religious achievements can be expected of a missionary whose thoughts are occupied largely with seal-skins, whalebone and blubber? . . . We must notice that Egede was not fully possessed with the true idea of evangelization. He entertained the mistaken theory that civilization must precede Christianity" (Thompson, *Protestant Missions,* p. 251; see also p. 246). See also Jas. M. Alexander, *The Islands of the Pacific: From the Old to the New,* p. 74.

34. Richard Lovett, *The History of the London Missionary Society: 1795– 1895,* p. 269.

35. Ibid., p. 470.

36. Ibid., p. 471.

37. E. G. Parrinder, *West African Psychology: A Comparative Study of Psychological and Religious Thought,* p. 225.

CHAPTER 7: THE STRUCTURE AND VALIDITY OF PEOPLE MOVEMENTS

1. Walter Lawry, *Friendly & Feejee Islands, Missionary Visit, 1847, &c.,* p. 257. See also correspondence in *Wesleyan* magazine.

2. Lawry, pp. 75-76.

3. A dig at the doctrinal emphases of other missions at a time when denominational harmony in New Zealand (where Lawry lived) had been disturbed by the advent of a high church bishop. The Wesleyan view of history was that God was the Actor, and men were His agents (not mere instruments). He was overwhelmed by the changes in Tonga.

4. For instance, Prof. Harvey of Dublin University was so impressed that he urged authorities in Britain to send medical supplies for the use

of missionaries in Tonga and Fiji. This led to the establishment of the
Protestant Missions' Medical Aid Society (Thos. Williams and Jas.
Calvert, *Fiji and the Fijians*, pp. 313-14). The impressions of Dr.
Coulter and Charles Darwin have been cited elsewhere, but also apply
here. Also, Capt. Fitzroy of the Royal Navy, cited in George Pritchard,
The Missionary's Reward . . . , p. 57.

5. Criticisms of the Sabbatarians have never been quite fairly evaluated.
Wilkes, who was impressed by the general effects of missionary work
in the Pacific (Chas. Wilkes, *Narrative of United States Exploring Expedition during the Years 1838-1842*, 1:135), says of this policy, "The
success of the missionaries in introducing this strict observance of a
Sabbath, is ascribed by themselves in a great degree to its analogy to
the taboo-days of heathen times" (ibid., p. 136). Anthropologically it
was a functional substitute.

6. In many Oceanic societies, in that he worships a foreign spirit in opposition to the tribal deity, he would most likely place himself in the
category of sorcery. This would expose him to the tribal magic of the
priest or medicine man, the bitter enemy of the sorcerer, and bring
him under the tribal laws for dealing with sorcerers. It would certainly strengthen the tribal resistance to Christianity.

7. F. J. H. Grattan, *An Introduction to Samoan Custom*, p. 17; Erich
Schultz, "Samoan Family Life and Law of Inheritance," in *Journal of
the Polynesian Society*, p. 45.

8. W. Butler, "South Sea Islands," in *Cyclopedia of Missions*, ed. Harvey
Newcomb, p. 698; Wm. Ellis, *Polynesian Researches* . . . , 1:138; and
John Davies, *The History of the Tahitian Mission: 1799—1830*, p. 138.

9. Butler, p. 704; John Williams, *A Narrative of Missionary Enterprises
in the South Sea Islands*, pp. 432-36.

10. Jos. Waterhouse, *King and People of Fiji*, pp. 257-58; Alan R. Tippett,
The Christian (Fiji: 1835-67), pp. 17-18.

11. Ellis, pp. 191-92. The theme of unobserved ritual has been developed
by Radcliffe-Brown, in 1939 Fraser Lecture, "Taboo" (in *Reader in
Comparative Religion*, ed. Wm. A. Lessa and Evon Z. Vogt, pp. 99—
111).

12. Williams, p. 435.

13. Ellis, p. 254.

14. Ezekiel 26:15—the oracle of Jehovah against Tyre, and the text on the
title page of this vol.

15. Further developed by the writer of this book ("Growth by Multi-individual Decision" and "Biblical Awareness of Social Units"), where
the biblical basis of both multi-individual action and awareness of
social units are dealt with.

16. Homer G. Barnett, *Innovation: The Basis of Cultural Change*, pp.
116-17.

17. For a good description of these experiences in Irian, see Jas. Sunda,
Church Growth in West New Guinea.

18. On pp. 177-78 it is noted that Russell, at the beginning of the preface
of his volume in favor of colonization (*Polynesia* . . .), made this
claim. I also point out that there were many references to negative
movements out of Christianity in Tahiti in the sources he is supposed
to have used.

19. For a good listing of this type of symbolism in Oceania, see Cyril S.
Belshaw, "The Significance of Modern Cults in Melanesian Develop-
ments," in *Reader in Comparative Religion*, ed. Wm. A. Lessa and
Evan G. Vogt, pp. 486-92.

20. Anthony F. C. Wallace, "New Religions Among the Delaware Indians,
1600—1900," in *Southwestern Journal of Anthropology*, pp. 1-21.

21. H. W. Tucker, *Memoir of* . . . *Selwyn* . . . , 1:103-4.

22. John Collier, *Indians of the Americas: The Long Hope*, p. 170.

23. Ralph L. Beals and Harry Hoijer, *An Introduction to Anthropology,* p. 504.

APPENDIX A: The Complexity of the Conversion of the Tahitians

1. Peter H. Buck, *Anthropology and Religion,* pp. 65-67.
2. Rbt. Hall Glover, *The Progress of World-wide Missions,* pp. 437-38.
3. Jos. King, "Oceania," in *Christianity Anno Domini 1901,* p. 378.
4. As, for example, in W. W. Howells, *The Heathens: Primitive Man and His Religions,* pp. 256-57.
5. Richard Lovett, *The History of the London Missionary Society: 1795–1895,* pp. 196-97.
6. Letter of the seven missionaries dated Oct. 21, 1812, cited in ibid., p. 198.
7. Letter of Jan. 14, 1815, cited in several sources, including Lovett, p. 205.
8. Account of the event written three days later and cited in Lovett, pp. 219-20. All these references (nn. 5-8) are here shown to have appeared in the official published L.M.S. centenary volume, so that there could be no doubt about their availability to the three writers.

APPENDIX B: Note on Io, the Maori Supreme God

1. See S. Percy Smith, trans., *The Lore of the Whare-wananga . . . ,* 2:110.
2. Ibid., Commentary, p. 111.
3. Ibid., pp. 129-30.
4. Ibid., pp. 136-37.
5. Ibid., p. 140.
6. Ibid., p. 92.

BIBLIOGRAPHY

This bibliography is confined to material used by the writer of this book and cited in his references.

Alexander, James M. *The Islands of the Pacific: From the Old to the New.* New York: Am. Tract Soc., 1908.

Amos, Richard. Correspondence in *Wesleyan* (Nov. 3, 1853).

Annual Field Reports: Cited in *Wesleyan* magazine, *Missionary Register, Australian Methodist Missionary Review*; *see also* Calvert, James; Colwell, James; Lovett, Richard; Newcomb, Harvey; and Stock, Eugene.

Australasian Wesleyan General Conference Minutes, 1856–1900. Sydney, Aus.: Jos. Cook, n.d.

Babbage, S. Barton. *Hauhauism: An Episode in the Maori Wars, 1863-66.* Wellington, N.Z.: A. H. & A. W. Reed, 1937.

Barnett, H. G. *Innovation: The Basis of Cultural Change.* New York: McGraw-Hill, 1953.

Beach, Harlan P. *Geography.* A Geography and Atlas of Protestant Missions, vol. 1. New York: Student Vol. Movement for Frgn. Msns., 1901.

Beals, Ralph L. and Hoijer, Harry. *An Introduction to Anthropology.* New York: Macmillan, 1954.

Beechey, Captain. *A Narrative of the Voyage and Travels of Captain Beechey to the Pacific, &c., Performed in the Years 1825–1828, &c.* London: W. Wright, 1836.

Belshaw, Cyril S. "The Significance of Modern Cults in Melanesian Developments." In *Reader in Comparative Religion*. Edited by William A. Lessa and Evan Z. Vogt, pp. 486-92. New York: Row, Peterson, 1958.

Benedict, Ruth. "Religion." In *General Anthropology*. Edited by Franz Boas, pp. 627-65. New York: Heath, 1938.

Bennet, George. *See* Montgomery, James.

Bliss, Edwin Munsell, ed. *The Encyclopedia of Missions*. Vol. 2. New York: Funk & Wagnalls, 1891.

Boas, Franz, ed. *General Anthropology*. New York: Heath, 1938.

Bowers, John. Address at the annual meeting of the Wesleyan Missionary Society. Reported in *Wesleyan* (1832).

Brittan, S. J.; Grace, G. F.; Grace, C. W.; Grace, A. V., eds. *A Pioneer Missionary Among the Maoris—1850–1879—Being Letters & Journals of Thomas Samuel Grace*. Palmerston North, N.Z.: G. H. Bennett, n.d.

Buck, Peter H. *Anthropology and Religion.* New Haven: Yale U., 1939.

———. *The Coming of the Maori.* Wellington, N.Z.: Whitcombe & Tombs, for the Maori Purposes Fund Board, 1950.

———. *Vikings of the Sunrise.* Philadelphia: Lippincott, 1938. Later published as *Vikings of the Pacific.* Chicago: U. of Chicago, Phoenix, 1959.

Buddle, Thomas. "The Aborigines of New Zealand." *Wesleyan* (1852), 457-66, 552-57.

———. Correspondence in *Wesleyan* (Oct. 9, 1851).

Buller, James. Correspondence in *Wesleyan* (April 18-19, 1851).

———. *Forty Years in New Zealand.* London: Hodder & Stoughton, 1878.

Bulu, Joeli. *Ai Tukutuku ni Noqu Bula.* Autobiographical manuscript vol. n.d.

———. *Joel Bulu: Autobiography of a Native Minister in the South Seas.* Translated by Lorimer Fison. London: Wes. Msn. House, 1871.

Bumby, John. Correspondence in *Wesleyan.*

———. "Itineration Journal." *Wesleyan* (1840).

Bunzel, Ruth. "The Economic Organization of Primitive Peoples." In *General Anthropology.* Edited by Franz Boas, pp. 327–408. New York: Heath, 1938.

Burton, J. W. *The First Century: The Missionary Adventure of Australian Methodism, 1855–1955.* Sydney, Aus.: Meth. Overseas Msns., 1955.

Butler, W. Correspondence in *Wesleyan,* cited from C.M.S. pub.

———. "New Zealand." In *Cyclopedia of Missions: Containing a Comprehensive View of Missionary Operations Throughout the World.* Edited by Harvey Newcomb, pp. 569-76. New York: Scribner, 1854.

———. "South Sea Islands." In *Cyclopedia of Missions: Containing a Comprehensive View of Missionary Operations Throughout the World.* Edited by Harvey Newcomb, pp. 678–725. New York: Scribner, 1854.

Calvert, James. Address at London Conference. In *Report of the Centenary Conference on Protestant Missions of the Lord: London 1888.* Edited by James H. Johnston. 3d ed. New York: Revell, n.d.

———. *Fiji and the Fijians.* Mission History, vol. 2. London: Alexander Heylin, 1860. *See also* Williams, T., and Calvert, James.

Carleton, Hugh. *The Life of Henry Williams.* 2 vols. 1874 and 1877. Revised (2 vols. in 1). Wellington, N.Z.: A. H. & A. W. Reed, 1948.

Catlin, George E. C. Introduction to *The Rules of Sociological Method* by Emile Durkheim. Translated by Sarah A. Solovay and John M. Mueller. Edited by George E. C. Catlin. New York: Macmillan, Free Press, 1962.

Cheever, Henry T. *The Island World of the Pacific.* New York: Harper, 1871.

————. *Life in the Sandwich Islands.* New York: Barnes, 1851.
Church Growth Bulletin. Vols. 1-5 (1963-68). Official organ of the
    Institute of Church Growth, now at Fuller Theological Seminary,
    Pasadena, California.
Collier, John. *Indians of the Americas: The Long Hope.* New York:
    New Am. Lib. of World Lit., Mentor, 1959.
Colwell, James, ed. *A Century in the Pacific.* London: Chas. H. Kel-
    ley, 1914.
Cooper, H. Stonehewer. *Coral Lands.* Vol. 2. London: Richard Bent-
    ley & Son, 1880. See in particular the section relating to Tonga.
Coulter, John. *Adventures on the western coast of South America . . .
    & . . . Islands in the Pacific Ocean.* London: Longman, Brown,
    Green & Longmans, 1847.
Cowan, James. *The New Zealand Wars: A History of the Maori Cam-
    paigns & the Pioneering Period.* 2 vols. Wellington, N.Z.: R. E.
    Owen, gov. printer, 1956. See especially vol. 2, on Hauhau.
Creed, Charles. Correspondence in *Wesleyan.*
Cross, William. Correspondence in *Wesleyan.*
Cust, Roger. *Essay on the Prevailing Methods of Evangelization of
    the Non-Christian World.* London: Luzac, 1894.
Danks, Benjamin. "Samoa." In *A Century in the Pacific.* Edited by
    James Colwell, pp. 477-505. London: Chas. H. Kelly, 1914.
Darwin, Charles. *The Voyage of the Beagle.* New York: Bantam,
    1958.
Davies, John. *The History of the Tahitian Mission: 1799–1830.* Edited
    by C. W. Newbury. New York: Cambridge U., for Hakluyt Soc.,
    1961.
de Bres, P. H. Pasadena, Cal. Correspondence at the Inst. of Church
    Growth, Fuller Theological Seminary.
Durkheim, Emile. *The Rules of Sociological Method.* Translated by
    Sarah A. Solovay and John M. Mueller. Edited by G. E. C. Catlin.
    New York: Macmillan, Free Press, 1962.
Dyson, Martin. *My Story of Samoan Wesleyanism: or, A Brief His-
    tory of the Wesleyan Mission in Samoa.* Melbourne, Aus.: Fergus-
    son & Moore, 1875.
Eggleston, John. Sydney, Aus.: Meth. Overseas Msn. Archives. Secre-
    tarial correspondence to Tonga, re Samoa Mission. Lot 30.
Elder, John Rawson. *The Letters and Journals of Samuel Marsden:
    1765–1838.* Dunedin, N.Z.: Coulls, Somerville, Wilkie Ltd., and
    A. H. Reed, for Otago U. Council, 1932.
Ella, Samuel. "Samoa." In *Proceedings*, pp. 620-45. Hobart, Aus.:
    Austral. Assoc. for Advancement of Science, 1892.
Ellis, William. *Polynesian Researches during a Residence of Nearly
    Six Years in the South Sea Islands, &c.* 2 vols. London: Fisher,
    Son & Jackson, 1829.
Erskine, John E. *Journal of a Cruise Among the Islands of the Western
    Pacific, &c.* London: John Murray, 1853.

Fancourt, H. C. *The Advance of the Missionaries: Being the Expansion of the C.M.S. Mission, South of the Bay of Islands, 1833–1840.* Wellington, N.Z.: A. H. & A. W. Reed, 1939.

Fanning, Edmund. *Voyages of Discovery in the South Seas, 1792–1832.* Salem, Mass.: Marine Research Soc., 1924.

Farmer, Sarah H. *Tonga and the Friendly Islands.* London: Hamilton, Adams, 1855.

Fison, Lorimer. *See* Bulu, Joeli.

Gill, William Wyatt. *Gems from Coral Islands.* London: Ward, 1856.

Gillman, E. W. Address at London Conference. In *Report of the Centenary Conference on Protestant Missions of the World: London 1888.* Edited by James Johnston. 3d ed. New York: Revell, n.d.

Glover, Robert Hall. *The Progress of World-wide Missions.* Rev. ed. New York: Harper, 1960.

Grace, T. S. *See* Brittan, S. J. et al.

Grattan, F. J. H. *An Introduction to Samoan Custom.* Apia, W. Samoa: Samoa Prntg. & Pub., 1948.

Greenwood, William. "The Upraised Hand." *Journal of the Polynesian Society* 51 (1942): 1-81.

Gudgeon, Thos. W. *The History & Doings of the Maoris 1820–1840.* Auckland, N.Z.: *Evening Star* ofc., 1885.

Handy, E. S. Craighill. *Polynesian Religion.* Honolulu, Hawaii: Bishop Museum, 1927.

Howells, W. W. *The Heathens: Primitive Man and His Religions.* New York: Doubleday, Nat. Hist., 1948.

Hunt, John. *Memoir of William Cross, Wesleyan Missionary to the Friendly & Feejee Islands, &c.* London: J. Mason, 1846.

———. *Typescript Journal, 1838–1848.* London: Methodist Missionary Soc.

———. *Letters on Entire Sanctification.* London: Wesleyan Conf. Office, n.d.

Im Thurn, Everard, and Wharton, Leonard C. *Journal of William Lockerby and Other Papers, &c.* London: Hakluyt Soc., 1925. Contains the text of "Journal of the Voyage of the Hibernia Missionaries."

Johnston, James, ed. *Report of the Centenary Conference on Protestant Missions of the World: London 1888.* 3d ed. New York: Revell, n.d.

Keesing, Felix M. *Modern Samoa: It's Government and Changing Life.* London: Geo. Allen & Unwin, 1934.

King, Joseph. *Christianity in Polynesia.* Sydney, Aus.: William Brooks & Co., 1899.

———. "Oceania." In *Christianity Anno Domini 1901.* Vol. 1. Edited by William D. Grant, pp. 366-85. New York: Chauncey Holt, 1902.

Koskinen, Aarne A. *Missionary Influence as a Political Factor in the Pacific Islands.* Helsinki, Fin.: Suomalaisen Kirjallisuuden, Seuran Kirjapainon oy., 1953.

Kroeber, A. L., and Waterman, T. T., eds. *Source Book in Anthropology*. New York: Harcourt, Brace, 1948.

Latourette, Kenneth Scott. *The Great Century*. History of the Expansion of Christianity, vol. 5. New York: Harper & Bros., 1943.

Laulii. *The Story of Laulii, a Daughter of Samoa*. Edited by William H. Barnes. San Francisco: Jos. Winterburn, 1889.

Lawry, Henry. Correspondence in *Wesleyan*

Lawry, Walter. Correspondence in *Wesleyan*

———. *Friendly & Feejee Islands, Missionary Visit, 1847, &c.* London: Chas. Gilpin, 1850.

———. "Itineration Journal for 1845." In *Wesleyan*.

———. "Report for Missions, 1851." In *Wesleyan*.

———. *Second Missionary Visit to Friendly & Feejee Islands, &c.* London: John Mason & Chas. Gilpin, 1851.

Laurenson, G. I. Personal correspondence received, June 7, 1962.

Leigh, Samuel. Correspondence in *Wesleyan*.

Lessa, William A., and Vogt, Evon Z. *Reader in Comparative Religion*. Evanston, Ill.: Row, Peterson, 1958.

Lips, Julius. "Government." In *General Anthropology*. Edited by Franz Boas, pp. 487–534. New York: Heath, 1938.

Lovett, Richard. *The History of the London Missionary Society: 1795–1895*. Vol. 1. London: Oxford U., 1899.

Lowie, Robert H. *Primitive Religion*. London: Peter Owen, 1960.

Lundie, Mrs. George Archibald, ed. *Missionary Life in Samoa as exhibited in the Journals of George Archibald Lundie during the Revival in Tutuila in 1840-41*. Edinburgh, Scot.: Wm. Oliphant & Sons, 1846.

McArthur, A. Address at London Conference. In *Report of the Centenary Conference on Protestant Missions of the World: London 1888*. Edited by James Johnson. 3d ed. New York: Revell, n.d.

McFarlane, S. Address at London Conference. In *Report of the Centenary Conference on Protestant Missions of the World: London 1888*. Edited by James Johnston. 3d ed. New York: Revell, n.d.

McGavran, Donald A. *The Bridges of God: A Study in the Strategy of Missions*. New York: Friendship, 1955.

———. *How Churches Grow: The New Frontiers of Mission*. London: World Dominion, 1959.

McNab, Robert. *Historical Records of New Zealand*. Wellington, N.Z.: John McKay, gov. printer, 1908.

Maning, F. E. *Old New Zealand and a History of the War in the North Against the Chief, Heke*. London: Whitcombe & Tombs, 1912.

Mariner, William. *Account of the Natives of the Tonga Islands in the South Pacific Ocean, &c.* 2 vols. Edited by J. Martin. London: Constable, 1827.

Marsden, J. B. *Life and Work of Samuel Marsden*. Christchurch, N.Z.: Whitcombe & Tombs, 1913.

Marsden, Samuel. *See* Elder, John Rawson; *also* McNab, Robert.

———. Journal excerpts published in *Wesleyan* (1822).

Martin, Lady. *Our Maoris*. London: Soc. for Promoting Chr. Knowledge, 1888.

Martin, William. Pamphlet on Land Tenure in New Zealand.

Masterman, Sylvia. *The Origins of International Rivalry in Samoa: 1845-84*. Stanford, Cal.: Stanford U., 1934.

Mead, Margaret. *Coming of Age in Samoa*. London: Penguin Books, 1954.

———. "A Lapse of Animism Among a Primitive People." In *Psyche* 9 (1928): 72-77.

———. "The Role of the Individual in Samoan Culture." In *Source Book in Anthropology*. Edited by A. L. Kroeber and T. T. Waterman, pp. 545-61. New York: Harcourt, Brace, 1948.

———. "Samoa." In *Co-operation and Competition Among Primitive Peoples*. Rev. ed. Edited by Margaret Mead. Boston: Beacon, 1961.

Meade, Herbert R. *A Ride Through the Disturbed Districts in New Zealand, &c.: Selections from the Journals & Letters of Lieut. Hon. Herbert Meade, R. N.* London: John Murray, 1870.

Methodist Church in Australia. *A Brief Account of Methodist Missions in Australsia, Polynesia and Melanesia, &c.* Sydney, Aus.: Epworth, c. 1904.

Mishkin, Bernard. "The Maori of New Zealand." In *Co-operation and Competition Among Primitive Peoples*. Edited by Margaret Mead. Boston: Beacon, 1961.

Missionary Register. Reports and Statistics of various missions.

Moffat, John S. *The Lives of Robert & Mary Moffat*. New York: Armstrong & Son, 1885.

Moister, William. *A History of Wesleyan Missions, &c.* 3d ed. London: Elliot Stock, 1871.

Montgomery, James, ed. *Journal of Voyages and Travels by Revs. Daniel Tyerman & George Bennet, deputed from the L.M.S. to Visit the South Sea Islands, &c., between 1821—1829*. London: Frederick Westley & A. H. Davies, 1831.

Montgomery, H. B. *Christus Redemptor: An Outline Study of the Island World of the Pacific*. London: Macmillan, 1907.

Morley, William. "New Zealand." In *A Century in the Pacific*. Edited by James Colwell, pp. 375-407. London: Chas. Kelly, 1914.

Morris, James. *A Voyage through the Islands of the Pacific Ocean, &c.* New York: Carlton & Phillips, 1856.

Moss, Frederick. *Through Atolls & Islands in the Great South Sea*. London: Sampson Low, Marston, Searle & Rivington, 1889.

Moulton, J. Egan. *Moulton of Tonga*. London: Epworth, 1921.

———. "Tonga." In *A Century in the Pacific*. Edited by James Colwell, pp. 409-37. London: Chas. Kelly, 1914.

Murray, A. W. *Forty Years Mission Work in Polynesia & New Guinea*. London: Jas. Nisbet & Co., 1876.

Nadel, S. F. *The Foundations of Social Anthropology*. London: Cohen & West, 1958.

Newcomb, Harvey, ed. *A Cyclopedia of Missions: Containing a Comprehensive View of Missionary Operations throughout the World.* New York: Scribner, 1854.

Newbury, C. W. *See* Davies, John.

Parrinder, E. G. *West African Psychology: A Comparative Study of Psychological and Religious Thought.* London: Lutterworth, 1951.

Pomare. "Letters from Pomare, King of Tahiti, 1818-36." Misc. ms. 1396, Turnbull Library, Wellington, N.Z.

Pratt, George. "The Genealogy of the Kings and Princes of Samoa." In *Proceedings,* pp. 655-63. Melbourne, Aus.: Austral. Assoc. for Advancement of Science, 1890.

Pritchard, George. *The Missionary's Reward, or, The Success of the Gospel in the Pacific.* London: John Snow, 1844. Introduction, by J. A. James, on French activity in Pacific.

Prout, Ebenezer. *Memoirs of the Life of the Rev. John Williams.* New York: Dodd, 1843.

Pybus, T. A. *Maori & Missionary: Early Christian Missions in the South Island of New Zealand.* Wellington, N.Z.: A. H. & A. W. Reed, 1954.

Radcliffe-Brown, A. R. "Taboo." In *Reader in Comparative Religion.* Edited by William A. Lessa and Evon Z. Vogt, pp. 99-111. Evanston, Ill.: Row, Peterson, 1958. Frazer Lecture, 1939.

Ramsden, Eric. *Marsden & Missions: Prelude to Waitangi.* Sydney, Aus.: Angus & Robertson, 1936.

Reed, A. W. *The Impact of Christianity on the Maori People.* Wellington; N.Z.: A. H. & A. W. Reed, 1955.

Robson, R. W., ed. *Pacific Islands Year Book.* 8th ed. Sydney, Aus.: Pacific Pub. Pty., 1959.

Rogers, Lawrence M. *The Early Journals of Henry Williams (Senior Missionary in New Zealand of the Church Missionary Society) 1826-40.* Christchurch, N.Z.: Pegasus, 1961.

Rose, Rt. Hon. Sir George. Address at World Missionary Society Annual Meeting 1840. In *Wesleyan* (1840).

Rose, Ronald. *South Seas Magic.* London: Rbt. Hale, 1959.

Rowe, N. A. *Samoa Under the Sailing Gods.* London: Putnam, 1930.

Russell, M. *Polynesia: or, An Historical Account of the Principal Islands in the South Sea, including New Zealand; and the actual condition of the inhabitants in regard to Civilization, Commerce & the Arts of Social Life.* 2d ed. Edinburgh, Scot.: Oliver & Boyd, 1843.

Schultz, Erich. "Samoan Family Life and Law of Inheritance." *Journal of the Polynesian Society* 20 (1911): 43-53.

Selwyn, G. A. New Zealand Letters from a Bishop: Selwyn's Visitation Journal. Mss., War Memorial Library, Auckland, N.Z.

Selwyn, J. R. *Pastoral Work in the Colonies and on the Mission Field.* Brighton, Aus.: Soc. for Promoting Chr. Knowledge, 1897.

Sherif, Muzafer. *The Psychology of Social Norms.* New York: Harper & Bros., 1936.

Slade, William. "The Maori of New Zealand." In *A Century in the Pacific.* Edited by James Colwell, pp. 119-49. London: Chas. Kelley, 1914.

Smales, Gideon. Correspondence in *Wesleyan.*

Smith, George. *Short History of Christian Missions.* Edinburgh, Scot.: T. & T. Clark, 1906.

Smith, S. Percy. *The Lore of the Whare-wananga: Teachings of the Maori College, &c.* Memoirs, Vols. 2 & 3. New Plymouth, N.Z.: Polynesian Soc., 1913.

Smith, William. *Journal of a Voyage in the Missionary Ship, Duff, to the Pacific Ocean, 1796—1802, Comprehending Authentic and Circumstantial Narratives of the Disasters which Attended the First Effort of the L.M.S., &c.* New York: Collins, 1813.

South Sea Sketches. See under Manuscripts.

Stair, J. B. "Jottings on the Mythology and Spirit-lore of Old Samoa." *Journal of the Polynesian Society* 5 (1896): 33-57.

Stock, Eugene, ed. *History of the Church Missionary Society: Its Environment, Its Men and Its Work.* 4 vols. London: Church Msnry. Soc., vols. 1-3, 1899; vol. 4, n.d.

Strachan, Alexander. *The Life of Samuel Leigh.* London: Hamilton Adams, 1894.

Stuart, Bishop. Address at London Conference. In *Report of the Centenary Conference on Protestant Missions of the World: London 1888.* Edited by James Johnston. 3d ed. New York: Revell, n.d.

Sunda, James. *Church Growth in West New Guinea.* Eugene, Ore.: Inst. of Church Growth, 1962.

Sutherland, Alexander, and Sutherland, George. *The History of Australia and New Zealand from 1606—1890.* London: Longmans, Green, 1894.

Taylor, Richard. *The Past & Present of New Zealand with Its Prospects for the Future.* London: Wm. Macintosh, 1868.

Te Rangi Hiroa. *See* Buck, Peter H.

Thomas, John. Correspondence and reports in *Wesleyan.*

Thompson, Augustus C. *Moravian Missions.* New York: Scribner, 1904. Twelve lectures.

———. *Protestant Missions: Their Early Rise and Progress.* New York: Student Vol. Movement for Frgn. Msns., 1903.

Thomson, Basil. *The Diversions of a Prime Minister.* Edinburgh, Scot.: Wm. Blackwood & Sons, 1894.

———. *The Fijians: A Study in the Decay of Custom.* London: Wm. Heinemann, 1908.

Tippett, Alan R. "Biblical Awareness of Social Units." No. 4 in series The Biblical Basis of Church Growth. *Church Growth Bulletin* (1965).

————. *The Christian (Fiji: 1835-67)*. Auckland, N.Z.: Institute Prtng. & Pub. Soc., 1954.

————. "Growth by Multi-individual Decision." No. 3 in series The Biblical Basis of Church Growth. *Church Growth Bulletin* (1965).

Tolhurst, Leonard Philps. "The Religious Concepts of the Maoris in Pre-European Days & a Detailed Study of the Ringatu Church of Today." Master's thesis, Seventh-Day Adventist Sem., Wash., D.C., 1955.

Tucker, Charles. Correspondence and reports in *Wesleyan*.

Tucker, H. W. *Memoir of the Life and Episcopate of George Augustus Selwyn, Bishop of New Zealand, &c.* 2 vols. London: Wm. Wells Gardner, 1879. Many letters cited in full.

Tucker, Miss ————. *The Southern Cross and Southern Crown*. London: Jas. Nisbet, 1855.

Turnbull, John. *A Voyage Round the World in the Years 1800–1804 in which the Author visited the Principal Islands of the Pacific Ocean, &c.* Philadelphia: Ben. & Thos. Kite, 1810.

Turner, George. *Samoa: A Hundred Years Ago and Long Before &c.* London: Macmillan, 1884.

Turner, Nathaniel. Correspondence in *Wesleyan*.

Turner, Peter. Correspondence in *Wesleyan*.

Turton, H. H. Correspondence in *Wesleyan*.

Tyerman, Daniel. *See* Montgomery, James.

Tylor, E. B. Foreword to *Samoa: A Hundred Years Ago and Long Before &c.*, by John Turnbull. Philadelphia: Ben. & Thos. Kite, 1810.

Vine, Ronald. "Te Kooti's Church Continues Its Ministry: Biblical Beliefs of the Denomination in the Urewere Country." *Auckland Weekly News* (Apr. 20, 1938), p. 42.

Vogt, Evon Z. *See* Lessa, William A., and Vogt, Evon Z.

Walker, F. Dearville. *A Hundred Years in Nigeria*. London: Cargate Press.

————. *The Romance of the Black River: The Story of the C.M.S. Nigeria Mission*. London: Church Msnry. Soc., C.M.S., 1930.

Wallace, Anthony F. C. "New Religions Among the Delaware Indians, 1600–1900." *Southwestern Journal of Anthropology* 12 (1956): 1-21.

Ward, John M. *British Policy in the South Pacific (1786–1893)*. Sydney, Aus.: Australasian Pub. Co. Pty., 1948.

Warren, John. Correspondence in *Wesleyan*.

Waterhouse, Joseph. *King and People of Fiji*. London: Wesleyan Conf. Ofc., 1866.

————. Fiji. Meth. Msn. Archives. Typescript copies of correspondence. Ms. 203, Turnbull Library, Wellington, N.Z.

Watkin, James. Correspondence in *Wesleyan*.

Watson, Robert Mackenzie. *History of Samoa*. Wellington, N.Z.: Whitcombe & Tombs, 1918.

Wesleyan Conference Minutes (Australian).

Wesleyan magazine (1820—1860). A major source.

Wesleyan Missionary Register (1830—1840).

West, Thomas. *Ten Years in South-central Polynesia: being Reminiscences of a Personal Mission to the Friendly Islands, &c.* London: Jas. Nisbet, 1865.

Wheen, John G. "The Missions of Australian Methodism." *Australian Methodist Missionary Review* (Oct. 4, 1913).

White, Rev. ———. Correspondence in *Wesleyan*.

Whiteley, John. Correspondence in *Wesleyan*.

Wilkes, Charles. *Narrative of United States Exploring Expedition during the Years 1838—1842.* 2 vols. London: Ingram, Cooke, 1852.

Williams, F. W. *Through Ninety Years: 1826—1916: Life and Work among the Maoris of New Zealand.* Auckland, N.Z.: Whitcombe & Tombs, n.d.

Williams, H. Foreword to *Hauhauism: An Episode in the Maori Wars, 1863-66*, by S. Barton Babbage. Wellington, N.Z.: A. H. & A. W. Reed, 1937.

———. *See also* Carleton, Hugh.

Williams, John. Correspondence cited in *Wesleyan*.

———. *A Narrative of Missionary Enterprises in the South Sea Islands, &c.* London: John Snow, 1837.

———. *See also,* Prout, Ebenezer.

Williams, Thomas. *Fiji & the Fijians.* Mission History, vol. 1. London: Alexander Heylin, n.d.

Williams, Thomas, and Calvert, James. *Fiji & the Fijians.* Rev. ed. (2 vols. in 1, updated to 1870). London: Chas. H Kelly, n.d.

Williams, William. *Christianity Among the New Zealanders.* London: Seeley, Jackson & Halliday, 1867.

Williamson, Robert W. *Religion and Social Organization in Central Polynesia.* New York: Cambridge U., 1937.

Wilson, William. *A Missionary Voyage to the South Pacific Ocean, performed in the years 1796-98 in the ship, Duff, &c.* London: T. Chapman, for the benefit of L.M.S., 1799.

Wood, A. H. *History and Geography of Tonga.* Tonga: C. S. Summers, gov. prtr., 1932.

Woon, William. Correspondence and reports in *Wesleyan*.

———. *Journal.* In Turnbull Library. Wellington, N.Z.

World Council of Churches. *See* under Manuscripts.

Wright, Harrison M. *New Zealand, 1769—1840: Early Years of Western Contact.* Cambridge, Mass.: Harvard U., 1959.

Yate, William. *An Account of New Zealand: and of the Formation and Progress of the Church Missionary Society's Mission in the Northern Island.* London: R: B. Seeley & W. Burnside, 1835.

Young, Robert. *The Southern World: Journal of a Deputation from the Wesleyan Conference to New Zealand and Polynesia.* London: John Mason, 1858.

GENERAL INDEX

GEOGRAPHIC INDEX

PERSONS INDEX

POLYNESIAN CLASSIFICATORY
TERMS INDEX

(Some of these terms have local use only; others are universals for Polynesia. The spelling in this index follows the documents or the usage of the locality to which they apply in this book.)